GOING GLOBAL

Key Questions for the Twenty-First Century

Michael Moynagh and Richard Worsley

Where have we come from?
Where are we going?
What do we need to think about?

A & C BLACK • LONDON

First published in Great Britain 2008

A & C Black Publishers Ltd
38 Soho Square, London W1D 3HB
www.acblack.com

The Guardian is a registered trademark of the Guardian Media Group plc. Guardian Books is an imprint of Guardian Newspapers Ltd.

No responsibility for loss caused to any individual or organisation acting or refraining from action as a result of the material in this publication can be accepted by A & C Black Publishers Ltd or the authors.

A CIP record for this book is available from the British Library.

ISBN: 9-780-7136-8866-5

This book is produced using paper that is made from wood grown in managed, sustainable forests. It is natural, renewable and recyclable. The logging and manufacturing processes conform to the environmental regulations of the country of origin.

Design by Fiona Pike, Pike Design, Winchester
Typeset by RefineCatch Ltd, Bungay, Suffolk
Printed in the United Kingdom by Caligraving

CONTENTS

Going Global has been produced as one element of a partnership agreement between the Economic and Social Research Council and The Tomorrow Project, designed to aid the transfer of academic knowledge to business and other audiences.

The Economic and Social Research Council is the UK's leading research, training and knowledge exchange agency addressing economic and social concerns. It aims to provide high quality research on issues of importance to business, government, the public and third sectors. The issues considered include economic competitiveness, the effectiveness of public services and policy, and quality of life. The ESRC is an independent organisation, established by Royal Charter in 1965, and funded mainly by government.

The Tomorrow Project is an independent charity undertaking a programme of research, consultation and communication about people's lives in Britain in the next twenty years. Its aims are to help individuals and organisations to think and learn about the future of people's lives in order to gain a better understanding of the present and to learn about the choices which will influence the future. (For more information, see **www.tomorrowproject.net**)

ACKNOWLEDGEMENTS

We would like to express our thanks to the many people who have contributed to this book:

to the Economic and Social Research Council for their support and partnership, and particularly to Dr. David Guy;

to the Centre for the Study of Globalisation and Regionalisation at the University of Warwick, who worked in partnership with us and provided Michael Moynagh with a visiting fellowship for the duration of the project;

to those who reviewed our emerging texts: Dr. Chris Hughes of the Centre for the Study of Globalisation and Regionalisation, Alan Wright, author of *Organised Crime*, Professor Albert McGill of Victoria University, Melbourne, Professor Chris Ogan of Indiana University, Professor Robin Cohen of Oxford University, Graham Leicester of the International Futures Forum, Professor Tom Ling of Rand Europe, Dr. Mayer Hillman of the Policy Studies Institute, London, Anthony Foottit of the Tindall Centre at the University of East Anglia, Angela Wilkinson of the James Martin Institute, Oxford University, Dr. Heribert Dieter of the Free University of Berlin, Dr. Ann Pettifor of Advocacy International and Professor John Driffill of Birkbeck College;

to those who served as members of a steering group for the project, helping to guide our work: Jonathan Flint of Oxford Instruments, Dr. David Guy of ESRC, Tony Gerrard of the Department for Trade and Industry, Graham Leicester of the International Futures Forum, Jill Mortimer of the Local Government Association, Professor Jim Norton of the Institute of Directors and Professor Jan Aart Scholte of the Centre for the Study of Globalisation and Regionalisation;

to Celine Tan of Warwick University, who assisted our research, to Juliet Kauffmann of Librios, who edited our texts and undertook much of the electronic handling of our material; to Hal Robinson of Librios for his constant advice and support;

to A & C Black, our publisher, and particularly to Lisa Carden, our editor;

to Guardian Books;

to all those who took part in the consultations that so helpfully informed our work, and

to our Tomorrow Project Trustees, under the wise chairmanship of Patrick Coldstream, for their encouragement and guidance.

The book owes much to all these people, while its shortcomings are, of course, our own.

Michael Moynagh and Richard Worsley

JOIN THE TOMORROW NETWORK – *for individuals with an interest in futures – free of charge. Members receive invitations to The Tomorrow Project's Network events involving distinguished speakers and regular briefings on emerging trends. To join the Network simply email* **richard.worsley2@btinternet.com**

CHAPTER 1
GETTING YOUR MIND ROUND GLOBALISATION

- You need to define it clearly
- ...to think about it concretely
- ...to accept its complexity
- ...to view it in context
- ...to view it critically

'Globalisation' has become the buzzword of our time. For some people it is a description of forces that are transforming our lives. For others it is a hate word, denoting much of what is destructive and unfair about today's world. For still others it is a source of hope – globalisation promises a better future.

Perhaps for most people it is a term of confusion: what exactly does it mean and how does it work? In this chapter we suggest five ways of getting your mind round globalisation.

First, you need to define it clearly – important when the word is used in multiple ways.

Some people, for example, equate globalisation with the market-based economy that has been sweeping across the planet. Others see globalisation as the process of spreading various products and experiences to all parts of the world: 'the car industry is globalised', or 'we are witnessing the globalisation of Western values'. *We define globalisation as the world becoming more interdependent and integrated.* Globalisation describes the processes involved. It affects every aspect of life – economic, political, social, cultural and environmental. It entails:

- *The multiplication of networks.* Better communications mean that civil servants, businesses, non-governmental organisations, professionals, computer games players, individuals on social network sites, criminals and many others are increasingly well connected;
- *The stretching of relationships.* Shopping malls offer consumers who can afford them products from all corners of the earth. A computer contains components that were manufactured in different countries. It can collect messages from the other side of the world. Organisations, from charities to al-Qaeda, use the Internet to stretch their activities across the planet;

■ *The intensification of human contact.* The idea that 'globalisation compresses time and space' simply means that things are getting faster and that you can jump distances far more easily than before. In an hour, you can send scores of messages to people who are miles away – look at all the e-mails that have piled up after your holidays! People are spending more time communicating with each other in their jobs and their spare time.

The important result is that spheres of life are emerging over and above geography. For part of their lives, people are beginning to inhabit a world that is not bound by territory.

During your working day, you may spend hours talking to colleagues in different countries. Back home, you have a long conversation with a Bangalore call centre to change your holiday flights. You then go to MySpace to catch up with friends from around the UK and overseas.

In the background are countless international gatherings setting product standards that will influence how your employer develops its business, agreeing rules for the sale of international airline tickets and negotiating protocols for the development of the Internet.

The World Globalisation Index, 1982–2004

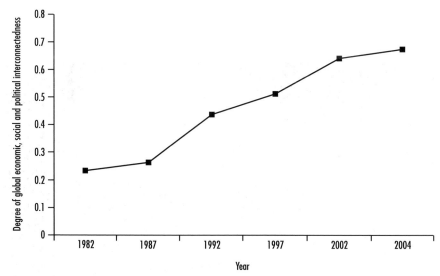

The world is becoming more interconnected.
Source: Ben Lockwood & Michela Redoano, *The CSGR Globalisation Index: an Introductory Guide*, Centre for the Study of Globalisation and Regionalisation Working Paper 155/04, 2005.
Note: Index is an aggregation of individual country indices, based on economic, social and political variables.

There is a growing world out there that has a huge impact on everyday life, a world that leaps national borders and has its own conventions and codes of behaviour.

Increasingly, this world 'out there' lies at the heart of globalisation. It is the result of individuals and representatives of organisations drawing together across distances and spending time with each other. A more integrated world is creating spheres that transcend the world itself — a world above the world.

Secondly, you need to think about globalisation concretely. The term suffers from being rather abstract, and many books on the subject make it even more so by generalising about it. To get a handle on the concept, it helps to think about globalisation in concrete terms. What does it mean in this particular situation for the world to be drawing together?

The experience will be different in different places. In the City of London, traders will be doing deals across the world, business people will be jetting in and out from one country to another and there will be wide acceptance of different national cultures.

In Tower Hamlets, a few miles away, young Muslims may also have a strong sense of being part of a wider world. But in their case, it will mean belonging to *umma*, the global Muslim community. Some may be suspicious of British culture.

Much further away in the suburbs of Manchester, on the other hand, residents may have little sense of belonging to a global world, even though the clothes they buy, the ethnic restaurants they visit, the global branding of the Manchester

United football team and other aspects of their lives mean that they are surrounded by globalisation. Their identities are local and regional rather than international.[1]

Globalisation is not a monolithic force sweeping all before it. It is a collection of processes that interact with specific contexts. A world above the world is emerging, but people are still rooted in the world below. The interaction of the two is what counts.

Another way of thinking about specific contexts is to identify, as we do in this book, issues that challenge the world today – how to feed the planet's growing population, how to tackle climate change, conserve energy, increase security and so on.

These issues have long histories, to which globalisation gives a new twist.

In the case of global hunger, there is a history of population growth, of consumer taste, of changing industry organisation and of attempts to raise food production. To these, globalisation is adding new dimensions, such as food supply chains with a worldwide reach.

Thirdly, you need to accept globalisation's complexity. When the world of physical boundaries meets the world that jumps boundaries, complicated situations arise. They can be difficult to understand.

For those who like things simple, this complexity can be hard to accept. There is a big appetite for books that sum up globalisation in simple terms, such as *The World is Flat*, the best-selling book by *The New York Times* journalist Thomas Friedman.[2]

The danger is that authors squeeze things into a framework that doesn't fit, or leave out more significant items because they sit awkwardly with the theme.

We don't think that the world can be understood by reducing its complexity to one overarching idea. The interaction between the 'world above' and the 'world below' is too complex.

We prefer, instead, to offer a simple *framework* for thinking about global issues:

- Where have we come from?
- Where are we going?
- What do we need to think about?

Though there are other ways to structure your thoughts, these questions have a strong intuitive appeal: they are what most people want to know. They encourage you to look backwards, to look forwards and to take stock.

Accordingly, in each of the main chapters that follow we have taken some of the best academic and other research, and put it into the same outline shape:

- 'The story so far' – which describes recent and current trends;
- 'What will shape the next 20 years?' – drivers that will mould the future;
- 'What might be the implications?' – the all-important 'so what?' question.

This offers a mental map of each topic and includes a much stronger, forward-looking dimension than most academic research provides. The result is a fuller picture than if you stop with the present.

Individuals and organisations all make some assumptions about the future – that it will be much the same as today, perhaps. Systematically thinking about the future can help you to test those assumptions. Are they valid?

Researchers often hesitate to speculate about the future. Their work may be strongly evidence based, which discourages them from stepping outside what they know – 'We can't collect evidence about the future in the way that we can about the present and the past.'

But this is not entirely true. It is possible to have an evidence-based approach to the future. You can collect evidence about recent trends (in global migration for example) and about what has caused those trends. From this you can build a model of how migration works, and then infer what will drive migration in the years ahead.

These inferences won't be complete. There may be shocks outside the migration system. As you peer further into the future it will get harder to know how much weight to put on each influence. But at least you will have a better idea of what is probable and what is uncertain. You may have to talk about possible futures ('scenarios') rather than one set future.

> 'You can have an evidence-based approach to the future'

Uncertainty is typical of knowledge, whatever the field. In history, for example, events may be recorded by only one person, with a slanted view. Other highly relevant events, which if we knew about them would change our take on what happened, may not have been recorded at all.

Yet, though our understanding of the past is limited, we still see it as valid. Likewise, our limited knowledge about the future is also valid. It is better than no knowledge.

Fourthly, you need to view globalisation in context. Globalisation itself has a history, and it can be helpful to see where we stand in the story.

One way of thinking about modern globalisation, which some people date from the Second World War and others from the 1970s, is to see it as developing through three overlapping phases:

Physical globalisation has involved the phenomenal expansion of world trade (cross-border trade soared from 8% of world output in 1950 to 25% in 2000),[3] and a massive increase in the movement of people – not just migration, but travel of every kind.

It includes the explosive growth in worldwide flows of capital. (Though largely intangible today, money was once highly physical, evolving from barter to coinage. It still retains a characteristic of the physical world in that it is constantly measured.)[4]

'China could eventually account for a third of all California's air pollution'

Physical globalisation ranges from networks that link people together, to global supply chains, to cross-border pollution – some experts predict that one day China could account for a third of all California's air pollution.[5]

It relies on global rules. Rules that were originally set by local communities, then by national governments with responsibility for defined physical territories, are now less geographically tied. Physical globalisation is about people, things and the rules governing them jumping physical boundaries.

Cultural globalisation is more about the worldwide movement of ideas and values, helped by the increasing use of global English. It includes, for example, the spread of:

- *consumer values,* as the world becomes more prosperous and hundreds of millions of people become modern consumers. Choice becomes a highly prized value, individuals increasingly construct their identities through consumption and ideas about fashion shoot round the globe, with an enormous impact on people's lives;
- *organisational values,* as more people assume that to organise in a modern way is the best means of getting things done. As we note in chapter 9, all over the world people's lives have been getting more organised. Ideas of good practice in how to organise, such as target-setting and accountability, spread ever more quickly across the earth;
- *religious values.* Modern means of communications have helped many Muslims to be far more aware of themselves as part of a global Islamic community. Christian denominations have acquired a stronger sense of global identity – with one part of the Anglican church, for instance, more ready to intervene in the life of another part thousands of miles away;

- *political values,* as from one corner of the earth to another people exchange information about climate change, the Iraq war, global poverty, human rights and other issues.

Though physical globalisation continues apace, the movement of ideas and values across countries is having a growing impact on people's lives. Often this impact goes unnoticed because we take these shared notions for granted. While I might have a different outlook to my neighbour, both our outlooks will increasingly be shared by others round the world.

As cultural globalisation assumes greater importance, it can be seen as a second – though overlapping – phase of globalisation. First globalisation was mainly about the movement of things and people; now it is increasingly about the exchange of ideas and values.

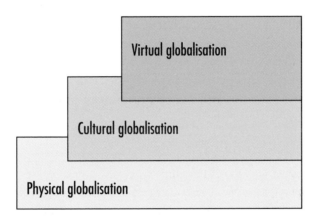

Virtual globalisation could emerge as a third phase, alongside the other two. At its heart will be the virtual economy. This will comprise paid-for products that are created purely online.

Specially important will be virtual reality. Even now, virtual reality is enabling computer-simulated worlds to be inhabited by people from around the globe. Users interact with each other via avatars (computer-generated representations of the individuals involved).

Virtual Magic Kingdom, for example, reproduces Adventureland, Fantasyland and Tomorrowland from Disney's theme parks. Users can build their own characters, mixing Disney costumes to create their own unique look and create their own rooms in the kingdom. The more they hang out and play, the more credits they earn to spend on furnishings. Credits are a typical in-world currency.

Second Life takes this a big step further. Inhabitants have their own avatars and are surrounded by the creations of other participants. They can buy software that enables them to perform a range of functions, from making exotic clothes to setting up a business. Individuals can buy land, build a house and then rent it.

Trading takes place using Linden dollars (named after the company that created *Second Life*), which can be converted to US dollars at several thriving online currency exchanges.

In 2006 one Second Lifer had created a bingo-like game called Tringo, which was licensed to Nintendo for sale in the real world. Someone else employed 17 people part time in the real world to manage her property empire in *Second Life,* then worth $250,000.[6]

In early 2007 about $2 million of real money was being traded every day. *Second Life's* annual gross domestic product (GDP) was estimated to be around $220 million.[7]

There is evidence from South Korea that virtual worlds lose their attraction after a while. But these tend to be online computer games rather than graphical chat rooms with the chance to make money.

The long-term allure of *Second Life* and its successors may lie in:

- *Advancing technology,* which will make it easier for novices to enter virtual worlds – the time initially involved is a large barrier for many people today.

  Second Life has opened its source code to software developers, encouraging them to invent new applications. For example, people are talking about worlds that mimic the seasons, so that plants grow as if in real life.

  Sensory feedback, using haptic interfaces, will eventually be common. Your hands – and in time other parts of your body – will feel objects as if they were real.

- *The social attractions.* It is easy to make virtual friends in *Second Life* by chatting to someone in a virtual art gallery or museum and finding that you have a common interest. If the other person doesn't want to talk, they don't have to type anything on their keyboard. So striking up a conversation is less intrusive than in real life.

  A three-dimensional space to meet up with friends or go out together would bring a new dimension to social network sites such as MySpace. For many employees, working in a virtual world could be more attractive than their current experience of sitting behind a computer all day.

■ *The economic opportunities.* Second Lifers can transfer money from their bank accounts into their *Second Life* accounts and then pay for very small items without incurring bank charges. This creates a market for low-cost products, which users can supply as part of having fun – 'Would you like to buy this piece of furniture for a dollar?'

These markets could become very large, allowing more and more people to earn part or full-time livings in virtual reality.

In 2005, an estimated 100,000 Chinese people earned their livelihood by playing Massively Multiplayer Online Games seven days a week. They sold their characters and other virtual assets to more affluent gamers in the West. Some characters can command hundreds of dollars depending on their 'levels' and other accomplishments.[8]

Will virtual economies take off? Rivers Run Red, a London company, employs two dozen people full time building projects in *Second Life* for clients.[9] Dell allows visitors in *Second Life* to customise computers that will be delivered to their real-life addresses.

A few corporations are selling virtual goods, such as shoes or cars. IBM has an island for internal meetings. Edinburgh University has students from all over the world in tutorial groups round a camp fire on a virtual beach.[10]

But it is still early days, and many organisations are adopting a wait and see approach.

If, as seems likely, these virtual economies do catch on, there will be many new spaces in the 'world above the world' for people to inhabit. Globalisation could acquire a whole new dimension.

The implications could be far-reaching. Will leisure become less distinct from work, as people use their spare time to develop virtual hobbies that also yield an income? If economic activity starts to migrate into the virtual sphere, would this ease some of the environmental constraints on growth? How would today's economic models be revised?

Finally, to get your mind round globalisation you need to view it critically. Much of the debate about globalisation has centred on whether it is a good or bad thing.

But in a way this doesn't get you very far. If you think globalisation is a bad thing (perhaps because it leaves the poor behind and damages the environment), what can be done about it? Most of those who think globalisation is a good thing (for instance, because it has raised living standards and spread human rights) also believe that it needs some reform.

So really the debate becomes: what changes are needed to maximise the benefits of globalisation and minimise its disadvantages? This forces you to look at globalisation critically.

One way to do this is to explore some of the tensions within globalisation: how might they be managed?

There is a particular tension between reducing poverty and widening inequality. Those who are positive about the current form of globalisation point to how the proportion of people in the most extreme poverty has fallen – from 27.9% worldwide in 1980 to 21.1% in 2002.[11]

This shows, they claim, that the benefits of global economic growth have trickled down to the bottom. They argue that this growth depends on skilled people having the financial incentives to use their abilities most effectively. To provide these incentives, incomes at the top may rise faster than those at the bottom.

Critics point to the widening gap between high and low incomes within countries most plugged into the global economy. They argue that inequality damages the confidence of people at the bottom, makes them feel powerless and produces frustration. This gives rise to stress, which often leads to ill health.

'Developing countries with lots of young people are more prone to armed conflict, violence and riots'

Individuals are also more likely to resort to violence, which may help to explain why developing countries with a high proportion of young people are more prone to armed conflict, terrorism and riots.[12] Unable to get jobs, young adults are frequently at the base of the economic pile.

Might both views be right? To reduce absolute poverty you need a form of economic growth that increases inequality, which in turn has high social and human costs. Is this a tension at the heart of globalisation? If so, for how long can it be maintained? Can inequality keep getting wider and wider before society snaps?

Post-war China, for example, has been a relatively equal society, but its leaders are concerned about the widening income gap as its economy powers ahead: how much inequality will people tolerate? Given the country's global footprint, if rising inequality made China politically unstable, the rest of the world would experience the fallout.

Can we find new ways of getting economic growth to cut absolute poverty, without widening the gap between the rich and the poor?

There is a tension between global economic growth and human well-being. China and India, for example, desperately need rapid economic growth to meet the ballooning demand for jobs.

Yet this growth has made air pollution so bad in New Delhi, Kolkata (Calcutta) and Beijing (Peking) that the UN considers these cities to have life-threatening environments. As noted in chapter 3, in some parts of China pollution is stoking public resistance to new factories. Many observers fear that environmental constraints will slow both countries' economic growth, causing unemployment to rise.

In the West, human relationships – often described as social capital – are increasingly important for organisational success. Companies rely on teamwork, knowledge-sharing between employees and other forms of collaboration to compete in the global economy. High-order relationship skills ('soft skills') are in ever greater demand.

Yet in many countries, workplace demands on employees have intensified concerns about the work/life balance. Many parents complain that they are too exhausted to spend quality time with their children, or that their job keeps them away from their family for too long.

Could it be that the demands of modern business are making it difficult for parents to equip children with the emotional capacities that companies will increasingly need?

There is a tension between the global and the local. To take just one example, global and national politics are entwined to an unprecedented degree.

To many people this feels like a loss of national sovereignty: national governments seem less in control than they were. Citizens resent being forced to accept decisions made by some distant international body or by a regional grouping like the EU. They expect their politicians 'to stand up for the national interest' and resist outside interference.

Yet for much of the political élite, the situation feels rather different. Sovereignty appears to have been pooled. Although national governments have lost power, in that they are bound by numerous international agreements and have to consult scores of international actors, their power has also been extended.

Each state has new opportunities to influence the others and advance its interests. Global migration, for example, can be managed more effectively through international cooperation.

As the world draws closer together, will these contrasting perceptions polarise further? How will they be managed?

1 In-depth interviews with a sample in Greater Manchester revealed that only a very small proportion had a significant sense of global identity. Mike Savage, Gaynor Bagnall & Brian Longhurst, *Globalization and Belonging,* London: Sage, 2005, pp. 191–201.

2 Thomas L. Friedman, *The World is Flat: The Globalized World in the Twenty-First Century,* London: Penguin, 2005.

3 Philippe Legrain, *Open World: The Truth About Globalisation,* London: Abacus, 2002, p. 108.

4 By contrast, though you might measure the number of people who share an idea, you wouldn't measure the idea itself.

5 'China's Growing Pollution Reaches U.S', 28 July 2006, **http://abcnews.go.com.**

6 *The Times,* 29 July 2006.

7 Victor Keegan, 'Virtual worlds and second lives', *Prospect,* April 2007, p. 51.

8 *Global Innovation Outlook* 2.0, IBM, 2005.

9 Victor Keegan, 'Virtual worlds and second lives', *Prospect,* April 2007, p. 51.

10 *The Times,* 18 June 2007.

11 See chapter 4 – Will the gap between the richest and the poorest countries narrow?

12 Henrik Urdal, 'A Clash of Generations? Youth Bulges and Political Violence', *International Studies Quarterly,* 50, 2006, pp. 607–629.

CHAPTER 2
HOW FAST WILL THE GLOBAL ECONOMY GROW?
THE STORY SO FAR

- 'The world economy is in the midst of an extraordinary purple patch'
- There has been an enormous increase in the global supply of labour
- The world has become flush with money
- Global communications have improved
- The global economy is now better managed
- So how should we understand today's 'purple patch' of global economic growth?

'The world economy is in the midst of an extraordinary purple patch', the International Monetary Fund (IMF) noted in 2006.[1] Global economic growth was significantly above average for the third year in a row. The trend is expected to continue till at least 2008 (see chart below).

Real GDP growth (%), 1960–2005

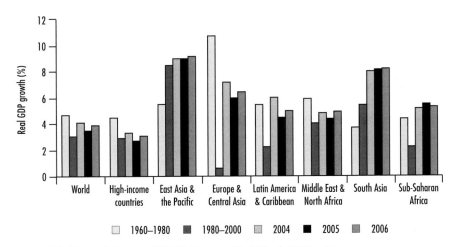

Source: *Global Economic Prospects 2007*, Washington: World Bank, 2007, p. 3.
Note: GDP is measured in dollars, at 2000 prices and market exchange rates. If GDP is measured at 2000 PPP (purchasing power parity) weights (i.e. using an exchange rate which means that buying a basket of products costs roughly the same wherever in the world it is bought) rates of growth would be higher – e.g. 5.1% for the global economy in 2006.

This growth has benefited lots of people — in China and India especially millions have escaped extreme poverty.[2] But before cheering, it's worth noting some big caveats.

- *This stellar performance is still not as good as 1960 to 1980*, before today's globalisation took off. East and South Asia and sub-Saharan Africa are doing distinctly better than in the earlier period.

  But the 'high-income countries', 'Europe and Central Asia' and 'the Middle East and North Africa' are doing less well. South America is much the same.

- *Economic growth has not kept up with population growth in much of the world.* Incomes per head, which really count, have crawled along at a slower rate, particularly in Africa, Latin America, and South and East Asia (see table below).

  In most of Africa per capita incomes actually fell between 1980 and 1995. Though they have recovered since, they are still rising at a modest pace.

- *The gap between top and bottom incomes has widened*, both across the globe and within most countries.

  At the same time, as we highlight in chapter 4, there appears to have been a slight bunching of incomes around the middle. Economic growth is a rising tide that lifts luxury yachts.

Per capita GDP growth (%) in selected regions, 1960–2004

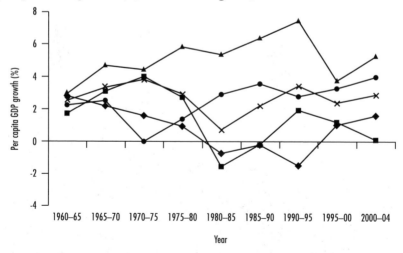

Source: *Trade and Development Report, 2006*, New York & Geneva: UNCTAD, 2006, p. 47.

With these caveats in mind, four developments have transformed the world economy in the past 20 years.

The first has been the enormous increase in the global supply of labour. Population growth has enlarged the planet's workforce. The opening up particularly of China, India and the former communist bloc has made available to the world labour that was once shut behind national borders.

The fall of the Berlin Wall, for example, was followed by reforms that brought hundreds of millions of workers into the international economy. Dismantling trade and other barriers has enabled low-cost workers to pour into Chinese factories at wages below those in the West. Rich countries have outsourced to India, which is beginning to outsource to its Asian neighbours and Africa.

> 'The planet has become awash with cheap labour'

According to the International Monetary Fund (IMF), bringing these new sources of labour into the market economy has effectively *quadrupled* the global labour force in the last quarter of a century.[3]

The planet has become awash with cheap labour, which has helped to fragment the production process. Producers are splitting the supply chain into smaller and smaller units, locating each in the area of the world with strongest competitive advantage.

A country can make a small part and ship it abroad, where it can be included in a larger component. The component may then be sent to a third country to be assembled in the finished product. Developing countries no longer need to build a whole factory to join a global supply chain.

Cheap labour has combined with the over-supply of products to keep prices down. From 1992 to 2002 a 40% rise in the volume of cooking appliances sold worldwide lifted the value of sales by just 8%.[4] The average prices of shoes and clothing in the United States fell by 10% between 1995 and 2005.[5]

With much the same happening for many other products, the lid has remained reasonably tight on inflation as the global economy has surged ahead.

Secondly, the world has become flush with money. This is the culmination of a long story.

It began with the 1971 break in the dollar's link with gold. Instead of paying its debts by selling exports and earning gold, America promised to meet its obligations in the form of US Treasury bills – government-backed IOUs that pay interest.

Broadly, if the United States ran a trade deficit before 1971, it could borrow money to finance its excess imports only so long as it had enough gold to repay the loans. Issuing IOUs has enabled the US to run up much larger deficits – 'Don't worry, we can't pay now but we'll find the money later.'

The government can effectively print money to pay for its imports. Because the American economy is so large, this has increased the global supply of money by a massive amount. Today the US imports half as much again as it exports.[6]

Abandoning gold was followed by the liberalisation of financial markets in the 1980s. Money could flow much more easily from economies with a surplus to countries that wanted to borrow. Global financial flows have never been greater.

In 1985 companies invested a mere $50 billion in factories, equipment and offices abroad: by 2000 this foreign direct investment came to $1.3 trillion. Americans' transactions of shares and bonds with foreigners soared from 4% of US GDP in 1980 to 230% in 1999.[7]

In particular, liberalisation brought lighter regulation of financial markets and encouraged more competition. Both have produced a host of new financial instruments. Many of these instruments involve leveraging large loans for relatively small down payments.

For instance, you might buy an option to purchase so many tons of coffee at a given price in six months' time. Your down payment could be the interest on the option. If the price of coffee rises above the agreed selling price, you could sell the option for a profit.

For relatively small interest payments, you might make a killing – or of course, if the price falls, a loss. In a similar vein, private equity firms borrow large sums to buy a company, turn it round and sell it off at a profit.

These sorts of devices have vastly increased the liquidity of the financial system. Outstanding credit derivatives, a form of insurance against a loan default, increased from $12 trillion worldwide in 2005 to $26 trillion in 2006.[8]

Money is at the heart of modern economies as never before. Its increased availability has brought many benefits.

It has allowed companies to invest in China, India and other emerging economies. It has enabled the United States to borrow vast sums – some $850 billion in 2006[9] – to pay for imports the country could not otherwise afford, creating a market for new factories in China and elsewhere. The world is far richer than it would otherwise have been.

But there has been a cost. At the heart of finance is speculation – people make a bet on shares, commodity prices or building a factory. This makes the whole system volatile.

Investors may pile into stock markets, as they did in the late 1990s. Markets soar. Then shares come crashing down when buyers realise that profits won't be as big as they had hoped.

Are we now on the threshold of another bubble? One view stresses how China's army of cheap labour has kept down inflation. As a result, the US Federal Reserve and other central banks have been holding interest rates at historically low levels.

In particular, the bursting of the dotcom bubble and the 9/11 terrorist attacks encouraged this cheap money – 'make it easy to borrow', central bankers thought, 'and the world won't plunge into recession'.

Money has been so cheap that American consumers have been having the time of their lives. They have bought Asian imports, supporting rapid economic growth in the region and pushing up the price of oil.

A tide of money has poured round the world – far more than can be invested sensibly in new factories and the like. So the money has been gushing into property, the world's stock exchanges and speculation based on commodity prices.

An alternative view is that the world had a savings glut. Oil exporters can't spend all the revenue generated by higher oil prices and are feeding their excess income into the global financial system.

At the same time, the Chinese are saving some 40% of their income, but are not allowed to invest in foreign assets. Many of their savings are held by the banks, which channel the funds to the rest of the world by buying foreign currency.

High levels of savings have kept down interest rates. This has encouraged borrowing, which has fuelled the inflation in house and other asset prices. Often the borrowing has been unwise.

On either view, concerns have been mounting that rising stock markets and higher house prices round the world are unsustainable. Were crashing stock markets in summer 2007 a wake-up call? Is the world due for another 'correction', akin to the 1997 crisis in Asia or the start-of-the-century slump in share prices?

The third major development has been the improvement in global communications. According to Market Intelligence Centre, the number of mobile phone subscribers worldwide hit 2.3 billion in 2006 and is expected to climb to 3.3 billion by 2011.[10]

> 'Mobile phone subscribers worldwide hit 2.3 billion in 2006'

Mobile phone users in Shanghai sent over 180 million text messages in a mere two days to celebrate the 2006 New Year.[11]

Add in the growth of Internet users (from 45.1 million in 1995 to an estimated 1.36 billion in 2007[12]), the development of Internet telephony (which is bringing video phones and slashing the cost of calls) and you have an unprecedented degree of global connectivity.

Information, ideas and fashions are spreading at breakneck speed. The result? Numerous opportunities are being created to improve efficiency.

As just one example, Tesco uses the latest techniques in film animation like Shrek to e-mail virtual samples between designers and buyers in the UK, and manufacturers 6000 miles away. This chops out the four-week delay in physically moving clothing samples backwards and forwards.[13]

Fourthly, in some respects the global economy is now better managed. It has become the norm for central bankers to set targets for inflation and use interest rates to achieve them.

By restraining prices, the world's abundance of cheap labour has enabled bankers to set their targets and gain credibility in meeting them without having to raise interest rates to politically difficult levels. A global framework, in effect, for managing inflation has begun to take root.

This framework has been key to the rediscovery of active demand management. Central banks and governments use interest rates and other tools to avert recessions, minimise unemployment and keep economies growing as close as possible to their long-run productive potential.

Much could still be done to improve economic management, but the widespread acceptance of some basic tools has made it easier for the global economy to weather shocks like 9/11 when they occur.

So how should we understand the 'purple patch' of global economic growth? Optimists wonder if the flood of cheap labour, the liquidity of the financial system, technological advance and better economic management are combining to usher in a 'long boom' of growth that will outdo the last quarter of the twentieth century.

Pessimists foresee all sorts of shocks that could push us off track. Who is more likely to be right?

1   *World Economic Outlook April 2006*, Washington: IMF, 2006, p. xi.
2   See for example Martin Wolf, *Why Globalization Works*, New Haven: Yale, 2004, pp. 157–163.
3   *World Economic Outlook April 2007*, Washington: IMF, 2007, p. 162.
4   Theo Nichols & Surham Cam, 'The World of White Goods – Markets, Industry Structure and Dynamics' in Theo Nichols & Surham Cam (eds.), *Labour in a Global World*, Basingstoke: Palgrave, 2005, p. 5.
5   'From T-shirts to T-bonds', *The Economist*, 30 July 2005.
6   Ann Pettifor, *The Coming First World Debt Crisis*, Basingstoke: Palgrave, 2006, p. 43.
7   Philippe Legrain, *Open World: The Trust About Globalisation*, London: Abacus, 2002, pp. 108–110.
8   Global Financial Stability Report. Market Developments and Issues, Washington: IMF, 2007, p. 50.
9   *Global Financial Stability Report. Market Developments and Issues*, Washington: IMF, 2007, p. 15.
10 'Global Mobile Phone Subscribers Expected to Reach 3.3 Billion by 2011', 31 January 2007, **http://mic.iii.org.**
11 'Festive text messages become new tradition', 5 January 2006, **http://www.chinadaily.com.**
12 'Internet User Forecast by Country', **http://www.etforecasts.com.**
13 *The World in 2010 and Beyond. BLU St. George's House Consultation, 7–8 September 2005 – Summary*, BLU, 2005, p. 4.

HOW FAST WILL THE GLOBAL ECONOMY GROW? WHAT WILL SHAPE THE NEXT 20 YEARS?

- Global demand will be a key driver
- Supply bottlenecks will be a limited constraint
- Resources will be used with greater efficiency
- Financial imbalances are unlikely to cause a major upheaval
- The main risk to the global economy is a series of crises

Global demand will be a key driver. Increased trade over the past 20 years has fed economic growth by raising demand. Entering the market economy has given low-cost workers more to spend.

At the same time, cheap labour has depressed prices. This has allowed every consumer dollar to buy more products, boosting output. Trade has created wealth.

If there are no economic shocks, demand is likely to continue to grow robustly. The World Bank expects the global middle class – roughly people with per capita incomes between the average of Brazil and Italy – to double by 2030, reaching more than a billion.

Nearly all this growth will be in developing countries, notably China and India.[1] As a result, these countries won't need to rely so heavily on exports to propel their economies. Their businesses will thrive by selling to expanding home markets.

These markets will also suck in imports from rich nations, giving the advanced economies a fillip.

But will new trade barriers punch a hole in this rosy scenario? Despite cutting trade restrictions over the past 20 years, the current regime has wobbly legs. Poorer countries struggle to export their farm products to the protected markets of Europe and North America, while a variety of rules makes it hard for them to support their infant industries and diversify.

Rich nations complain about lack of access to emerging markets in Asia, particularly for financial products. Fears are widespread that the United States especially will pull down the shutters on cheap manufacturing imports to protect its workers.

Protectionist pressures in the United States are indeed strong, and growing. Many in Congress are angry with China for, as they see it:

- threatening US jobs by undervaluing its currency;
- stealing American intellectual property;
- closing its markets to US financial institutions;
- banning imports of US beef;
- deploying a host of 'unfair trade practices' to sustain its $232 billion trade surplus.

Add in suppressing human rights and developing long-range missiles that could hit the United States, and you have a potent anti-China trade lobby.[2]

Yet several factors will work against greater protectionism:

- *Rich countries could face a series of legal challenges to their farm subsidies* under the World Trade Organization (WTO) rules, if the 'Doha' round of trade negotiations collapses. Europe and the US may want to keep negotiating to avoid this.
- *The US government will face pressure to get concessions on financial services.* Advancing the cause of these interests, which are very important to the American economy, may keep the government plugged into the WTO process.
- *Technology has done more than freer trade to lower the rich world's blue-collar wages.* That seems to be the consensus of academic research.[3] Liberalising trade may actually improve pay by forcing companies to raise productivity, which lifts wages.

  If this research continues to be confirmed, protectionism might seem increasingly unattractive: why face all the disadvantages if there are few benefits?

- *Might protectionist pressures in agriculture weaken?* If farmers in Europe, North America and elsewhere move heavily into biofuels, as some have started to do, less land would be available for food.[4] Tighter food markets would reduce European and American farmers' dependence on subsidies.

Here are two possibilities. The first is that WTO-led trade liberalisation will continue, albeit at a slow and faltering pace.

The US will take the heat out of its protectionist debate through a series of symbolic measures. High-profile initiatives to limit some imports will be celebrated in the press, but the small print will limit their impact. A few industries may get genuine protection for a limited period, provided they show that they are adjusting to a more open regime.

Alternatively, WTO-led liberalisation will stall for a period and then resume. If the Doha round fails, for example, countries would reach bilateral agreements, as they have increasingly been doing.

But they would be aware of the disadvantages:

- developing nations would struggle to prize open the rich economies because they would be acting individually rather than together;
- bilateral agreements would discriminate against third parties, who might have sold the product more cheaply if the playing field had been level;
- multinationals would find the sheer number of agreements a logistical nightmare.

The clincher could be regional agreements in Asia, which would arouse rich country fears that they will be shut out. In time, America and Europe would come running back to the WTO.

Will rising demand face bottlenecks in supply? There is a fear that demand will grow faster than the ability to meet it – with at least three possible constraints:

> '230 million Chinese could migrate from the countryside to the towns in 10 years'

Tight labour supply is the first. Wages are rising quite sharply in China and India, for example. Does this herald labour shortages? The population is also ageing in the global North, which means that fewer people could be available to work in rich nations.

Yet it is hard to see the recent four-fold expansion of the global labour force turning into a general scarcity – for several reasons:

- *China has a queue as long as the Great Wall waiting to climb the skills ladder.* Firms are moving west to draw on the vast reserves of labour still in the countryside.

    These workers start in low-skilled jobs. Then, as they get more skilled, they or their children shift into more demanding occupations.

    Goldman Sachs expects 230 million Chinese to migrate from the countryside to the towns over the next 10 years.[5]
- *The reservoir of cheap labour in other countries is potentially huge.* India could have 300 million ready to move.[6] Plenty of labour is available elsewhere in Asia and Africa.

The worldwide supply of youth labour is at least 400 million – young people who are unemployed, discouraged from seeking work (because jobs don't exist), or who earn less than the equivalent of $2 a day and would readily move into higher paid 'market' jobs.[7]

- *The world's workforce will be better educated.* In 1960, 30 million students were enrolled in higher education worldwide. The number had jumped to 115 million in 2004.[8]

 With Asia leading the way, the total will continue to mount. Higher skills will support more sophisticated processes and products.

- *The global North will find ways to ease its labour shortages,* caused by an ageing population. As we discuss in chapter 6, immigration could well increase, attracted by vacant jobs. Later retirement is likely, with Britain and other countries now planning to phase this in.

Raw materials shortages could be a second constraint. Oil is the most obvious but, as we argue in chapter 13, reserves are likely to keep growing over the next 20 years, gas supplies will be plentiful and coal will eventually become cleaner. If oil prices shoot higher, renewable alternatives and conservation will become more attractive.

The same principles apply to other raw materials. Though possibly disruptive in the short term, in the long run higher prices would encourage greater efficiency of use, the recycling of worn-out products and the search for alternatives.

Spikes in commodity prices will remain part of economic life, with some sectors especially hard hit. But it is interesting that the global economy has grown particularly fast just as oil prices (and the price of other commodities) have reached record highs. Resource squeezes are unlikely to derail growth over the long term.

Pressure on ecosystems will be a mounting constraint. The UN's Millennium Ecosystem Assessment found that two-thirds of the benefits that humans obtain from ecosystems were coming from ecosystems which were being degraded or used unsustainably.

For example, 5–20% of the world's freshwater use exceeds long-term sustainable supply.[9] Companies will face tighter water supplies and tougher regulations when they mine raw materials in areas where ecosystems are fragile.

With tourism becoming the world's largest employer, businesses will be expected to manage ecosystems with ever more care. Environmental concerns will keep pushing up costs, but these rises will continue to be incremental, while new technologies and processes should enable firms to manage ecosystems better.[10]

Resources will be used with greater efficiency – a third factor supporting economic growth. In particular, global productivity – the value added per hour worked – will continue to rise.

Developing countries will improve existing technologies and develop their own, as they are already doing. Taiwan has become a world centre for the semiconductor industry, while Korea is a leader in consumer electronics and automobiles, as well as in semiconductors.

By investing in higher education and attracting foreign research and development (R & D), countries like China and India will move into higher-value products and become world beaters in many of them.

The rising value of each worker's output will spur on the global economy by supporting higher wages. These higher incomes will increase the consumption of other products, giving a further push to economic growth.

Yet compared to the rich countries, pay will remain low. So as China and other emerging economies extend their reach up the value chain, the lower prices that we have seen in clothing and other low-end manufactures will be repeated for more sophisticated goods and services.

Even if prices of textiles and the like do not keep falling, the prices of computers, cars, travel advice and some banking services will. Consumers will have more in their accounts to spend on other goods.

The value added by rich-country workers will also continue to increase. Though others would disagree, Goldman Sachs's Andrew Tilton argues that the US productivity boom is far from over.

Since the mid 1990s, US productivity has surged by an average of 2.9% a year, the best decade since the 1960s. This has been driven by heavy investment in information technologies, plus more recent improvements in organisation and processes to exploit these technologies.

America's productivity spurt should last a lot longer.

- Continuing, rapid innovation in the IT industry suggests that this part of the equation has much more to contribute.
- History teaches that it takes decades for companies to tap the full potential of major, 'disruptive' technological improvements.
- In the long term, nanotechnology, biotechnology and brain sciences could prove just as disruptive as IT, especially as these four technologies combine together.[11]

Asia will scale the value ladder, but rich nations will harness the latest technologies to keep ahead. The whole world will become wealthier.

Will financial imbalances cause a major upheaval? In 2006 the US had an estimated current account deficit of $848 billion, 6.4% of GDP.[12] In other words, every day of the year it was borrowing more than $2 billion to pay for imports that were not financed by earnings from exports. Many think that this is unsustainable. There are two questions.

The first is a general one about what is happening to the world economy. Is there, as we have noted, a money glut caused by excessively low interest rates, or is there a savings glut because oil exporters and China cannot spend all their earnings?[13]

If there is a money glut, the world could face a period of rising inflation, followed by much higher interest rates to get inflation under control. The global economy would slow dramatically.

> 'In 2006 the US borrowed over $2 billion a day to pay for imports'

This would make it almost impossible for the US to reduce its current account deficit by boosting exports. The dollar might crash as investors lost confidence. Devalued dollars would buy fewer imports, damaging exporters in the rest of the world and prolonging a possible world recession.

But if there is a savings glut, the excess savings will eventually be spent – oil exporters will build more infrastructure and Chinese households will probably be allowed gradually to invest in expanding businesses overseas.

Instead of the world economy grinding to a halt for a period, its productive capacity would actually grow. Managing the US trade deficit would be much easier.

At present, the savings glut view seems more likely. Wages in the United States are not roaring ahead, which is what one would expect if the country was entering a period of inflation. Though prices have crept up, cheap Asian imports and a fairly tight monetary policy seem to be keeping prices reasonably stable.[14]

Circumstances today seem very different to the late 1970s, when oil prices last rocketed and inflation soared.

The second question is how well America's trade deficit can be managed till it is significantly reduced. The deficit is currently financed mostly with loans from China. Some commentators fear that China may switch these loans to other countries, causing the dollar to nosedive.

Though this must be a possibility, at present it seems highly unlikely. China would have much to lose by moving rapidly out of dollars. A falling dollar would reduce the value of its remaining US holdings.

Significantly, $300 billion of China's foreign currency is owned by households and businesses. A marked drop in the value of these holdings would leave companies and individuals with fewer assets to back their loans. Corporate credit ratings would suffer, undermining confidence.[15]

This is one reason why China is unlikely to revalue its currency sharply, which would effectively devalue the dollar. The risks would be too great. Instead, China seems to be allowing its currency to appreciate gently and is slowly reducing the proportion of its overseas holdings in dollars.

This gently, gently approach, typical of China, bodes well for stability in the long run.

So what are the main risks to the global economy? Possibilities range from another 9/11, to upheavals in the Middle East, to Russia's use of the 'energy weapon', to a clash between China and the United States. But if you look at the next 20 years as a whole, these sorts of event – though disruptive at the time – would be unlikely to blow the economy off course completely.

> 'China's gently, gently approach to currency bodes well for stability in the long run'

In economic terms, the world recovered pretty quickly after 9/11. The global economy has weathered a series of storms in the Middle East. Russia might conceivably throttle gas supplies to Europe, but not if this damaged its economy for long. The Chinese and American economies are so interdependent that if a military conflict occurred (over Taiwan for example), they would be likely to call a rapid halt to it:

Might a flu pandemic be a serious risk? This is widely expected, now that Avian flu (the H5N1 virus) is firmly entrenched among birds in Asia. The World Health Organization believes that there is a serious risk that the virus will spread from birds to humans and then between humans.

The 1918–19 'Spanish flu' pandemic killed at least 40 million people, twice as many as died in the First World War.[16]

Though 'Spanish flu' was exceptional, high death rates from a new pandemic are entirely possible.

- Infectious diseases can spread more quickly now that half the world's population live cheek by jowl in urban areas and more people travel across the globe – they made over 800 million journeys in 2006.[17]
- Developing an effective vaccine is difficult when you cannot know in advance the exact strain of virus that will emerge.
- Current plans to contain the disease may well not work, though they could buy time.[18]

A 2005 assessment by the US Congressional Budget Office concluded that in a severe flu pandemic, equivalent to 1918-19, roughly 90 million people would become sick in the United States and 2 million would lose their lives.

Real GDP would be 5% lower over the subsequent year than if the pandemic had not taken place. That would be 'comparable to the effect of a typical business-cycle recession in the United States during the period since World War II'.[19]

Allow for comparable effects round the world, and the global economy would receive a severe jolt, but not a mortal blow. On a 'mild scenario', the effects would be much less.

Climate change is a larger threat. Unfortunately perhaps, the risk here is not that measures to tackle global warming will slow economic growth. Such an outcome seems highly unlikely, as we discuss in chapter 12.

Rich-world consumers remain reluctant to change lifestyles to mitigate climate change – talk to US motorists about higher fuel prices! This reluctance is even stronger in the developing world, where material possessions matter a lot (cars and 'white' goods are still relatively scarce) and the environment has a lower priority for many people than in the West. Faced with consumer resistance, governments are unlikely to adopt measures that dampen the economy.

More likely is that storms, droughts and other climatic disturbances will intensify. They will cause more and more damage, and raise the costs of disaster-relief and insurance.

Over the next 20 years, these costs will be an increasing drag on the world economy, but not enough to change its trajectory.

Crises in China and India could be an even bigger risk because these countries now play such a large part in the world's economic system.

China and India need to drive their economies forward to provide jobs for their fast-growing populations and meet rising middle-class aspirations. But as we discuss in chapter 3, there is a real danger that economic growth will hit the buffer of environmental degradation. (This is where climate change *is* a risk.)

Will their governments be able both to sustain rapid growth and tame its environmental effects? Many fear not. Governments could be squeezed between environmental protests on the one hand ('Clean up the water!' 'Our children are dying from air pollution') and economic demands on the other ('We want jobs!' 'Where are the schools and hospitals?' 'Help us build better homes!').

Will political support ebb away, leaving governments increasingly precarious? And in either country (or both), might instability undermine growth, stalling the global economy?

Might the greatest risk be several crises in quick succession, such as the disruption of oil supplies in the Middle East, rapidly followed by another 9/11, with a major upheaval in China soon after? The world is so connected and many issues are so linked that one crisis could precipitate another.

1   *Global Economic Prospects 2007*, Washington: World Bank, 2007, p. 73.
2   Irwin Steizer, 'Can big rivals talk their way out of trouble?' *The Times*, 28 May 2007.
3   Some of this literature is referred to by Jagdish Bhagwati, *In Defense of Globalization*, Oxford: OUP, 2004, pp. 123–127.
4   The size of the impact on agriculture would partly depend on how much additional land was brought into cultivation by clearing forests, a major concern for a host of environmental reasons.
5   Jim O'Neill, Sun Bae Kim & Mike Buchanan, 'Globalisation and Disinflation – Can Anyone Else "Do a China"?' *Global Economics Paper No. 147*, London: Goldman Sachs, 2006, p. 6.
6   David Smith, *The Dragon and the Elephant*, London: Profile Books, 2007, p. 148.
7   *Global Employment Trends for Youth*, Geneva: ILO, 2006, p. 9.
8   Joachim Tres, 'Higher Education in the World 2007', 23 February 2006, **http://web.guni2005.upc.es.**
9   Millennium Ecosystem Assessment, *Ecosystems and Human Well-Being. Opportunities and Challenges for Business and Industry*, Washington, DC: World Resources Institute, 2005, pp. 2, 10.
10 Millennium Ecosystem Assessment, *Ecosystems and Human Well-Being. Opportunities and Challenges for Business and Industry*, Washington, DC: World Resources Institute, 2005, pp. 24–29.
11 This third point is not made by Tilton, but the rest of these two paragraphs is based on a resume of his argument by Gary Duncan, 'A productivity cure for America's blues', *The Times*, 7 August 2006.
12 *Global Financial Stability Report*. Market Developments and Issues, Washington: IMF, 2007, p. 15.
13 The terms 'money glut' and 'savings glut' were used by Martin Wolf in 'Villains and victims of global capital flows', *Financial Times*, 13 June 2007.
14 This was the conclusion of a detailed study of global inflation data contained in a UBS report, 'Crisis, what crisis', 12 June 2007, summarised by David Smith, 'Boom times and doom mongers', *The Sunday Times*, 17 June 2007.
15 Laixiang Sun, 'China in International Trade: Achievements and Future Challenges', paper presented to *Goodenough/ESRC Conference on China and Globalisation*, Goodenough College, London, 11 May 2007.
16 World Health Organization, 'Avian flu frequently asked questions', 5 December 2005, **http://www.who.int.**
17 World Health Organization, 'International Travel and Health 2007', 1 January 2007, **http:/www.who.int.**
18 Christina Mills et al., 'Pandemic Influenza: Risk of Multiple Introductions and the Need to Prepare for Them', PLoS Medicine, 21 February 2006, **http://medicine.plosjournals.org.**
19 *A Potential Influenza Pandemic: Possible Macroeconomic Effects and Policy Issues*, Washington: Congressional Budget Office, 2005, pp. 1–2.

HOW FAST WILL THE GLOBAL ECONOMY GROW? WHAT MIGHT BE THE IMPLICATIONS?

- The World Bank is fairly optimistic
- Poor people will continue to be left behind
- Tackling the income gap will remain an urgent priority

The World Bank has produced a fairly optimistic scenario for the period up to 2030.[1] In view of what we have said, the scenario seems sensible, though slightly hopeful. It relies on China and India maintaining healthy rates of economic growth, for example.

The Bank's 'baseline' projection is for the world economy to more than double between 2005 and 2030, growing from $35 trillion to $75 trillion. Global growth would be slightly faster than in the previous 25 years.

> 'The world economy could more than double between 2005 and 2030'

With accelerating growth, developing countries would triple output from $8 trillion to $24.3 trillion, and increase their global share from 23% to 33%.

But growth rates would fall marginally in the developed economies, mainly due to their ageing populations.

On a purchasing power parity (PPP) basis, countries' average incomes per head would rise across the board:

- the income of an average developing-country resident would rise from $4,800 to $12,200 in today's prices;
- in rich countries, the average income would climb from $29,700 to $54,000;
- instead of receiving 16% of the average rich-world income, the average developing-country person would get 23%;
- Chinese incomes would leap from 19% of the average level in rich nations to 42%, reaching close to the poorest of today's high-income economies;
- sub-Saharan Africa would fall further adrift, and Latin America would see little if any convergence.

So, if you want to imagine what the world will be like in 2030, think what it would mean for people to increase their incomes by nearly or more than double. This has roughly happened in the past 25 years. What difference has it made for someone in a developing country or in a rich one?

What would it mean for this to happen again? How might fashions, entertainment, travel and other aspects of life change? With millions more tourists from Asia, for example, what would it be like to visit the Pyramids?

Poor people would continue to be left behind. This is the most urgent message from the World Bank's projections.

Under its 'baseline' scenario, sub-Saharan Africa would miss by miles the world's 'millennium' target of cutting the proportion of the global population in extreme poverty to just under 14% by 2015. The target would be met for the world as a whole, but not for Africa. The region would fail to reach the target even by 2030.[2]

Economically, all the pressures will be to widen the gap between top and bottom incomes within countries, despite the possibility of greater bunching round the middle, noted in chapter 4.

Masses of cheap labour worldwide will tend to hold down wages at the bottom end of national economies. If pay rose rapidly, organisations would simply outsource to cheaper parts of the world.

At the top end, a global market for talent will enable people with the best skills to command higher and higher salaries. The demand for these skills will continue to rise as new high-value activities emerge, not just in the global North but increasingly in the South as well.

If people in the middle of the income range improve their skills, more workers would compete for better-paid jobs, which would moderate salary pressures at the higher end. But expanding global demand for the best skills, which by definition will be in short supply, will continue to push up earnings at the pinnacle.

Tackling the income gap will remain an urgent priority. Strong evidence exists that the size of this gap really matters.

A wide gap damages the confidence of people at the bottom, undermines their self-esteem, leaves them feeling powerless and produces frustration. Individuals are more likely to feel that others disrespect them and resort to violence. They also tend to feel anxious and isolated. All this gives rise to stress, which often leads to ill health.

Egalitarian societies, on the other hand, appear to be more cohesive and cooperative.[3]

The world is doing a reasonable job of increasing wealth: will it find politically acceptable ways to spread this wealth more evenly?

1 *Global Economic Prospects 2007*, Washington: World Bank, 2007, pp. 38–42.
2 *Global Economic Prospects 2007*, Washington: World Bank, 2007, p. 59.
3 Some of this evidence is summarised by Richard G. Wilkinson, *Mind the Gap: Hierarchies, Health and Human Evolution*, London: Weidenfeld, 2000 and Michael Marmot, *Status Syndrome*, London: Bloomsbury, 2004.

CHAPTER 3
WILL THE EMERGING ECONOMIES CATCH UP WITH THE WEST?
THE STORY SO FAR

- The global balance of power is changing
- Emerging economies had favourable circumstances before growth took off
- The state has strategically led development in most of these economies
- Countries have followed different development paths
- Many emerging economies have been growing faster than rich ones
- Their experiences have helped to shape ideas about development

How profoundly will the global balance of power change? Today's rich nations are increasingly having to share power with the 'emerging economies'. These are developing countries that are expanding their markets, have experienced rapid economic growth and offer lucrative, if sometimes risky, investment opportunities.

They include many of the once-communist countries in Europe and the former Soviet Union, Latin American nations like Brazil and Mexico, Asian 'tigers' such as Korea that are chasing Japan up the economic ladder, Malaysia and Singapore, and the big beasts, China and India.

This is a hugely diverse group. What generalisations can we make about these countries' economic growth? Have they got the capacity to catch up with the rich world? How big a threat do they pose to Europe and North America? Our bird's eye view focuses mainly on Asia, and on China and India in particular.

Most of these economies had favourable circumstances before growth took off. For example:

- *Geographical features helped.* Unlike poor landlocked countries such as Bolivia, Burundi and Kyrgyzstan, China's long coastline has kept down transport costs. The median landlocked country has transport costs 55% higher than the median coastal economy.[1]
- *Food production per head has been higher in Asia than Africa in recent decades,* thanks partly to the famous Green Revolution. 'This performance has provided a platform for Asia's extraordinary growth.'[2]

- *80% of China's workforce (mainly in the countryside) did not depend on the state.* They poured into new factories without the government having to release workers by reforming the over-manned public sector.

    Russia, by contrast, had very few workers outside state-owned farms and other state organisations. To shake out surplus labour and make it available to the market sector, the government privatised faster than was sensible.[3]

- *Numbers in education tended to be larger* than in countries that have remained poor. By 1960, enrolment in secondary education was considerably higher in East Asia than most of sub-Saharan Africa. These countries also had more scientific and technical manpower by the mid 1960s.[4]

    The Indian Institutes of Technology (IIT) have turned out high-quality graduates since the late 1940s. Many of them worked abroad – a third of the engineers in Silicon Valley are Indians. By providing firms that were outsourcing with information and contacts in India, expatriates helped kick-start India's IT industry. Two-thirds of IIT graduates now stay in India.[5]

The state has strategically led development in most of Asia's emerging economies. Governments have protected 'infant' industries till they could stand on their own feet. Sometimes they have given them export subsidies and other forms of support, allowing them to grow and achieve economies of scale. (China created Special Economic Zones for this purpose.)

Integration into the global economy has been sequential: sectors too weak to compete have been protected; protection and subsidies have then been withdrawn as sectors have become stronger.

Foreign investors have been required to transfer technology and train local workers: Malaysia's government-owned oil company, Petronas, is now in a position to train other developing countries.

Though they have opened their markets for long-term investment, China and India have restricted short-term capital flows to reduce instability. To an extent, fruits of growth have been shared with poorer regions.[6]

Market reforms have been introduced within this framework of state-led development. China announced its open-door policy in 1978 and gradually liberalised trade in the 1980s, as did Korea and other Asian countries. India began to loosen trade restrictions from the early 1990s, as did the former Soviet bloc countries. China, India and others have cautiously welcomed foreign investment.

Going much wider than trade, China replaced its communes with the 'household responsibility' system. Collective land was assigned to individual households who kept most of the proceeds.

State enterprises have been privatised – damagingly fast in Russia, very slowly in India, with China in between: since the late 1990s China has rapidly transferred small and medium-sized enterprises to their managers, but has moved in a more phased way to privatise larger ones.

Despite some commonalities, countries have followed different development pathways.
Some have relied on natural resources – including much of the Middle East, parts of Russia and large chunks of Latin America. But raw materials don't always translate into development. Exports of natural resources can push up the exchange rate, for example, making it harder for new manufacturing industries to compete with foreigners.

Most emerging economies have started with a 'complementing' model. They have contributed to multinationals' supply chains. Complementary relationships have been established with companies selling into rich markets, cutting costs of production.

Singapore, for instance, encouraged electronics firms to set up assembly plants; it next moved into the more sophisticated end of the industry, and then in the 1990s began to attract biomedical companies. China now manufactures a vast range of products for multinationals. India has followed a similar path, but in services.

As they have developed, some countries have moved towards a 'substituting' model. Rather than feeding the supply chains of foreign-owned companies, they have begun to establish multinationals that compete with foreigners in their own right.

In 2005, Hong Kong-based Li & Fung had over 24,000 employees in 40 countries and a turnover of more than US$8.5 billion.[7] Having generated exports mainly by its own rather than foreign companies,[8] India's fast-growing companies, like Infosys in software, Rambaxy in pharmaceuticals and Bajaj Auto in automobile components, are establishing a global presence.

Korea was exceptional in trying to leapfrog its forerunners and compete with them directly in chemical and heavy industries. These industries relied on integrated forms of production and depended on economies of scale, which – with Korea's small home market – could be obtained only through exports.

In the 1960s, using export subsidies and other forms of support, the Korean government actively promoted shipbuilding and other companies that would compete with the rich world.[9]

Japan caught up with the West through companies like Sony and Toyota that took on firms in Europe and North America. India and China hope to do the same.

India has some companies that are becoming a global force, but China is further behind. Processing and assembling imported components account for over half China's exports.[10] Yet these exports are dominated by foreign-owned companies, often Taiwanese.[11] How quickly will this change?

Many emerging economies have been growing faster than rich ones as a result of their development strategies, and this is illustrated in the table below.

But some countries like Mexico have been losing out to Asia's new economic powers. Having been ahead of the pack, their cheap labour is no longer a selling point – other countries are even cheaper – and they are struggling to find an alternative. They are getting squeezed between rich nations on the one hand and the newly emerging economies on the other.

As China and India bound ahead, might other countries find themselves in the same boat as Mexico?

GDP growth (%) in selected regions of the world, 1980–2006

Regions	1980–2000	2004	2005	2006
High income countries	2.9	3.3	2.7	3.1
East Asia & Pacific	8.5	9.0	9.0	9.2
China	n/a	10.1	10.2	10.4
Indonesia	n/a	5.1	5.6	5.5
South Asia	5.4	8.0	8.1	8.2
India	n/a	8.5	8.5	8.7
Europe & Central Asia	0.6	7.2	6.0	6.4
Poland	n/a	5.3	3.4	5.4
Russian Federation	n/a	7.2	6.4	6.8
Turkey	n/a	8.9	7.4	6.0
Latin America & the Caribbean	2.2	6.0	4.5	5.0
Argentina	n/a	9.0	9.2	7.7
Brazil	n/a	4.9	2.3	3.5
Mexico	n/a	4.4	3.0	4.5

Source: *Global Economic Prospects 2007: Managing the Next Wave of Globalisation*, Washington: World Bank, 2007, p. 3.

The experiences of emerging countries have helped to shape ideas about development. Three models have competed for influence.

The 'Washington Consensus' dominated much official thinking during the 1980s and 1990s. The World Bank and the IMF in particular argued that minimising the role of government, privatising state enterprises, liberalising trade and capital markets, and sweeping away red tape were the core policies needed to develop an economy.

A 'post-Washington Consensus' has gained ground since the late 1990s, partly as a result of the 1997 crisis. East Asia was badly hit by sudden outflows of capital. Currencies fell, investors called in their loans, massive bankruptcies

occurred and a currency crisis turned into a banking crisis, which extended to Russia, Argentina and Brazil.

Those who backed the 'Washington consensus' blamed 'crony capitalism' – banks had made too many unwise loans because they were too close to their borrowers. But supporters of state-led development argued that the sudden withdrawal of foreign capital illustrated the dangers of integrating into the global economy too closely too fast. Speculators could bring growth to a juddering halt.

After 1997 Korea introduced IMF-led market reforms, which included making bank loans to industry more arms-length. But these reforms seem to have been counter-productive. Corporate finance fell sharply, cutting investment, which in turn will make the economy less dynamic.[12]

The post-Washington Consensus calls for a more balanced approach. Market reform should be part of a broader package that recognises the limitations of markets. Economists like Joseph Stiglitz argue that democratic politics can prevent development, leaving the poor behind, damaging the environment and allowing corporations to flourish at the expense of individuals.[13]

Today, these views are widely shared, even within the IMF and World Bank. Disagreements focus on what sort of government action would correct market imperfections.

The 'Beijing Consensus' has now begun to emerge. This is a term – not originating in Beijing – for a number of ideas that reflect China's current approach to development.

First, innovation is key to long-term success. Letting technologies trickle down to catch-up countries will not be enough: emerging economies must develop their own.

> 'Will the Beijing Consensus become the new orthodoxy?'

Secondly, chaos is a constant in development but should be minimised. Addressing quality-of-life issues, like environmental sustainability, can help to do this. So can a step-by-step approach to political reform, since rapid democratisation may create instability.

Thirdly, states should follow their own paths to development, free from outside intervention.

Now widely debated, the Beijing Consensus is having a growing influence, especially in Africa. China is becoming more than a banker to Africa: it's a role model. Will the Beijing Consensus become the new orthodoxy?

1   Anthony J. Venables, 'Shifts in Economic Geography and their Causes', *CEP Discussion Paper No. 767*, London School of Economics Centre for Economic Performance, December 2006, p. 10.

2   Jeffrey Sachs, *The End of Poverty*, London: Penguin, 2005, p. 70.

3   Gang Fan, 'The Dual-Transformation of China: Past 20 Years and 50 Years Ahead' in Grzegorz W. Kolodko (ed.), *Emerging Market Economies. Globalization and Development*, Aldershot: Ashgate, 2003, p. 172.

4   Ha-Joon Chang, *The East Asian Development Experience: The Miracle, the Crisis and the Future*, London: Zed, 2006, pp. 148–152. Chang notes this within an argument that 'initial conditions' were relatively unimportant. But he fails to consider a number of the conditions discussed here.

5   David Smith, *The Dragon and the Elephant: China, India and the New World Order*, London: Profile, 2007, pp. 137–138.

6   These strategies have been summarised by Joseph Stiglitz, *Making Globalization Work*, London: Allen Lane, 2006, pp. 30–35.

7   **http://www.lifunggroup.com** (accessed 27 April 2007).

8   Prasenjit K. Basu, 'India and the Knowledge Economy: The "Stealth Miracle" is sustainable' in Prasenjit K. Basu et al (eds.), *India as a New Global Leader*, London: Foreign Policy Centre, 2005, p. 49.

9   Jang-Sup Shin, 'Substituting and Complementing Models of Economic Development in East Asia', *Global Economic Review*, 34(1), 2005, pp. 103–105.

10 *The Economist*, 31 March 2007.

11 88% of the high-tech products China exported in the mid 2000s were produced by either foreign joint ventures or wholly owned foreign enterprises. Kerry Brown, 'General Economic Development in China', paper presented to *Goodenough/ESRC conference on 'China and Globalisation'*, Goodenough College, London, 11 May 2007.

12 Ha-Joon Chang, The East Asian Development Experience: The Miracle, the Crisis and the Future, London: Zed, 2006, pp. 279–308.

13 Joseph Stiglitz, *Making Globalization Work*, London: Allen Lane, 2006.

WILL THE EMERGING ECONOMIES CATCH UP WITH THE WEST? WHAT WILL SHAPE THE NEXT 20 YEARS?

- Emerging countries will have plenty of scope to catch up with the rich
- One constraint will be social instability
- Another will be 'soft infrastructure'
- A third could be lack of sufficient knowledge
- A fourth constraint could be the environment

Emerging countries will have plenty of scope to catch up with the more developed ones, narrowing the gap between them in terms of average incomes per head.

Rural China and India will have huge surpluses of labour that can move from low-productivity agriculture to higher-productivity manufacturing and services.

As these workers climb the skills escalator, they will boost the size of the middle classes. China's middle class, for example, is expected to double to 40% of the population (568 million people) between 2003 and 2020.[1] This will provide a massive domestic market to support further development.

Investment will produce comparatively large returns because it tends to have a bigger impact in the early stages of development than later on. A single new road does far more to open up an area than an extra road within a dense network.

When developing countries invest they can leap from nowhere to state-of-the-art equipment, whereas leading economies get productivity gains more slowly: their investments often merely improve technology.

Emerging economies will continue to benefit from these early-stage advantages. Investment in technology is the life force of economic growth.

Adequate funds are likely to be available for investment, though the World Bank has put a question mark on this: might emerging economies have access to fewer savings as baby boomers in the rich countries retire, live off their savings rather add than to them, and switch to safer investments?[2]

More likely is that:

- later retirement will prolong the period during which older workers save;
- Asia's expanding middle classes will fill any savings hole left by the rich world;

■ persistent growth will make emerging markets less risky places to invest.

China has funded its development largely from domestic savings, Taiwanese capital and (to a smaller extent) foreign direct investment, which remains tightly controlled. There have been concerns about over-investment and the country is now becoming a major investor abroad. None of this suggests a future shortage of savings.

Some emerging countries are likely to gain economic momentum. True, extra investment may not boost incomes by as much as in the early phases. But the experience gained from each stage of development will support further advance.

Incomes, consumption patterns and production systems will slowly converge with rich nations, making it easier to borrow more sophisticated technologies. Growing home markets will offer economies of scale (potentially huge in China and India), which will encourage specialisation that can be turned into exports.[3]

Some countries may reach a point where they get increasing returns to investment. They may develop clusters of expertise that draw in more capital, which strengthens these clusters and in turn makes them even more attractive to investors. Bangalore's strength in IT is a good example.

The global economy is likely to keep growing, despite occasional hiccups, as discussed in chapter 2. This will provide a friendly context in which emerging countries can develop.

As these factors help emerging economies develop, social capacity will be increasingly important. Social capacity comprises factors that enable a country to realise its development potential – not just the quality of labour, but things like social stability, adapting to change and good policies.

Social capacity permits an economy to build new competitive strengths. These strengths can offset its declining advantage in cheap labour, allowing the country to climb the development ladder.

Four dimensions of social capacity will be pivotal. Will they put a cap on development?

One potential cap will be social stability. Commentators often point to the danger of social unrest, especially in China and India. But could the risk be even greater than they fear?

Mounting unemployment could be a problem. A number of emerging economies have drawn workers from low-productivity farming into higher-productivity manufacturing. The trouble is that these higher-productivity sectors create fewer jobs than low-productivity ones. The industrial sector becomes the main motor for productivity increases but not for job creation.[4]

'Employment in Chinese manufacturing actually fell between 1995 and 2002'

For example in China, despite the country's boom in exports, higher productivity in state-owned enterprises has contributed to an *overall fall* in the country's manufacturing employment, possibly from 98 million in 1995 to 83 million in 2002.[5]

More job losses are to come. China's domestic economy (which is much, much larger than its export sector) is notoriously inefficient. The government is opening it up slowly to foreign competition.[6] As it does so, productivity will rise, shaking out jobs.

India's service sector, which accounts for about half of the GDP, shot ahead at approximately 8% growth a year between 1985 and 2005, but grew jobs at less than 1%.[7] The number of jobs created for each unit of growth has declined substantially in almost all India's productive sectors, largely due to the capital intensive nature of development.[8]

Yet the working age population will continue to rise for several decades, and 60% of this demographic bulge will come in five of the poorest states.[9]

Improved productivity is great if it leads to higher incomes that are spent on labour-intensive activities, which create jobs. But strong competition between emerging economies, combined with large supplies of labour, are likely to moderate the increase in wages. Competition in consumer markets could squeeze profits. If earnings and profits rise quite slowly, might growth in demand fail to take up the jobs slack?

Between now and 2030, 8–10 million young people will enter the labour force annually both in China and India, and more women may want to work as well.[10]

'China has to create some 24 million new jobs a year for migrants leaving the countryside, for students leaving schools and colleges and for people left newly unemployed by the rationalisation of state-owned enterprises.'[11]

Will there be enough jobs for them all? Governments will be under escalating pressure to invest in job-creation schemes and other forms of support, especially in the poorer villages.

Middle-class demands will rise at the same time, however. China and India's middle classes will continue to expand rapidly. India's 40 million middle-class households — which typically contain five people, have a bank account and own a TV, fridge and a motorcycle or small car — are growing by about 10% a year.[12]

Aspiring households will press their governments to spend more on providing health care, cleaner streets, more reliable electricity, less air pollution and so on (all of which will create jobs, but nowhere near enough to absorb the growing labour force). China's middle classes worry about the costs of housing, education and health.

Will governments have enough resources to satisfy both the middle classes and the poor?

Compounding the problem will be the demographic shift. By 2025–30, urban China will see its elderly dependency ratio converge to levels seen in the more industrialised world. Hong Kong, Korea and Singapore will follow suit around 2030. Rural China and Thailand will come next between 2035 and 2040. Malaysia will follow closely in about 2045, and India, Indonesia and the Philippines will bring up the rear some time after 2050.[13]

In China, mandatory pension schemes cover only half the urban workforce (and far less in rural areas), self-funding accounts have been diverted to existing retirees and corrupt practices have come to light in some schemes. In addition, China's 'one child' policy is producing a generation of urban workers anxious about who will care for their ageing parents in the countryside – and who will pay.

Pension reform could include extending the coverage of mandatory schemes, and raising contributions or taxes to make good assets that have been lost from self-funded accounts.[14] This would leave less room to tax urban workers and use the proceeds to support the poor.

How will all these challenges be met? Over the next 20 years, China will face the herculean task of preventing unemployment, meeting the aspirations of its burgeoning middle class and making provision for the future. For a while, India will 'just' have to prevent unemployment and satisfy its expanding middle class.

Both countries will face these challenges as their rates of economic growth decline. If Chinese manufacturing exports, for example, kept forging ahead at their current pace, by 2012–14 every ship in the world could be involved in the China trade![15]

Of course, this won't happen. As economies grow, their rate of growth tails off – that's been the story of the rich nations. It is easier to add an extra $1–10 than $10–100.

Will the Chinese and Indian economies have become sufficiently large for slower growth to yield enough extra income to satisfy expectations all round? Or will a diminished rate of growth be inadequate to square the circle of unemployment, rising middle-class aspirations and (in China) an ageing population?

Could social unrest – already a problem in both countries[16] – become a serious threat? Might internal strains even cause China to break apart, as some fear?

'Soft infrastructure' could be a second cap on development. Emerging countries require the rule of law, secure property rights (including intellectual property), evenhanded treatment of all parties and transparent governance in both the public and private sectors.

These are often under-developed, which puts off investment:

- Weak legal systems can mean that the theft of intellectual property is rampant, so that multinationals have to be wary lest their technology, designs and processes are stolen.
- China's lax disclosure rules require listed companies to provide a bare minimum of information, which puts off foreign investors.
- Giving favours ('you're family') rather than transacting business on merit ('you've got the best qualifications') creates inefficiencies that can cost a country billions.

Transparency is at the heart of 'soft infrastructure' – and extends to politics. It enables people to be held to account, which checks abuses.

Some argue that authoritarian governments are best able to keep order and drive economic reform, advantages that outweigh their lack of transparency. India, for instance, has found it difficult to set up special economic zones (following China's example) because of protests from people who would lose their land. As a democracy, the government can't ride roughshod over the opposition.

While authoritarian politics may be helpful in the early stages of development, in the long run it cannot guarantee the transparency required by global capitalism. Democracy has a better chance of creating the checks and balances that transparency needs. One organ of the system can be overseen by another, and the whole edifice is then supervised by the voting public.

Creating 'soft infrastructure' may be a greater challenge than many suppose. As we will discuss in chapter 9, standards of transparency in rich nations are likely to rise. Emerging economies will be chasing countries that are rushing ahead.

Not joining the race would be expensive: global corporations might find that keeping corrupt officials sweet in the modernising world does mounting damage to their reputations in rich markets. This could deter investment.

Improving transparency usually involves an initial trade-off with stability. Political risk consultant, Ian Bremmer, argues that when a country moves from being politically closed to being more open it follows a J curve.

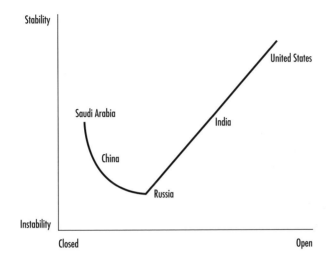

It descends the left of the J into more instability before rising up the right stroke to greater stability. As it climbs the right of the J, more openness and more stability go hand in hand.[17]

Chinese officials fear that if they were to introduce democracy quickly, disharmony would be so great – the dip of the J so deep – that the country might not cope. On one reading, they prefer a cautious, step-by-step approach: 'We'll allow the election of local government officials so long as they belong to the Communist Party, but we are not going any further yet.'

They hope that a little more openness can be combined with continuing stability, which will allow another small relaxation of controls later.

Whether China can steadily increase openness without a social earthquake (whether the J remains shallow) is one of the world's big uncertainties.

Might reducing 'corruption' follow a similar path? If the global economy requires increasing transparency, the incentives to reduce corruption – and move down the left of the J – will strengthen.

Yet what the West calls corruption in emerging countries is often a deep-seated mindset: individuals with ties to one another feel an obligation to support each other. Inevitably, this creates powerful vested interests.

So, cracking down on corruption could produce widespread resentment and lead to unrest. It's worth remembering that mounting complaints about corruption can reflect a feeling that corruption is not extensive enough! 'Other people are getting favours but I'm missing out.'

Which countries will successfully move through the dip in the J curve, ending up with less corruption and enhanced stability?

Insufficient knowledge could be a third development cap. Countries can move from medium-tech to high-tech development by expanding secondary education, and especially universities.[18]

China and India are currently in this phase of development. They are experiencing double-digit wage inflation in many skilled jobs and acute shortages of senior managers. To ease these pressures, they are growing their universities – India starting rather earlier than China.[19]

But if they and other parts of Asia want to join the super-league economies, increasing university students will not be enough: raising the quality of universities will be vital. Then, instead of being consumers of knowledge produced by the rich world, they would become producers of knowledge themselves.

Patents, licensing agreements, consulting and other forms of knowledge transfer have become major sources of income for rich countries, and a significant cost to developing ones. Righting this trade imbalance is central to the Beijing Consensus.

Despite impressive advances, storming the knowledge economy may be more of a challenge than many suppose.

A number of countries will be starting from a long way behind. The McKinsey Global Institute reckons that just 10% of China's engineering and IT graduates are able to compete with their peers abroad.[20]

In India, only one in four engineering graduates is said to be employable in the IT-enabled services sector. The remainder lack the required technical competences, English fluency, team-working skills and oral presentation ability.[21]

Educational standards in the rich world will pull ahead, with new pedagogies based on advances in brain science, better sharing of good practice among teachers, improved responses to learners' feedback, and greater self-monitoring and self-teaching by learners, all enabled by IT. Learning will be more collaborative and less hierarchical.[22]

Will emerging countries have the resources to keep up, let alone catch up? In particular, will they be able to improve secondary education so that university entrants are better qualified, push up university enrolment nearer to the levels seen in rich nations and improve the overall quality of universities, all at the same time?

Getting the most able graduates to teach in higher education will be difficult. As now, the brightest students will be tempted to study, research and then teach in centres of excellence overseas. If you are among the best, you will want to live among the best.

From 1978–2007, 1.06 million Chinese left to study overseas, but only 275,000 have returned. The rest preferred to stay abroad because of higher living standards, brighter career prospects and the freedom to have as many children as they wish.[23]

Will more and more Chinese boys in the 'one child' generation, who heavily outnumber girls, remain overseas to find a wife?

Graduates remaining at home will be enticed out of universities by companies offering higher salaries to attract scarce talent. It will be hard to raise standards if the most capable graduates continue to leave the university system.

How will Asia respond to this challenge?

- China has allotted extra funds to selected universities it wants to become world class.
- American and European universities are setting up campuses in Asia, which may help to improve standards in the long run.
- Privately run institutions could be increasingly important. Along with India, China has been attracting corporate research institutes, such as one of Microsoft's three global research centres.
- Schemes to attract graduates back from abroad already exist in many countries and are likely to be extended.

Will developments like these enable emerging countries to multiply enough top-flight research centres to enter the heart of the global knowledge economy? Or will they produce insufficient global leaders to punch their weight?

A fourth cap on development could be the environment. More than ever before, social capacity today includes environmental capacity. Given this, commentators often note that emerging economies will be unable to sustain the current model of development because of environmental constraints. They then write about the future as if little will change. But 'business as usual' will *have* to change.

On current trends, for example, China alone could have 1.1 billion cars in 2031, compared to the world's 800

> 'China could have 1.1 billion cars in 2031, compared to the world's 800 million now'

million now, and its consumption of paper would be twice current global production.[24] Desertification means that China's northern cities are having to dig deeper and deeper for water, with growing doubts about how much further down they can go. In addition, 90% of China's water is polluted.

Some have argued that China's environment is so bad that cleaning it up would wipe out all the benefits of the last three decades of development.[25] India faces similar strains. Something will have to give.

The problem for both countries is that their political stability depends critically on economic growth. What would happen if the environmental costs of growth created a public backlash?

In May 2007 a text message campaign in the eastern Chinese city of Xiamen blocked construction of a chemical plant.[26] Imagine if China experienced many more such campaigns: could the country sustain its rapid economic growth? And if growth slowed, would rising unemployment cut away support for the Communist Party?

It is entirely possible that the government will become trapped between a cascade of environmental protests and mounting discontent from unmet economic aspirations. For all its skill, will the government be able to steer a path between the two or will it be brought crashing down?

Optimists hope that environmental technologies will square the circle. But will these technologies come on stream quickly enough and at a cost the country can afford?

1   Chinese Academy of Social Science report quoted in *China Daily News*, 27 October 2004.

2   *Global Economic Prospects 2007. Managing the Next Wave of Globalization*, Washington: The World Bank, 2007, pp. 48–50.

3   Moses Abramovitz, 'Catching up, Forging Ahead, and Falling Behind', *The Journal of Economic History*, 46(2), 1986, pp. 385–406.

4   Cadrina Rada & Lance Taylor, 'Developing and Transition Economies in the Late 20th Century: Diverging Growth Rates, Economic Structures, and Sources of Demand', *DESA Working Paper No. 34*, 2006, p. 9.

5   Dirk Pilat et al., 'The changing nature of manufacturing in OECD economies', *STI Working Paper 2006/9*, OECD, 2006, p. 12.

6   Yang Yao & Linda Yueh, 'Introduction' in Yang Yao & Linda Yueh, *Globalisation and Economic Growth in China*, Singapore: World Scientific Publishing, 2006, p. 26.

7   'Jobless growth in India', 10 March 2005, Association of Indian Progressive Study Groups, **http://aipsg.blogspot.com.**

8   Swati Narayan, 'Unemployment and migration', *India Together*, March 2004, **http://www.india together.org.**

9   'India's Economy', *The Economist*, 3 February 2007.

10 *Global Economic Prospects 2007: Managing the Next Wave of Globalisation*, Washington: World Bank, 2007, p. 43.

11 Will Hutton, *The Writing on the Wall. China and the West in the 21st Century*, London: Little, Brown, 2007, p. 29. Hutton cites estimates in 2005 from China's Development Research Council.

12 David Smith, *The Dragon and the Elephant. China, India and the New World Order*, London: Profile, 2007, p. 162.

13 Peter S. Heller, 'Is Asia Prepared for an Ageing Population', *IMF Working Paper 06/272*, 2006, pp. 4–7.

14 Peter S. Heller, 'Is Asia Prepared for an Ageing Population', *IMF Working Paper 06/272*, 2006, pp. 9–10, 18.

15 Estimates by European Futures Observatory, June 2007.

16 Ethnic clashes in India are being fuelled by the influx of migrant labourers from poorer provinces looking for work. In China, the numbers involved in public protests increased from 740,000 in 1994 to 3.7 million in 2004. Will Hutton, *The Writing on the Wall. China and the West in the 21st Century*, London: Little, Brown, 2007, p. 30.

17 Ian Bremmer, *The J Curve. A New Way to Understand Why Nations Rise and Fall*, New York: Simon & Schuster, 2006, esp. ch. 1.

18 Katarina R. I. Keller, 'Education Expansion, Expenditures per Student and the Effects on Growth in Asia', *Global Economic Review*, 35(1), 2006, pp. 28–31.

19 In the late 1990s the number of tertiary students in India was rising by over 13%. In China, the number increased by 24% to 29% a year between 2001 and 2004. *The Global Education Digest 2006*, Montreal: UNESCO Institute for Statistics, 2006, p. 22.

20 Cited by David Smith, *The Dragon and the Elephant. China, India and the New World Order*, London: Profile, 2007, p. 113.

21 Jane E. Shukoske, 'Bringing foreign universities to India', *The Hindu*, 14 November 2006. Shukoske is the Executive Director of the US Educational Foundation in India.

22 Anne Grocock, 'Universities in the Future', *Journal of the Royal Society of Medicine*, 95(1), 2002, pp. 48–49.

23 Chinese Academy of Social Sciences report, quoted by Jonathan Watts, 'China fears brain drain as its overseas students stay put', 2 June 2007, **http://education.guardian.co.uk.**

24 David Smith, The Dragon and the Elephant. China, India and the New World Order, London: Profile, 2007, p. 218.

25 Kerry Brown, 'General Economic Development in China', paper presented to *Goodenough ESRC conference on 'China and Globalisation'*, Goodenough College, London, 11 May 2007.

26 '"Text protest" blocks China plant', 30 May 2007, **http://news.bbc.co.uk.**

WILL THE EMERGING ECONOMIES CATCH UP WITH THE WEST? WHAT MIGHT BE THE IMPLICATIONS?

- Emerging economies will grow at very different rates
- New powers will begin to dominate the global economy
- Rich countries should not over-react
- Rich nations will compete by supplying products that help emerging ones develop

Emerging economies will grow at very different rates – inevitably because they are so varied. How each performs will depend on how much economic momentum it gathers and whether its social capacity will limit growth – in particular whether insufficient stability, transparency, knowledge and sustainability will constrain growth.

It is easy to point to the immense problems that China and India in particular will face. It is entirely possible that the environmental effects of growth will prevent either or both countries meeting their economic aspirations. There are real fears that the resulting stresses could cause China to disintegrate.

Yet neither country should be underestimated. Both have long track records of maintaining stability despite internal strains. Their governments are aware of the problems they face and are seeking to tackle them – India is investing more in infrastructure, for example, and China is seeking to develop its universities.

China has shown remarkable resourcefulness and determination in addressing priorities – a sixth ring road is being completed round Beijing whereas London has only one!

'A sixth ring road is being completed round Beijing, compared to London's one'

Many Chinese are not clamouring for more democracy. They express fears that democracy will produce instability, undermine the economy and create opportunities for the West to exploit Chinese divisions as it did in the nineteenth century.

China has already managed one transformation – from a state-owned to market economy. Might it not manage future transitions?

If China and India forge ahead, life could be difficult for some of the other emerging economies. The two giants' vast supplies of cheap labour and their massive home markets could give them advantages that other countries will struggle to match.

Chinese exports are already a threat to some Latin American countries. Asian and East European economies could suffer as well. By 2030, might China and India have broken away from the herd and be occupying a position somewhere between the rich nations and the rest of the emerging world?

New powers will begin to dominate the global economy. A 2006 study compared today's seven largest emerging economies (China, India, Brazil, Russia, Indonesia, Mexico and Turkey), known as the E7, with the current G7 (US, Japan, Germany, UK, France, Italy and Canada). It concluded that, given stable trading conditions, the E7 will move from being 75% of the size of the G7 to being 75% *bigger* by 2050.[1]

This will be due mostly to their faster population growth and their high levels of investment. Mainly because of its booming population, India has the potential to grow the fastest.

However, per capita incomes in the E7 will still lag far behind the G7. Despite impressive rates of investment, spending on R & D, in absolute terms, will also remain only a fraction of the rich countries' for many years: China currently devotes roughly just 10% of what the US spends.[2]

Like other emerging economies, most of China's 'advanced technology' exports are easy-to-copy products such as mobile phones and DVD players. Though clusters of innovation are emerging in cities like Beijing, Bangalore and Greater Seoul, general standards of education will have to rise a lot before emerging countries produce more complex exports on a large scale.

At 5% a year (unusually high, admittedly), America's growth in the first quarter of 2006 was half the rate of China's. Yet its much larger economy meant that the US was adding about twice as much in absolute terms to global output as was the Middle Kingdom.

In total dollar numbers, the US will keep growing by a larger amount than top-of-the-league China for at least the next decade.[3] The E7 will narrow the gap with the G7, but by 2030 will be far from catching up.

Will emerging economies threaten the rich ones? On the downside:

- rich societies will face mounting competition for raw materials;
- their low-tech and, increasingly, high-tech manufacturing will become uncompetitive;
- they will lose banking and other tradeable services to emerging countries;

- their low- and medium-skilled workers will be squeezed by lower-cost workers overseas;
- their dominance of global politics will face intense challenge.

Equally, the developed world will have plenty to celebrate. Huge, growing markets abroad (if they are sustained) will create new business opportunities and should allow companies to specialise more in their strengths. This will boost incomes and propel further economic growth. Emerging economies may leap ahead, but the rich ones won't stand still.

Consumers in advanced countries will continue to benefit from imports of cheap manufactures and, increasingly, services.

Ever more dependent on rich-world markets, emerging countries will have a strong incentive to collaborate with the G7 in tackling global problems. Collaboration will be at least as important as competition.

All of which means, as many commentators are saying, that developed countries would be wise not to 'demonise' their new competitors – 'What a threat to jobs!' 'You can't trust them because they are so corrupt!' 'Look at China's growing military strength!'

> 'A defensive response from rich countries may produce a defensive reaction from emerging ones'

A defensive response from rich nations may bring about a defensive reaction, creating the very tensions the rich world fears.

A better approach would be to help the new powers navigate through choppy waters as they continue to develop. Their stability and growing prosperity will be vital for the rest of the world. If China and India stumble, rich countries' overseas investments, export markets and cheap imports could all be at risk.

The biggest threat to rich nations will not be the success of emerging economies, but that the largest ones falter.

Rich countries will compete by supplying products that help emerging ones develop, and by growing their specialised strengths.

Initially, easy-to-copy products and processes will continue to migrate to the emerging nations, while more complicated tasks will stay within the rich world.

In time, as emerging countries acquire skills in complex activities, rich economies will build on their lead in other fields. Expanding middle classes in China, India and elsewhere will create vast markets for products that were first sold in the affluent world.

The UK will have several advantages:

- *It is strong in quite a few services that rely on complex skills,* which are not easily codified and imitated. These include the skills of drawing together knowledge from different sources, and combining them creatively to produce something new or highly specific to the customer.

  As the global economy goes up-market, the demand for these non-commoditised services will grow. Britain's services may be exactly what China and India want in the next stage of their development.

- *London will build on its clusters of skills,* particularly in financial and business services and in 'creative' industries such as advertising. Companies wanting a European base often choose London for this very reason.

  The next two decades will see global corporations emerging from India, perhaps China and from other newly industrialised countries. They will want a presence in Europe, and many will opt for London because of its specialist skills.

  This in turn will encourage computer programmers, graphic designers and other skilled workers to move to London from the emerging, as well as rich economies. If you are top of the tree, London will be one of the best places to be.

  These overseas skills will help to improve existing services and build new ones for export. With London able to import from all over the world, the challenge for Britain's regions will be to become the capital's suppliers of choice.

- *Sterling's value could well fall significantly within the next decade.* The UK already has a substantial balance of payments deficit. Without a lower exchange rate, this deficit is likely to balloon unsustainably as the UK moves from being a net exporter to a net importer of energy.

  Though temporarily lowering the country's standard of living, a carefully managed devaluation of the pound would strengthen the export sector. The economy would re-balance away from consumption to investment and exports.

---

1 John Hawksworth, *The World in 2050*, London: PriceWaterhouseCoopers, 2006, pp. 3–5. These figures are at purchasing power parity rates, a measurement currently preferred by economists when comparing living standards. If market exchange rates are used, the 'E7' are currently 20% of the size of the G7 and will be 25% larger in 2050. The World Bank (*Global Economic Prospects 2007. Managing the Next Wave of Globalization*, Washington: World Bank, 2007, pp. 36–46) has

produced estimates for 2030, but these aggregate all the developing countries, including the least developed ones.

2 C. Fred Bergsten et al., China: the Balance Sheet. What the World Needs to Know Now about the Emerging Superpower, New York, Public Affairs, 2006, p. 4.

3 Figures cited by Gerard Baker, 'America's economic hegemony is safe', The Times, 25 April 2006.

CHAPTER 4

WILL THE GAP BETWEEN THE RICHEST AND THE POOREST COUNTRIES NARROW?

THE STORY SO FAR

- Fewer people now live in extreme poverty
- Overall, inequality has been getting worse
- Africa suffers from some important physical disadvantages
- Inflation in the rich countries during the 1970s brought Africa's growth to a halt
- African economies had to be 'adjusted' to generate hard currency for debt payments
- During the 1990s adjustment policies were modified in the light of this dismal experience
- At last globalisation seems to have begun to work for Africa

Fewer people now live in extreme poverty. This herculean summary of the last quarter of a century glides blissfully over hard questions: should we talk about income or assets, for example?

In many parts of the world, a family may be better off owning a plot of land and growing subsistence crops (which yield no income) than having the head of the household in a low-paid job one minute and unemployed the next.

Income is only one aspect of well-being. Other dimensions include life expectancy, education, the environment and the quality of human relationships. How much of the story do comparative incomes tell?

Even so, if we take the conventional definition of extreme poverty – people living on less than a dollar a day – numbers have indeed fallen, from a little over 1.2 billion in 1980 to just over a billion in 2002.

This has happened while the global population has been growing, so that the proportion of the world on less than a dollar a day has dropped more sharply – from 27.9% to 21.1%. The proportion on less than $2 a day shrank from 60.8% to 49.9% (see table below).

Before celebrating, however, we should note that the bulk of the decline is accounted for by China: in sub-Saharan Africa, the total on under $1 increased by over a third (and by more for people under $2).

As much as half the world's population still lives on less than $2 a day, which is a pitiful amount. Many don't have access to clean water, electricity, health care and other things that richer people take for granted.

Poverty in developing countries – millions of people (and %)

Region	Less than $1 per day		Less than $2 per day	
	1980	**2002**	**1980**	**2002**
East Asia & the Pacific	472 (29.6)	214 (14.9)	1,116 (69.9)	748 (40.7)
China	375 (33.0)	180 (16.6)	825 (72.6)	533 (41.6)
Rest of East Asia & the Pacific	97 (21.1)	34 (10.8)	292 (63.2)	215 (38.6)
Europe & Central Asia	2 (0.5)	10 (3.6)	23 (4.9)	76 (16.1)
Latin America & the Caribbean	49 (11.3)	42 (9.5)	125 (28.4)	119 (22.6)
Middle East & North Africa	6 (2.3)	5 (2.4)	51 (21.4)	61 (19.8)
South Asia	462 (41.3)	437 (31.3)	958 (85.5)	1,091 (77.8)
Sub-Saharan Africa	227 (44.6)	303 (46.4)	382 (75.0)	516 (74.9)
Total	**1,218 (27.9)**	**1,011 (21.1)**	**2,654 (60.8)**	**2,611 (49.9)**
Total — excluding China	844 (26.1)	831 (22.5)	1,829 (56.6)	2,078 (52.6)

Source: *Global Economic Prospects 2006,* Washington: World Bank, 2006, p. 9.

They may worry about where the next family meal will come from or what will happen if one of the children is ill. They feel at the mercy of officials who boss them around. Anxiety and powerlessness can lead to stress, which damages the immune system and makes you more prone to disease.

Overall, inequality has been getting worse, though trends in inequality are complicated. Basically:

- *if you compare* **individuals** – average incomes per head of the world's richest and poorest people – the gap has narrowed, largely because China and India have made immense reductions in poverty;
- *if you compare* **countries** – the average income of one country and another – the gap has widened: more countries are lagging behind the rich nations than are catching up;

- *if you compare incomes* **within countries** – between the richest people and the poorest – then again the gap is widening: from within China to the US, the rich are pulling away from the poor.

One review of the literature looked at inequality from a variety of angles. It concluded that people round the centre of the income distribution worldwide have been drawing together to some extent, yet the extremes have been flying apart.

The gap between the richest and the poorest has been widening, but income differences for those in the middle have slightly narrowed. 'There is no sign at all that either the extreme impoverishment at the bottom or the extreme enrichment at the top of the world distribution are coming to an end.'[1]

It is against this background that we look at the world's poorest countries, focusing on sub-Saharan Africa, the poorest continent in the world. We do this because many people have a moral aversion to the widening income gap between rich and poor nations and because countries with low incomes per head tend to score badly on other measures of human welfare, such as literacy and health care.

While the rich nations got richer and many of the Asian economies sprang to life, between 1980 and 2001 sub-Saharan Africa largely stagnated. Thirty years ago the average income in the region was twice that of South and East Asia: now it is well below half.[2] Why has Africa done so badly?

Africa suffers from some important physical disadvantages. Much of the population lives in the interior without easy access to the coast, which shoves up the costs of trade. In many rural areas, low population densities – reflecting meagre farm yields – make linking up scattered villages relatively expensive.

South of the Sahara, the continent 'has an ideal rainfall, temperature, and mosquito type that make it the global epicentre of malaria, perhaps the greatest factor in slowing Africa's economic development throughout history.'[3]

Virtually everyone in tropical Africa contracts the illness at least once a year. This causes absenteeism from work and school. Loss of a key person can stop an investment project in its tracks.

When children die in large numbers, parents overcompensate by having more children. Too poor to educate all their children, they may pay for only one. The result? Children who survive malaria lack the schooling they need to escape poverty. AIDS adds another killer disease to one that has tormented the region for centuries.[4]

These disadvantages make it harder for Africa to develop, but they are far from making the task impossible. In much of sub-Saharan Africa, real incomes per head grew strongly in the 1960s, approaching rates in other developing countries by the end of the decade.[5] The region's performance then stalled. What happened?

Inflation in the rich countries during the 1970s brought Africa's growth to a halt. Hikes in the oil price, plus 'printing money' by the central banks, caused prices to shoot up in the rich world.

To prevent inflation getting worse, the West encouraged low-income countries to syphon off – in the form of loans – some of the excess funds flowing into the banks from oil producers. These loans helped the poor countries pay the higher

cost of their oil imports and keep their development strategies on track.

Trouble began when the rich economies took steps to get inflation under control. Interest rates soared, which increased the cost to poor countries of servicing their debts.

At the same time, higher interest rates put a break on the West's economic growth and some economies actually shrank. The demand for coffee, copper, tea and other commodities fell, hurting Africa which relied on commodity exports.

Poor countries were squeezed between higher debt charges and lower export earnings. In the early 1980s many of them became unable to service their commercial loans. To avoid an international banking crisis, the IMF took the lead in helping poor countries finance their debts provided they adopted 'economic adjustment policies'.

African 'economies had to be "adjusted" to generate hard currency for debt repayments'.[6] The adjustment involved policies, forced on the poor countries by the IMF and World Bank, which became known as the Washington Consensus.

They included privatisation, less government intervention and a bigger role for market forces. In particular, debtor countries were encouraged to export so as to earn foreign currency to pay for their debts.

Many of these countries had strengths in the same range of commodities, so that commodity exports overall continued to grow. Inevitably prices fell, which prevented exporters earning enough to pay off their loans. Farm incomes dropped, increasing poverty. Africa's per capita income fell by an average of 0.4% in the 1980s.[7]

Countries found it increasingly difficult to pay for imported machinery and other goods needed to develop their economies. By 1992, each $100 of commodity exports bought 52% less manufacturing imports compared to 1980.[8] The position deteriorated further in the 1990s.

Though far from the only factor, falling commodity prices was the single biggest reason for Africa's massive debts by the turn of the millennium. For every $2 Africa received in aid in 2005, it sent back nearly $1 in debt payments.[9] (Calculating the figures differently, the Jubilee 2000 campaign and others estimated that debt repayments were *higher* than aid flows.)

During the 1990s adjustment policies were modified in the light of this dismal experience. Greater attention was paid to making the state and non-market institutions more effective. A new emphasis was placed on health, education and infrastructure. Protecting the poor through safety nets and targeted spending was given higher priority.

In 1996 the World Bank and IMF launched the Highly Indebted Poor Countries Initiative, which allowed for some debts to be written off. Yet despite an enhanced version in 1999, in practice few loans were cancelled: the conditions attached were frequently beyond the institutional capacities of the economies involved.[10]

There was mounting global concern that these countries were trapped in debt and had more and more people in extreme poverty. At the United Nations Millennium Summit in 2000 governments committed themselves to eight Millennium Development Goals (MDGs), which ranged from halving extreme poverty and halting the spread of HIV/AIDS to providing universal primary education, all by the target date of 2015.

How to achieve these goals has been intensely debated. There is a wide consensus on the need for increased official aid to help the poorest countries spend more on education, health and basic social infrastructure, though the United States has yet to match rhetoric with deeds.

Considerable agreement also exists that there is no one-size-fits-all package of successful policies, and that national governments should have a strong proactive role alongside market forces.

Disagreements centre largely on how big a part governments should play. Some experts doubt that poor country governments have the capacity to steer development in a highly active way: bureaucracies should work with the grain of market forces.

Others argue that the experience of both the rich and the emerging Asian economies is that constraining market forces can be vital in the early stages of development. For a while infant industries may need to be subsidised and protected from competing imports, for example.

At last globalisation seems to have begun to work for Africa. From 2004 to

> **'Is this the start of a new dawn for Africa?'**

2006, for the first time in over 30 years sub-Saharan Africa has experienced three successive years of economic growth above 5%; the World Bank expects this to continue to at least 2008.

China has been largely responsible. Its demand for commodities has pushed up African export earnings. China has also begun to invest heavily in the region. Is this the start of new dawn for Africa?

1   Bob Sutcliffe, 'World Inequality and Globalization', *Oxford Review of Economic Policy*, 20(1), 2004, p. 33.
2   Commission for Africa, *Our Common Interest*, London: Penguin, 2005, p. 16.
3   Jeffrey Sachs, *The End of Poverty*, London: Penguin, 2005, p. 58.
4   Jeffrey Sachs, *The End of Poverty*, London: Penguin, 2005, pp. 196–200.
5   Benno J. Ndula & Stephen A O'Connell, 'Governance and Growth in Sub-Saharan Africa', *Journal of Economic Perspectives*, 13(3), 1999, pp. 41–42.
6   Ann Pettifor, *The Coming First World Debt Crisis*, Basingstoke: Palgrave, 2006, p. 111.
7   UNCTAD, *Trade and Development Report, 2006*, New York and Geneva: United Nations, 2006, p. 46.
8   Martin Khor, *Globalization and the South: Some Critical Issues*, Penang: Third World Network, 2000, p. 18.
9   Commission for Africa, *Our Common Interest*, London: Penguin, 2005, p. 23. In 2004 sub-Saharan Africa spent $15.2 billion in debt payments. Alex Wilks & Francesco Odonne, 'Forever in your debt?' 2006, **http://www.socialwatch.org.**
10 UNCTAD, *Trade and Development Report, 2006*, New York and Geneva: United Nations, 2006, pp. 53–54. By the late 1990s an IMF Extended Fund Facility programme had between 74 and 165 conditions attached.

WILL THE GAP BETWEEN THE RICHEST AND THE POOREST COUNTRIES NARROW? WHAT WILL SHAPE THE NEXT 20 YEARS?

- Better understanding of what needs to be done will be vital for Africa
- More funds are likely to be available for investment in Africa
- The world economy is likely to provide a mixed context for development
- The quality of governance will be vital
- Climate change is probably the biggest threat to African development

Better understanding of what needs to be done will be vital for Africa. In the global knowledge economy, knowledge is not quite everything, but it is extremely important. The prospects for Africa look promising.

Aid is being better targeted and is less tied to donors' interests. For example, donors are allying aid more closely to performance. They are addressing – slowly – the problems caused by a multiplicity of aid channels and the lack of coordination.

They are conducting pilot studies for improving the quality of aid to fragile states, such as by building the capacity to govern, making longer-term commitments and paying greater attention to recipients' priorities.

Though much remains to be done, the direction of change is towards improving the quality of aid and this looks set to continue.[1]

Balanced approaches to development are now widely accepted, in contrast to the previous over-reliance on markets.

More is being spent on disease control, improving education, building infrastructure and supporting the poor. The need for both markets and government intervention is generally acknowledged, though – as we've noted – how much intervention is debated.

Context is now seen as vital. Instead of single models of development, donors have endorsed the need to distinguish between different circumstances and to customise how aid is given. Types of aid may include:[2]

- balance of payments support;
- general budget support;
- aid-funded debt relief;
- project aid through government;

■ project aid through NGOs or private providers;
■ multilateral aid.

Donors are doing more to tailor the mix of aid to the specific situation. *Disasters and dangerous diseases are being better managed.* Between the 1970s and the end of the century the number of natural disasters worldwide more than tripled, as did the number of people affected. But the reported death toll halved.[3] Better communications, even in the poorest countries, will be one factor improving the management of disasters in future.

More is now being spent on managing HIV/AIDS in Africa, while Country Strategy Plans have attracted new resources for beating malaria.[4] The World Health Organization continues to improve arrangements for monitoring and controlling the spread of infectious diseases.

Though such developments are drops in the ocean compared to what needs to be done, they are creating a trajectory of change that should bring increased benefits in future.

At its worst, for instance, a global pandemic could decimate Africa's urban poor but, should it occur, the longer it is delayed the better it is likely to be managed. *Efficiency will increase as good practice spreads and technology surges forward.* The First Mile Project, for example, encourages small farmers, traders, processors and others from isolated rural areas in Tanzania to build market chains linking producers to consumers.

Participants use mobile phones, e-mail and the Internet to share their local experiences, exchange good practice and come up with new ideas. Learning from one another increased farm incomes after just one season.[5]

Improved crop varieties, perhaps using genetic modification, will raise yields and bring other gains, such as biofortification. This is a process that nutritionally enhances – biofortifies – staple crop varieties with higher levels of vitamins and minerals.

When biofortified varieties are introduced, farmers don't have to change their existing practices and diets to get the benefits. Biofortification could do much to improve the health of the rural poor.[6]

With these and many other developments, might Africa have its own green revolution? Or will R & D be skewed towards the interests of the multinationals rather than small farmers? (See chapter 5.)

More funds are likely to be available for investment in Africa. Lack of investment has been a major constraint in the past, but the future looks more promising.

Debt relief seems to be finally arriving. Under the Multilateral Debt Relief Initiative, agreed at the 2005 Gleneagles summit of world leaders, the poorest nations will get full relief from their debts to the World Bank, IMF and the African Development Fund – the bulk of most African countries' debts.

Governments have to show economic competence to qualify. Twenty-two countries – not all in Africa – had fulfilled the conditions by 2007 and others were expected to do so in future.[7]

Debt cancellation can amount to 20% of a government's budget, which must be spent on development instead. It allows economies to grow faster, since debt payments no longer take money out of the country. It also improves a country's credit rating, increasing the confidence of foreign investors.

On the downside are the conditions attached to debt cancellation. The IMF, for example, imposes tight constraints on public spending, which prevents governments from recruiting and training the health staff needed to tackle HIV/AIDS – vital for economic development.[8]

Fears exist that rich countries will take the cost of debt cancellation from their overseas aid budgets, reducing the benefits to poor nations.[9] The G8 Finance Ministers have said that countries which have debts cancelled should get less from the World Bank in future, which would leave little net gain.

Official aid (on top of debt relief) is likely to increase, though at present the trend is gloomy. At the Gleneagles summit in 2005, the G8 world leaders promised to double aid to Africa by 2010. But they have resolutely refused to commit themselves to a year-by-year timetable.

Having been on an upward swing till 2006, financial help from governments and international bodies actually edged lower in the year after Gleneagles. It is forecast to fall again slightly in 2007.[10] Rich countries are still far from fulfilling their 2005 promises.

Two things could change this. The first is the arrival of new donors. Brazil, China, India, Russia and South Africa are all becoming important providers of support to poor countries. India, for example, has extended to Western Africa credit totalling over $0.5 billion to strengthen its commercial ties with the region.[11]

> **'China is transforming Africa'**

China is transforming Africa. In 2004 it invested more in the continent than all the Organisation for Economic Co-operation and Development (OECD) countries.[12] In return for guaranteed supplies of raw materials and support at the UN, China:

- builds infrastructure;
- offers soft loans;
- sells arms (so China is a mixed blessing).

Increasing levels of aid from China and the global South may take up slack from the North.

Secondly, the emergence of China as a rival in Africa is likely to spur America and Europe to step up their assistance. In the scramble for commodities and global influence, will the West want to be left behind?

Capital from private sources is set to grow. Some of this will be foreign direct investment (FDI), as companies seek to exploit raw materials for an expanding market and other opportunities. Flows from within Africa, especially South Africa as a regional leader, are becoming very significant. In the early 2000s, for the first time they were easily the largest component of FDI.[13]

However, commodity investments tend to create relatively few jobs directly, while South African supermarkets in the rest of Africa have actually hindered development. They have damaged the market for local products by importing so-called superior offerings from home.

An increase in domestic savings may be more significant in the long term. Micro finance institutions have proved effective, for example in the Cameroon and Burkina Faso.[14] Groups of impoverished recipients (usually women), whom the banks won't touch, borrow small sums for business ventures from others in the group. Or sometimes a bank extends credit if the group guarantees repayment. Group pressure ensures that debt payments are kept up.

This type of credit, which finances grassroots development, looks likely to spread over the next 20 years, but by how much?

Perhaps the largest growth in private capital will come through remittances from migrants overseas, discussed in chapter 6. These funds can be used to finance development. But on the other side of the coin, migration enables the West to hoover up health workers and other skilled labour from Africa, making development more difficult.

Officially recorded remittances to sub-Saharan Africa increased by 72% between 1990 and 2005, reaching $8.2 billion. Informal remittances (such as cash sent with a friend) were much higher – perhaps four times so according to household surveys in Uganda.[15]

Formal and informal remittances to Africa may well exceed foreign direct investment and overseas aid combined. They are likely to become even more important as rich countries get wealthier (lifting migrants' wages) and more people migrate.

A global development tax should not be ruled out. In 2006, France introduced an air tax to fund drug treatment for HIV/AIDS and other killer diseases. With Germany and other countries, it has pressed for a global tax on air travel to help finance development. Might the momentum for some form of international tax grow?

The world economy will provide a mixed context for development, with pluses, minuses and uncertainties.

On the plus side, the global economy looks set to surge ahead, fuelled especially by the expansion of China and India. As noted in chapter 2, plenty of disturbances could cause a bumpy ride, but – on a balance of probability – average growth is likely to at least equal the past two decades.

The demand for commodities should remain strong, which will benefit African exports. More than a third of Africa's export income comes from natural resources.[16]

Will commodity-led growth be an advantage? In the past, being rich in oil, diamonds and other natural resources has often been a curse. Rival groups have competed for a quick source of wealth, sometimes using violence.

Some groups have ignored political conventions to grab power, undermining political stability. They have then used their new-found wealth to buy arms, reward their supporters and keep control, instead of using it to finance development. Angola, Nigeria and former Zaire are often cited as examples.

Yet one review of the literature has warned against exaggerating the 'resource curse'. Botswana and Gabon are among notable exceptions. A lot depends on the context.[17]

If commodity exports flourish in the years ahead, at least some countries will seize the opportunities. They will:

- tax their export earnings to raise funds for development;
- use their extra foreign exchange to import what's needed for industrialisation;
- build industries based on their natural resources – confectionary using cocoa, for example.[18]

Though not inevitable, a 'resource blessing' is conceivable.

Will Africa be allowed to exploit fully the world's expanding markets? Despite exemptions, agricultural protection in the rich world loads the dice against poor economies. So does rich countries' protection of intellectual property rights, which makes technology transfers difficult.

The World Trade Organization's rules make it harder for poor countries to protect their infant industries, as many rich countries did when they first developed.

Yet recently there have been two intriguing examples of the global trade system bending in Africa's favour. Up to 2004, the multi-fibre agreement (MFA) gave Mauritian garment imports privileged access to OECD countries vis-à-vis Asia. Most unusually for a preferential tariff, it allowed entry for garments made with duty-free inputs from other countries.

The United States African Growth and Opportunities Act (AGOA) gives duty-free entry for a wide range of products from 38 African countries. Again unusually, it allows apparel imports to use fabric from a third country.

These exceptions have been highly significant. Global trade is increasingly fragmented, with several countries undertaking different tasks to produce the finished article. For manufacturing to develop in Africa, countries will have to concentrate on specific activities within the supply chain. They will need to import the required inputs duty free, which is not normally allowed under preferential tariffs' rules.

These two exceptions have proved their worth. Mauritius has transformed itself from a poor sugar island into one of Africa's richest countries. Apparel exporters under AGOA have expanded manufacturing considerably.[19]

But Mauritius's exemption under the MFA expired in 2004. AGOA applies only to the US market, whereas Europe is far more important for Africa.

To compete with China for influence, might the EU eventually go further than the United States? Might Europe allow third party inputs to be duty-free not only in garment imports, but in other manufactures it treats favourably from Africa?

Will China's giant footprint on the world economy be a plus or minus for Africa? China will provide a growing market for African commodities. Low-cost imports from China will improve African consumers' living standards, and in the case of capital goods cut the costs of development.

Chinese companies are using Africa to learn how to become multinationals, and more will invest in the continent in future, along with businesses from India and other emerging economies.[20]

Against this are fears – expressed by South Africa among others – that cheap Chinese imports will make it difficult for Africa to get on the bottom rung of the manufacturing ladder. How will African countries compete?[21]

When poor countries do have an advantage, will China pull up the ladder behind it by protecting its domestic market from cheaper African imports, and by giving tacit support to the global North if it does the same?

Even if African manufacturing exports do expand, will prices fall because there is a world over-supply? Africa's manufacturing exporters could face the same sort of problems that commodity exporters experienced in the 1980s and 90s.[22]

The global economy will create plenty of opportunities for Africa, but it is not all clear that Africa will be allowed to take full advantage of them. Richer nations may break the transition mechanism from agriculture to manufacturing to services in countries south of the Sahara .

The quality of governance will be vital for Africa. This is often presented in terms of the quality of African governance. But global governance will be at least as important.

Will global governance coalesce into something more purposeful, with a stronger focus on the poorest nations? In chapter 8, we consider the possibility that the G8 meetings of heads of state will expand to include the newly emerging powers and representatives of the poor world.

> 'Global governance will be at least as important as African governance'

Might an enlarged gathering become a vehicle for coordinating the multiplicity of international bodies that have overlapping and fragmented remits in the development field? With greater representation from the South, would it give a stronger lead on the Millennium Development Goals, many of which are unlikely to be achieved by the 2015 target?

Or will rivalries between the big powers prevent a more focused approach? Witness China's recent behaviour in Africa. China's trade safari to the continent (see table below) has provoked claims that it is undermining the West's efforts to improve governance in the region.

China has supported entrenched autocrats like Mugabe. In 2005 it gave a cheap $2 billion loan to Angola. This allowed the country to wriggle out from the West's demands that it reform governance in return for assistance. Many see China as a force for ill-discipline.

China–African Trade ($US billion), 1990–2010

1990	0.67
2000	12.30
2006	55.50
2010	100.00 (projected)

Source: Ian Taylor, 'Win-Win Situation? The Case of Africa and China', *Goodenough/ESRC Conference on China and Globalisation*, held at Goodenough College on 11 May 2007.

Yet Chinese diplomats say that they are learning as they go in Africa. They recognise that China's reputation has suffered from their country's lax approach to poor governance. They claim that there will be fewer negatives in future. In 2007 China began to play a more constructive role in Darfur.[23] Might a more coordinated international approach to Africa be possible in the years ahead? *Governance within Africa will remain a contentious issue.* Extensive corruption and other government failings are widely viewed as barriers to development, making it more difficult for sub-Saharan countries to get the external support they need.[24]

Some experts believe that the honeypot approach to politics ('let's grab the pot and dish out the contents to our friends') is so deep-seated in Africa that it will take years to root out, and development will suffer meanwhile.[25]

A more optimistic view hopes for better government:

- *Wider literacy,* for example, will enable more people to read the newspapers, which will increase public awareness and perhaps strengthen the pressure for good governance.
- *Urbanisation* will reduce people's dependence on family and village ties. It will broaden networks, possibly in time lessening traditional feelings of obligation ('I'll give you a job because you are my uncle'). Slowly, urbanisation will encourage modern attitudes towards efficiency and the equal treatment of people.
- *The human rights agenda* is bringing a consensus that social and economic rights are as important as political and legal ones. African leaders and international bodies are making greater reference to them in policy statements. These references will provide further yardsticks that citizens and non-governmental organizations (NGOs) can use to hold governments to account.
- *New networks of accountability* are influencing African governments, as we note in chapter 5. These networks include local civil society organisations, African nationals in international bodies, other African governments, the African Union, donor governments, international NGOs and official international development agencies. They can all put pressure on a government to raise its game.[26]

Climate change is probably the biggest threat to African development. Sub-Saharan Africa is heating up faster than the world as a whole. The maximum temperature in Kericho, the centre of Kenya's tea industry, has increased by 3.5 degrees in the past 20 years.

Droughts and desertification could wreak havoc on a vast scale. Even more problematic could be confusing changes in the seasons and violent, erratic and unpredictable weather. Farmers will find it increasingly difficult to know when and where to invest precious time and inputs, and what to plant.[27]

As we discuss in chapter 12, global warming *that has already occurred* will hit Africa disproportionately over the next 20 years. Famine and mass migrations could set development back by years.

Yet Africa can be helped to adapt to climate change by:

- switching crops;
- developing new varieties;
- combating desertification by planting trees to create micro-climates suitable for farming;
- reducing the risk of disaster – for example by storing rainwater better, diversifying livelihoods and developing systems that warn of sudden weather changes.[28]

Will enough resources be available for these and other approaches?

1 *Global Monitoring Report 2007*, Washington: World Bank, 2007, pp. 160–169.
2 Mick Foster & Jennifer Leavy, 'The Choice of Financial Aid Instruments', *Working Paper 158*, London: Overseas Development Institute, 2001, pp. 2–10.
3 *Living with risk: A global review of disaster reduction initiatives*, Geneva: International Strategy for Disaster Reduction, 2004, p. 3.
4 'Malaria in Africa', Roll Back Malaria, World Health Organization, **http://www.rbm.who.int.**
5 **http://www.ifad.org** (accessed 23 May 2007).
6 **http://www.ifpri.org** (accessed 23 May 2007).
7 *Global Monitoring Report 2007*, Washington: World Bank, 2007, p. 170.
8 Rick Rowden, *Changing Course. Alternative Approaches to Achieve the Millennium Development Goals and Fight HIV/AIDS*, Washington: ActionAid International USA, 2005, pp. 21–40.
9 Alex Wilks & Francesco Oddone, 'Forever in your debt?' 2006, **http://www.socialwatch.org;** *Global Monitoring Report 2007*, Washington: World Bank, 2007, pp. 170–171.
10 *Global Monitoring Report 2007*, Washington: World Bank, 2007, p. 150.
11 *Global Monitoring Report 2007*, Washington: World Bank, 2007, p. 154.
12 Ian Taylor, 'Win-Win Situation? The Case of China and India', *Goodenough/ESRC Conference on 'China and Globalisation'*, Goodenough College, 11 May 2007.
13 Abah Ofon, 'South-South co-operation: can Africa thrive with Chinese investment?' in Leni Wild & David Mepham (eds.), *The New Sinosphere*, London: IPPR, 2006, p. 26.
14 Ann Pettifor, *The Coming First World Debt Crisis*, Basingstoke: Palgrave, 2006, p. 118.
15 *Global Economic Prospects 2006: Economic Implications of Remittances and Migration*, Washington: World Bank, 2006, pp. 88, 91.
16 Joseph Stiglitz, *Making Globalization Work*, London: Allen Lane, 2006, p. 134.

17 Matthias Basedau, 'Context Matters – Rethinking the Resource Curse in Sub-Saharan Africa', *Working Papers: Global and Area Studies*, German Overseas Institute Research Unit: Institute of African Affairs, 1 May 2005, pp. 19–35.

18 Cocoa beans are increasingly ground in the countries where they are grown rather than where they are consumed. African countries accounted for 16% of cocoa grindings in 2004–05. 'The cocoa industry: From volume to value-based growth?' European Cocoa Association, 17 September 2005, **http//www.eurococoa.com.**

19 Paul Collier & Anthony J. Venables, 'Rethinking trade preferences: How Africa can diversify its exports?' *Discussion Paper Series No. 6262*, Centre for Economic Policy Research, May 2007, pp. 11–19.

20 Lindsey Hilsum, 'China, Africa and the G8 – or why Bob Geldof needs to wake up' in Leni Wild & David Mepham (eds.), *The New Sinosphere*, London: IPPR, 2006, p. 7.

21 Ian Taylor, 'Win-Win Situation? The Case of China and India', *Goodenough ESRC Conference on 'China and Globalisation'*, Goodenough College, 11 May 2007.

22 Jose Antonio Ocampo & Maria Angela Parra, 'The Dual Divergence: Growth Successes and Collapses in the Developing World since 1980', *DESA Working Paper No. 24*, New York: UN Department of Social and Economic Affairs, 2006, p. 15.

23 Ian Taylor, 'Win-Win Situation? The Case of China and India', *Goodenough/ESRC Conference on 'China and Globalisation'*, Goodenough College, 11 May 2007.

24 However, as an explanation for Africa's poverty, these shortcomings may well have been exaggerated. See Jeffrey Sacks, *The End of Poverty*, London: Penguin, 2005, pp. 311–315.

25 For example, Matthew Lockwood, *The State They're In*, Rugby: Intermediate Technology Publications, 2006, pp. 73–127.

26 Alex de Waal, *AIDS and Power. Why there is no political crisis – yet*, London: Zed Books, 2006, pp. 53–61.

27 'Africa – Up in smoke 2', The second report on Africa and global warming from the Working Group on Climate Change and Development, London: New Economics Foundation, 2006, p. 5.

28 Reducing the Risk of Disasters – Helping to Achieve Sustainable Poverty Reduction in a Vulnerable World: *A DfID Policy Paper*, London: DfID, 2006, pp. 9–10.

WILL THE GAP BETWEEN THE RICHEST AND THE POOREST COUNTRIES NARROW? WHAT MIGHT BE THE IMPLICATIONS?

- The prospects for sub-Saharan African are distinctly mixed
- Success may come by following a different path to Asia

The prospects for sub-Saharan African are distinctly mixed. Despite its many disadvantages, the continent has more going for it now than for many decades.

There is better understanding of what needs to be done, more funds will become available for investment, African export markets should remain perky, while China's looming presence will lift the region's profile in global politics, perhaps bringing more generous trade deals.

Big questions remain, however. The challenge is to scale up development so that it has a major impact. Will African leaders be able sufficiently to tame their honeypot politics to allow this? Will global warming throw up so many new problems that officials and experts have to run faster for the continent to stand still? Will cheap imports from Asia swamp Africa's nascent industries and prevent diversification?

Success may come by following a different path to Asia. Adrian Wood, an academic in development studies, has argued that Africa's development may be more like that of South America and eventually the United States than Asia. Africa has a ten-fold advantage over Asia in land area per worker, which more than offsets the continent's inferior quality of land. It is also rich in mineral resources.

Africa would do well to build on these comparative advantages by investing heavily in transport and other infrastructure and by applying knowledge to nature.

> 'Africa's development may be more like that of the US than Asia'

Chile and Costa Rica provide an example: the rapid growth and diversification of their primary exports in the 1990s owed much to investment in sector-specific research, training, extension services and education.

Were Africa to follow this path, it would end up with a larger primary sector and smaller manufacturing one than Asia. Perhaps more important, spending heavily on primary products would push up the average amount of capital invested for each worker, which would increase wages. This would make labour-intensive manufacturing unattractive.

Africa would be forced to miss out Asia's labour-intensive phase of industrialisation and follow North America's more capital-intensive route.[1] One study found that 'most developing countries that have been growing fast have been increasing market shares in mid- to high-technology exports.'[2]

What might this more capital-intensive journey look like?

- *Might Africa industrialise round its natural resources,* just as Finland industrialised on the basis of fish and timber, for example?
- *Could tourism give diversification a fillip?* One of China's African projects is a large tourism complex in Sierra Leone.[3] Though everything is currently sourced from China, for future ventures this might change as Chinese companies build manufacturing capacity in the region. Flying goods from Lagos to Freetown would be cheaper than from Shanghai, offsetting Africa's higher wages.
- *Migrants' remittances will boost local incomes* and expand the domestic market for manufactures.
- *Might regional trade agreements extend to domestic markets further?* If the African Union delivered its aim of lowering trade barriers on the continent, might Africa industrialise on the back of a coast-to-coast home market, as did the United States? Or might regional groupings, like the East African Community with over 100 million people, offer large 'domestic' markets?

1 Adrian Wood, 'Could Africa Be like America?' in Boris Pleskovic & Nicholas Stern (eds.), *The New Reform Agenda*, Washington: Annual World Bank Conference on Development Economics, 2003, pp. 163–200.

2 Jose Antonio Ocampo & Maria Angela Parra, 'The Dual Divergence: Growth Successes and Collapses in the Developing World since 1980', *DESA Working Paper No. 24*, New York: UN Department of Social and Economic Affairs, 2006, p. 19.

3 Lindsey Hilsum, 'China, Africa and the G8 – or why Bob Geldof needs to wake up' in Leni Wild & David Mepham (eds.), *The New Sinosphere*, London: IPPR, 2006, p. 7.

CHAPTER 5

HOW WILL THE WORLD FEED ITS GROWING POPULATION? THE STORY SO FAR

- Malnutrition remains a scourge on the planet
- World population growth has been slowing
- The planet has been unable to feed its growing population
- The rich have been over-eating while the poor have starved
- Tackling food shortages has become an international priority

Malnutrition remains a scourge on the planet. More than 800 million people do not have enough food. If they don't die, they are more prone to disease and they have less energy to work than do adequately nourished individuals. Extreme malnutrition in children causes long-term brain damage, making it harder for them to earn a living.

Poverty and hunger go hand in hand. Often poor people cannot afford sufficient food, which undermines their capacity to sustain a livelihood, leaving them even more underfed.

There is much more to food, of course, than feeding the poor. It is central to consumer lifestyles, and as such – in the West – a significant source of identity.

Arguably, though, food insecurity is the most important moral challenge facing the world. Using the UN Food and Agriculture Organization's definition, food insecurity occurs when people at some time do not have 'physical and economic access to sufficient, safe and nutritious food to meet their dietary needs and food preferences for an active and healthy life.'[1]

World population growth has been slowing, which has eased the pressure on food resources. In 1965-70 the growth rate reached an all-time high of about 2.0% a year, and then declined to 1.2%. This decline has been unprecedented because it has been caused largely by voluntary reductions in procreation.[2]

By the late 1990s it became clear that across the world people were choosing to have fewer children. Families of five, six or eight were becoming less common.

UN demographers suggest that if the percentage rate of population increase continues to fall as it has since the early 1970s, after 10,000 years of almost

Estimated world population (millions), 1950–2007

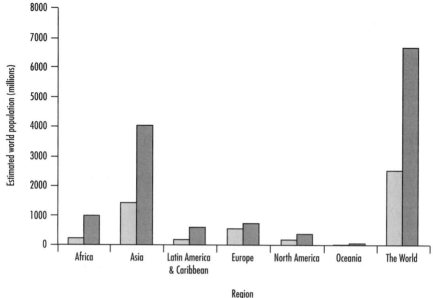

Source: *World Population Prospects: The 2006 Revision*, New York: United Nations, 2007, table 1.1.

uninterrupted, exponential growth, the world population will stabilise by around 2050. We are witnessing the 'most staggeringly important shift' in world demographic trends.[3]

Despite the slower pace of growth, current trends are adding 77 million people to the global population a year – equivalent to a country larger than the UK. The world's population grew from a little over 2.5 billion in 1950 to just under 6.7 billion in 2007 (see chart above).

Six countries will account for half the annual increase in global population from 2005 to 2010 – India, China, Nigeria, Pakistan, the US, Indonesia and Bangladesh. The American figure is due mainly to high immigration, which puts the US on a different demographic path to most of the developed world.[4]

The planet has been unable to feed this growing population. True, agricultural output has more than kept up with population growth – due, for example, to:

- better plant varieties;
- large increases in the use of fertilisers;
- a doubling of the irrigated area;

- more effective control of insects and pests;
- improved strains of livestock and poultry;
- wider use of nutritionally balanced feeds.

The global supply of food calories per person rose from 2420 kilocalories (kcal) per day in 1958 to 2808 kcal in 1999.[5] The proportion of undernourished people in the developing world fell from 20% to 17%.

Yet despite this huge achievement, the figures are not as encouraging as they might seem:

- more than 800 million people are still undernourished in developing countries;
- the figure remained stable between 1990–92 (823 million) and 2001–03 (820 million);
- this contrasted with the 8% decline in the proportion of underfed people between 1979–81 and 1990–92, which itself was lower than the 9% fall in the decade before that;
- a decline of 26 million undernourished people between 1990–92 and 1995–97 was followed by an increase of 23 million up to 2001–03.[6]

For years the world had been making slow headway against hunger. Has the trend now been reversed?

The International Food Policy Research Institute's Hunger Index shows that since the mid 1980s large parts of the Andean region in South America, African countries like Ghana, Mozambique and Angola, and South Asia have begun to escape the vicious cycle of poverty and hunger. But trends have been less encouraging in sub-Saharan Africa as a whole.[7]

The rich have been over-eating while the poor have starved. Is this significant? Some argue that poverty is the root cause of hunger. If you could get rid of poverty you would eliminate hunger. The eating habits of the rich have little to do with it. Others say that over-eating by the rich makes it much harder to reduce both poverty and hunger.

More than a billion adults – mostly rich people – are overweight, 25% more than the number of people who are underfed. Among the overweight are at least 300 million who are clinically obese.[8]

In the US, for example, the number of overweight adolescents trebled between 1980 and the early 2000s. In the mid noughties, 30% of US adults aged 20 and over – some 60 million people – were clinically obese.[9]

Obesity is not just a problem for the West. In 1995, 10% of Chinese were judged overweight or obese: by 1999 the figure was 15%.[10]

Overweight is largely a 'disease of affluence', even though many of those afflicted are among the poor in wealthier countries. It stems partly from lack of exercise, as more people do sedentary jobs in the service sector.

But it is also due to changes in diet. As poor people grow richer, they eat more meat. 'The general shift towards meat (and the saturated fat that comes along with it) is the greatest transition of modern times both in nutrition and in agriculture.'[11]

> **'The general shift towards meat is the greatest food transition of modern times'**

As a rule of thumb (though experts are divided), an individual requires an average of at least 40 grams of animal protein per day. Almost three-quarters of the world's population live in countries where animal protein consumption is less than 30g. Just 16% of people are in countries – mainly in the West – where consumption averages 50 to 80g.[12]

Richer countries are eating more meat than they need. Land is being used to support this surplus livestock instead of growing crops for human consumption.

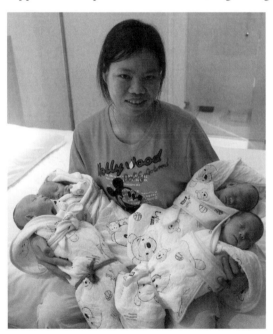

If land was switched from meat to grains for human food, many more people could be fed*. Food prices would be kept lower, helping the poor.

It is often pointed out that the world already produces enough to feed its population. The global supply of food kilocalories (around 2800 kcal per person per day) would be sufficient for everyone ifthe food was equally distributed. But because more affluent people tend to eat more than they need, the poorest go without.

Tackling food shortages has become an international priority. In 1996 the Rome World Food Summit set a target of halving the number of undernourished people by 2015. The United Nations Millennium Summit, in September 2000, set a less ambitious – but still stretching – target of halving the *proportion* of people who suffer from hunger by 2015.

With the other Millennium goals (including targets for extreme poverty, education, gender equality and health), this has galvanised action to meet the needs of the poor.

Though there is plenty of debate over specific strategies, communities of experts are widely agreed on what should be done about hunger. A twin-track approach is necessary.[13]

Long-term action is required to raise agricultural production in developing countries. This would boost rural incomes, benefiting the majority of the world's hungry who live in rural areas: they would have more money with which to buy food. It would also help to keep food prices low.

To increase agricultural production:[14]

- peace and stability is a bottom line. Conflicts are the cause of more than half of Africa's food crises;
- developed countries should remove farming subsidies and other barriers to food imports from developing countries;
- public investment in infrastructure, agricultural research, education and extension is vital. The state has a key role to play;
- the post-1980s decline in foreign assistance for agriculture and rural development should be reversed, with a stronger focus on the neediest countries;
- technology is critical. It should be adapted to local conditions and meet the needs of small farmers;
- better farming should be part of an holistic approach to development, guided by the 'triple bottom line' of economic, social and environmental sustainability;
- better-educated women have a key role. They tend to have fewer children, and those children themselves are better educated. Women play a vital part in agriculture in poor countries, so improving their education will make it easier for them to learn better husbandry.

Direct action against hunger is essential, alongside measures to improve food output.

'Escaping poverty seems much more difficult for hungry people, who are disadvantaged in their capacity to earn a livelihood. Accelerating hunger reduction requires direct measures to help people who are both poor and ill-fed to escape the hunger-poverty trap.'[15]

Priorities should include replacing stop-start food aid with a longer-term approach, improving the distribution of this aid and making sure that the right kind of food (rather than rich people's food) is distributed.[16]

1　Quoted by P. J. Gregory, J. S. I. Ingram & M. Brklacich, 'Climate change and food security', *Philosophical Transactions of the Royal Society*, 360 (2005), p. 2141.

2　Joel E. Cohen, 'The Future of Population' in Richard N. Cooper & Richard Layard (eds.), *What the Future Holds. Insights from Social Science*, Cambridge, Massachusetts: MIT, 2003, p. 36.

3　Colin Tudge, *So Shall We Reap*, London: Penguin, 2003, p. 25.

4　World Population Prospects: The 2006 Revision, New York: United Nations, 2007.

5　Bernard Gilland, 'World population and food supply. Can food production keep pace with population growth in the next half-century?', *Food Policy*, 27 (2002), pp. 47–48.

6　*State of Food Insecurity in the World 2006*, Rome: Food and Agriculture Organization, 2006, p. 8.

7　Doris Wiesmann, 2006 Global Hunger Index. A Basis for Cross-Country Comparisons, **http://www.ifpri.org.**

8　'Overweight and obesity', World Health Organization, **http://www.who.int** (accessed 13 December 2006).

9　'Overweight and obesity', 4 December 2006, Centers for Disease Control and Prevention, **http://www.cdc.gov.**

10　Colin Tudge, *So Shall We Reap*, London: Penguin, 2003, p. 111.

11　Colin Tudge, *So Shall We Reap*, London: Penguin, 2003, p. 139.

12　Bernard Gilland, 'World population and food supply. Can food production keep pace with population growth in the next half-century?' *Food Policy*, 27, 2002, pp. 50–51.

13　*State of Food Insecurity in the World 2006*, Rome: Food and Agriculture Organization, 2006, p. 6.

14　'Causing Hunger: an overview of the food crisis in Africa', *Oxfam Briefing Paper*, 91, July 2006.

15　*State of Food Insecurity in the World 2006*, Rome: Food and Agriculture Organization, 2006, p. 6.

16　'Causing Hunger: an overview of the food crisis in Africa', *Oxfam Briefing Paper*, 91, July 2006, pp. 2–3. It is obviously important that the right kind of food does not flood the local market, putting local farmers (whose produce should be bought first) out of business.

HOW WILL THE WORLD FEED ITS GROWING POPULATION? WHAT WILL SHAPE THE NEXT 20 YEARS?

- Demographic and economic changes will make it harder to feed everyone
- Resource constraints will be a big problem
- Maximising food resources will depend especially on good governance
- The global food supply chain will continue to favour the more affluent
- Will food fashions change?

Demographic and economic changes will make it much harder to feed everyone. Three developments will be especially important.

The first will be population growth. Though birth rates are falling, the momentum behind demographic trends will make the planet even more crowded than it is today.

More women in the developing world are entering their child-bearing years than ever before. Behind them are their children, who will reach parenting age in the next two decades.

A third of the developing world's population was aged 15 or under in 2000. For Africa, the figure was 43%. Hundreds of millions of young adults and children will keep the population growing.[1]

In addition, people will live for longer as the world becomes more wealthy, new medical treatments come on stream and the campaign against HIV/AIDS gathers strength.

The United Nations provides population projections till the mid century, which gives a helpful context for the next two decades. Its 2006 projections range from a 'low' of 7.8 billion in 2050 to a 'high' of 10.7 billion, reflecting the uncertainties that exist.

Its 'medium' projection (updated in 2007) suggests that the global population could grow from an estimated 6.7 billion in 2007 to 9.12 billion in 2050 – an increase of 2.5 billion people. This would represent about *40% growth* (see chart and table overleaf).

Most of the extra people will live in towns. Urban dwellers now equal the rural population for the first time ever, and are expected to comprise 60% of the global population in 2030.[2]

Estimated and projected world population (millions), 2007–2050

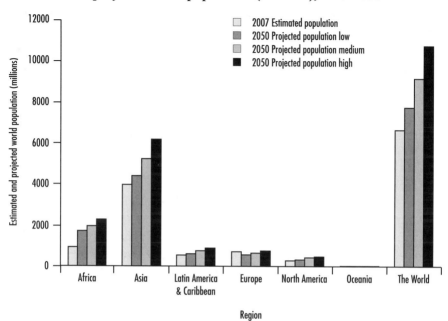

	2007	2050		
	Estimated pop	Projected pop		
		Low	Medium	High
Africa	965	1,718	1,998	2,302
Asia	4,030	4,444	5,266	6,189
Latin America & the Caribbean	572	641	769	914
Europe	731	566	664	777
North America	339	382	445	517
Oceania	34	42	49	56
The World	6,671	7,792	9,191	10,756

Source: *World Population Prospects: The 2006 Revision*, New York: United Nations, 2007, table I.1.

As hundreds of millions of people worldwide move from rural to urban areas over the next two decades, they will stop relying on subsistence farming and become food buyers instead.

Rising incomes will allow them to adopt the 'all-you-can-eat' habits of the West. They will buy more dairy products (global milk prices have soared as consumption in China, for example, has grown) and will switch to meat (which requires more land than traditional foods).

Population growth, urbanisation and rising incomes could push up the demand for food by 70–80% over the next half century.[3]

Resource constraints will make it more difficult to feed this growing population. Three constraints will be especially significant.

The first will be water.[4] Ninety per cent of the world's rainwater and natural underground water (aquifers) is used to produce food. In many areas the aquifers are running dry, largely because of irrigation. In the Punjab, a major agriculture success story, underground water is being pumped two times faster than rain is replacing it.

Worldwide, aquifers are being depleted by at least 160 billion tons a year. That is the amount of water needed to produce 160 million tons of grain – enough to feed half a billion people. Urban growth is making the situation worse by ratcheting up the demand for water.

> 'In our research in Northern Uganda we are increasingly encountering agriculturalists and pastoralists fighting over dwindling water supplies. Literally fighting, with AK47s.'[5]

There are solutions. Rainwater can be captured – at low cost – before it runs down the street. Crops will be developed that use water more efficiently. Rice that yields 4 tons an acre uses little more water than rice that yields 2 tons. Though controversial, protein crops may be genetically modified to produce higher yields with less water.

Rotating sprinkler systems, which waste water, may be replaced by electronic systems that take the right amount of water to the right plant at the right time.

These and other innovations would require considerable investment worldwide and higher farming skills. Investment and new skills were possible in the Green Revolution. Why should they not be feasible again?

Land will be a second constraint. Some studies suggest that the global area under cultivation could be more than doubled — to 3 billion hectares or more. But this would be extremely difficult:

- more forests would be cut down, which would damage the world's ecology;
- most of the best farmland has already been cultivated, which means that land cleared in future will be increasingly marginal;
- expansion of the cities is eating up agricultural land.

Raising yields on existing farms would feed the growing population more easily.[6] But this will be a challenge. In India, about a third of the irrigated land is damaged by salination and more than 12% has been abandoned.

In the US, a third of the original topsoil has gone and much of the rest is degraded. Though major efforts have been launched to restore soil and create new soil, American farmland is losing topsoil on average 17 times faster than topsoil is being formed.[7]

Climate change will bring hurricanes, flooding from rising sea levels and droughts, which will take land out of production. The Gobi Desert is marching south towards Beijing by 50 kilometres a year, reducing maize yields as it goes.[8]

Solutions to climate change could reduce the amount of land growing food. The US government, for example, is subsidising ethanol and biodiesel production from corn, sugar and other crops, much to the delight of American farmers. Mexican consumers were less pleased. In 2006–07 the price of tortillas doubled in 12 months.[9]

Research will respond to some of these challenges by seeking to help plants adapt to climate change, such as improving the genetic make-up of roots so that they use less water.[10] Better fertilisers have the potential to increase land productivity, especially in many poor parts of the world which do not use fertiliser.[11] Despite the constraints (and possible ecological damage), might agricultural land expand by nearly a fifth between the early 2000s and 2050? [12]

> 'Aquaculture may produce a Blue Revolution to rival the Green Revolution'

In some areas, land may be used in novel ways. China's rice paddies produce two-thirds of the world's pond fish. During the 1990s the country almost doubled yields per acre by growing multiple types of fish in the same pond.

'Aquaculture has such massive global potential that its future has been called the "Blue Revolution" and compared with the past Green Revolution. Two decades from now, more fish may come from aquaculture than ocean fishing. It could be an effective way for people in poor countries to obtain the nutrients they desperately need.'[13]

How far will these positive developments offset the threats to land under food? *A third constraint will be labour.* Many of the improvements needed to feed humanity will require higher levels of farm management.

Training has been crucial in many parts of the developing world. It could be highly effective in future if agricultural extension services, which have traditionally been provided by the state, were expanded. Poorer countries will continue to need external financial support to help with this.

Sub-Saharan Africa is home to 26 million people with HIV. As well as being a human tragedy, HIV/AIDS reduces the human resources available for farming:[14]

- sickness and ill health make it harder for people to tend their farms;
- death prevents parents passing on vital agricultural skills to their children;
- caring for others reduces time on the farm;
- the need to pay for medicines can force people to sell farm tools or even their land.

A 2004 World Bank study warned that without prompt action to tackle HIV/AIDS, the South African economy could face complete collapse within four generations.[15]

Maximising food resources will depend especially on good governance, which is discussed in chapter 8.

There is a strong need for capable government — at a very basic level to maintain law and order. Between 1990–92 and 2001–03, five war-torn countries in sub-Saharan Africa accounted for 29 million of the region's 36 million increase in underfed people.[16]

- Armed conflict deters investment and diverts resources.
- Many people flee their homes, join militias or are killed, leaving farms unattended.
- Insecurity restricts mobility and grazing, and often discourages people from tending their farms.
- Disruption of infrastructure and markets prevents cash crops from being sold and food being bought from outside the area.
- Sometimes warring factions deny food to groups thought to support the opposition.

Though the number of armed conflicts fell by 40% between the early 1990s and the mid noughties, continuing conflicts – as in Darfur and Iraq – help hundreds of thousands of people to remain trapped in poverty and hunger.[17]

More generally, but particularly in sub-Saharan Africa, which accounts for 13% of the developing world's population and 25% of its underfed people,[18] governments need to intervene in rural areas to offset weak, risky and inequitable markets. Unstable prices are a particular problem.

Appropriate action – like setting up grain reserves to stabilise prices or subsidising farm inputs – can nurture the private sector, enabling the state to become less involved in future.

But many African countries suffer from a culture of clientelism and 'winner takes all'. On one view, leaders focus more on retaining power than promoting development.

Government jobs are given to satisfy 'clients' (often people in the same family or tribe) rather than on the basis of merit, weakening state capacity. Client groups receive tax exemptions or are treated favourably within departmental budgets, reducing funds for effective development.[19] Extreme forms of clientelism can provoke armed retaliation by excluded groups, as in Sudan.

Could more hopeful circumstances be starting to emerge? Since the 1980s African governments have been enmeshed in new webs of accountability.

These networks reach down to domestic players through local representatives of international bodies and national civil society organisations: both can put pressure on their governments through their global contacts. ('Do you want us to tell people in the World Bank what you are doing?')

Networks also reach sideways to other African governments, the African Union and sub-regional organisations, and upwards to a permeable set of international institutions. These outside bodies can also put pressure on a government.[20]

Might emerging global networks begin to help politicians become more accountable, resist clientelism and build governing capacity? ('Your NGOs say that you've made virtually no progress in dealing with corruption. If we give financial assistance, how can we be sure the money will get to the right people?')

There is a long way to go before networks are highly effective in this sort of way. Meanwhile, conflicts might be contained (and food supplies increased):[21]

- if rich countries strengthened their support for UN peace-keeping missions and for the African Union's Africa Standby Force;
- if they controlled the supply of arms to the region;
- if they invested more heavily in poverty reduction and improving accountable governance.

Might growing Chinese influence in Africa encourage the West to become more deeply involved?

The global food supply chain will continue to favour the more affluent. In recent decades, the food chain (farming→manufacture→distribution→retail→ consumption→waste) has become more and more international.

Consumers in developed countries obtain a growing proportion of their food from countries miles away, drawing farming into this global chain. Owing largely to urbanisation, consumers in developing countries are following suit. In Kenya, supermarkets grew from a tiny niche in 1997 to over 20% of urban food retailing in 2004.[22]

Globalisation of the food chain has increased the power of retailers. A 2003 study of selected European countries found that the food chain had some 160 million consumers, 90,000 food processors and manufacturers, but just 100 supermarket chains.[23]

Supermarkets are powerful because consumers like what they offer. Consumers find them convenient (everything is in one place), they think their products are good value for money, advertising encourages them to spend and supermarkets are a low-cost way of maintaining social status.

Status can be enhanced by eating foods that are similar to those that wealthy people like – foods that look perfect (bananas are the right size), are exotic (avocados all the year round) or echo a cuisine fashionable among the rich. Buying food that friends would approve of is particularly important — 'he shops at Waitrose'.

As these trends continue, urbanisation and expansion of the Asian middle class will hugely increase the demand for supermarkets, as well as for restaurants and take-aways.

Growth is an imperative for these businesses – it is what their shareholders expect. But healthy individuals can eat only so much food. So, to grow the market, just as they do now food retailers will constantly add value to their products – through packaging, enhancing taste so that people buy more and developing innovative lines. Global

> 'The world's livestock could eat as much grain as 4 billion people in 2050'

sales of high-value agricultural products were growing by 8–10% a year in 2005.[24]

As sales increase, the food supply chain will continue to skew production away from the needs of the hungry.

- *Land will be diverted to crops for the rich.* Land that could grow food for underfed people locally will produce crops for those who are over-eating miles away. In 2002 Senegal devoted half its agricultural land to peanuts for Western margarine.[25]

The plus is that this generated an income that could be used to import food. But when lots of countries are producing for the more affluent, land worldwide and other resources to support crops for the poor become limited. Prices go up and shortages increase.

- *Grain that could have fed poor people will be diverted to cattle feed* to satisfy the growing urban demand for meat. If present trends in meat-eating continue, the world's livestock will consume as much grain in 2050 as would feed 4 billion people in 2050 (over two-fifths of the predicted global population).[26]

- *Farms will be amalgamated and smallholders squeezed out,* due to pressure from retailers to cut costs and meet industry standards.[27] More people will drift from the land (and subsistence farming) to the towns, where they will have to rely on purchased food.

- *Food research will benefit mainly the rich.* Research, funded largely by multinationals, will be geared more to adding value than developing food for poor people. Most food science is paid for by commercial interests. These firms make the bulk of their profits from 'middle class' foods and so invest most heavily in them.[28]

- *Genetic engineering may benefit rich people more than the poor.* Crops that are genetically modified most easily, like rapeseed (which is used for animal feed, vegetable oil and diesel fuel), tend to support the consumption habits of the more wealthy.

According to some experts, genetic engineering is unlikely to increase significantly the yields of wheat, rice and maize, the staple foods of most poor people, since these crops do not lend themselves readily to genetic modification (GM).[29]

However, GM could play a role in improving the vitamin content of cereals, which would benefit the diets of a large number of poor people, especially in Africa.

- *Further developments in monoculture could put food supplies at risk.* Due to the Green Revolution, India's 30,000 native varieties of rice are in the final stages of being replaced by one super-variety, showing the direction in which monoculture is headed.'[30]

Despite new ways of protecting species, the loss of diversity will increase the chance of a disease or insect doing widespread damage within a single breed or crop. Who would go without food if a pest mutated and swept through India's rice fields?

Will food fashions change? The global food chain's bias to the rich may be offset by mounting opposition to industrial farming. Ethical consumption, concerns about business ethics and the desire for healthy eating are all growing.

Scores of animal welfare, organic, vegetarian, fair trading and ethical movements are springing up. Will their combined weight push global food production in directions that make it easier to feed the undernourished, or will their objectives remain too diverse?

Measures to tackle climate change may shove up the costs of transport, encouraging consumers to switch to local suppliers. As a straw in the wind, some UK food retailers have decided to use an aircraft symbol when perishables have been imported by air. Might demand for local food boost production in rich countries and expand global food supplies?

Will the middle classes eat more healthily, aware that this is a smart thing to do? This would slow the increase in meat consumption, releasing land for crops to feed the poor. London's Food Strategy, for example, contains a strong emphasis on healthy eating and supporting small farmers.[31] Will buying from small farmers through 'secondary food hubs' become fashionable?

At present a revolution in eating habits seems unlikely. A 2006 survey of 12 million UK shoppers using Tesco's loyalty card found that only 8% had moved to a healthier diet in the past four years, while the same number were eating *more* junk food.[32] But might this change?

For instance, nutrigenomics (roughly the study of diet-gene interactions) may create a fashion for personalised diets, based on each person's genetic make-up, as a form of health promotion and disease prevention. Services are being advertised on the Internet.[33] As consumers become better informed about diet and health, might larger numbers change their behaviour?

1   Source: *World Population Prospects: The 2006 Revision*, New York: UN, 2007.
2   'World Urbanization Prospects: The 2006 Revision', United Nations Population Division, 2007, **http://www.un.org.**
3   'Millennium Ecosystem Assessment', *Ecosystems and Human Well-being: Opportunities and Challenges for Business and Industry*, Washington: World Resources Institute, 2005, p. 25.
4   Data in this section is drawn from James Martin, *The Meaning of the 21st Century*, London: Eden Project Books, 2006, pp. 66–71.
5   Peter Walker, 'Human Security and the Critical Role of Science in Achieving It', Boston, Feinstein International Centre, November 2006, **http://fic.tufts.edu.**
6   Colin Tudge, *So Shall We Reap*, London: Penguin, 2003, pp. 36–37.
7   James Martin, *The Meaning of the 21st Century*, London: Eden Project Books, 2006, p. 72.
8   Colin Tudge, *So Shall We Reap*, London: Penguin, 2003, p. 40.
9   Brittany Sauser, 'Ethanol Demand Threatens Food Prices', *Technology Review, 13 February 2007*, **http://www.technologyreview.com.**

10 P. J. Gregory, J. S. I. Ingram & M. Brklacich, 'Climate change and food security', *Philosophical Transactions of the Royal Society*, 360, 2005, p. 2144.

11 Bernard Gilland, 'World population and food supply. Can food production keep pace with population growth in the next half-century?' *Food Policy*, 27, 2002, p. 56.

12 C. Ford Runge, Benjamin Senauer, Philip G. Pardey & Mark W. Rosegrant, *Ending Hunger by 2050. Crucial Investments and Policies*, Washington: International Food Policy Research Institute, 2003.

13 James Martin, *The Meaning of the 21st Century*, London: Eden Project Books, 2006, p. 75.

14 'Causing Hunger: an overview of the food crisis in Africa', *Oxfam Briefing Paper*, 91, July 2006, p. 23.

15 Cited by Alex de Waal, *AIDS and Power. Why there is no political crisis – yet*, London: Zed Books, 2006, pp. 86-87. This conclusion, while underlining the impact of HIV/AIDS, should be treated with caution since many economists doubt that existing economic models adequately capture the impacts of the disease.

16 *State of Food Security in the World 2006*, Rome: Food and Agriculture Organization, 2006, p. 23.

17 Reported by Human Security Center in 2005, cited by Joachim von Braun, 'The World Food Situation. An Overview', December 2005, International Food Policy Research Institute, **http://www.ifpri.org.**

18 *State of Food Security in the World 2006*, Rome: Food and Agriculture Organization, 2006, p. 23.

19 Matthew Lockwood, *The State They're In: An Agenda for International Action on Poverty in Africa*, Rugby: ITDG Publishing, 2006, pp. 73–97.

20 Alex de Waal, *AIDS and Power. Why there is no political crisis – yet*, London: Zed Books, 2006, pp. 53–61.

21 Causing Hunger: an overview of the food crisis in Africa', *Oxfam Briefing Paper*, 91, July 2006, pp. 22–23.

22 P. J. Gregory, J. S. I. Ingram & M. Brklacich, 'Climate change and food security', *Philosophical Transactions of the Royal Society*, 360, 2005, p. 2141.

23 P. J. Gregory, J. S. I. Ingram & M. Brklacich, 'Climate change and food security', *Philosophical Transactions of the Royal Society*, 360, 2005, p. 2141.

24 Joachim von Braun, 'The World Food Situation. An Overview', December 2005, International Food Policy Research Institute, **http://www.ifpri.org.**

25 *The Ecologist*, November 2002, p. 41.

26 Colin Tudge, *So Shall We Reap*, London: Penguin, 2003, pp. 145–146.

27 Hartwig de Haen et al., 'The World Food Economy in the Twenty-first Century: Challenges for International Co-operation', *Development Policy Review*, 21, 2003, pp. 687–690.

28 For example, see Christian J. Peters, 'Genetic engineering in agriculture: who stands to benefit?' *Journal of Agricultural and Environmental Ethics*, 13, 2000, pp. 313–327.

29 Colin Tudge, *So Shall We Reap*, London: Penguin, 2003, pp 268–269.

30 James Martin, *The Meaning of the 21st Century*, London: Eden Project Books, 2006, p. 78.

31 *Healthy and Sustainable Food for London, The Mayor's Food Strategy 2006*, London: London Development Agency, 2006, p. 75.

32 Reported in *The Times*, 11 December 2006.

33 Albert E. J. McGill, 'Nutrigenomics: A Bridge Too Far, For Now?' paper presented to the *Ethics & Politics of Food Conference*, Oslo, 2006.

HOW WILL THE WORLD FEED ITS GROWING POPULATION? WHAT MIGHT BE THE IMPLICATIONS?

- Will food supplies keep up with the population?
- Food security will be more important in global politics
- Global food companies will face intense scrutiny
- Might the middle classes develop new ideas about food?

Will food supplies keep up with the population? An estimated 40% more people by mid century (many getting richer), huge constraints on water, land and labour, fragile governance in many countries and the global food industry's middle class bias will make this a tall order.

But on the positive side will be the slowing down of population growth (perhaps stabilising after 2050), technological answers to resource limitations, support from global networks for better governance and the possibility that town dwellers will eat a healthier diet, releasing land for staple crops.

Recently, the number of undernourished people has remained constant while the population has kept going up. Is this the likely scenario for the next 20 years? The total who are underfed would stay at around 800 million, but this would represent a falling percentage of the planet's population.

Food security will be more important in global politics. With 90% of humanity living in areas that share water supplies with other countries, 'water wars' have been widely predicted. Yet it is at least as likely that water shortages will *strengthen* international cooperation.

> 'China has a fifth of the world's population on just 7% of the world's cultivable land'

In the past 50 years countries have negotiated over 200 water treaties, whereas violence between states over water has been reported in just 37 cases (all but seven in the Middle East).[1] Too much may be at stake for nations to fall out with each other.

China's need to import food will have global implications. China is not blessed with abundant farm land. One fifth of the world's population is crowded on to just 7% of the world's cultivable soil.[2] As China's population grows and becomes more wealthy, food consumption will soar. The country has a history of famines leading to rebellion, and its leaders will want to avoid a repetition at all costs.

This could be as important to Beijing's foreign policy as the economy's need for oil. It could be one reason why the government is stacking up foreign currency reserves. Faced by a food crisis, China would have enough foreign exchange to secure supplies.

But importing food will not be enough. In 2006, 400 out of 668 large Chinese cities were short of water and rationing was getting more common.[3] Widespread water shortages, coupled with high unemployment, could threaten the country's political stability. The whole world would feel the effects.

Global food companies will face intense scrutiny – even more than today. Sustainable farming, fair trade and healthy eating will attract more attention, not least from the expanding middle classes in Asia, Africa and South America. In a globalised world, these new graduates and professionals will share many of the concerns of their counterparts in the West.

They will adopt more affluent diets on the one hand, but – in many cases – have sympathy for the poor on the other. They will support a flood of international NGOs, who will exert strong pressure on business and governments to address global food concerns. In an increasingly transparent world, food companies will face mounting demands to justify their activities.

Might the middle classes develop new ideas about food? Though the food industry influences consumers through advertising, it largely responds to consumer demands. Might concerns about poverty, climate change and personal health encourage new ideas about what is fashionable to eat?

Perhaps led by celebrities, might the notion of eating *enough* (rather than too much) gain ground?[4] Fashionable consumers would eat just enough to keep themselves and the planet healthy, and leave more resources to feed the poor. The food industry would respond by developing ways to make 'enough' food attractive and satisfying.

Could this be the future of food in the next two decades?

1 United Nations Development Programme, *Beyond Scarcity: Power, poverty and the global water crisis*, Basingstoke: Palgrave, 2006, p. 221.

2 James Kynge, *China Shakes the World. The Rise of a Hungry Nation*, London: Weidenfeld, 2006, p. 126.

3 James Kynge, *China Shakes the World. The Rise of a Hungry Nation*, London: Weidenfeld, 2006, p. 143.

4 We are grateful to Dr. Albert McGill for this thought.

CHAPTER 6
WHAT WILL HAPPEN TO GLOBAL MIGRATION?
THE STORY SO FAR

- People are on the move
- The nature of international migration has been changing
- The growth of short-term migration has been especially important
- Remittances are now a major component of the global economy
- Migration illustrates the tensions between globalisation and nation states

Across the planet, people are on the move. Huge numbers have been flowing into the towns.

To give some idea of the scale, cities contained 750 million people – nearly 30% of the world's population – in 1950. Today the total is over 3 billion, with projected growth to 5 billion by 2030. By then, 60% of the world will live in cities.[1] Migration within countries is mostly responsible.

Much smaller in total, but still highly significant, has been the expansion of international migration, which is our focus. According to the UN, the number of international migrants leapt from 75 million in 1965, to 175 million in 2000 and to 191 million in 2005.

These were people living outside their country of birth or citizenship for 12 months or more.[2] Though just 3% of the global population, they are equivalent in size to the fifth most populous country in the world.[3]

They include people with permission to work, their families, refugees (7% of the world's international migrants)[4] and those who are unauthorised. Migration continues to polarise between people with high and low skills.

The nature of international migration has been changing – for example:[5]

- *Migration from the global South to the North has been growing fast.* In 1960 57% of all migrants lived in less-developed regions: in 2005 just 37% did so. Europe had the largest number of immigrants in 2005 (64 million), followed by Asia (53 million) and North America (44 million).
- *More countries now host a significant number of migrants.* Between 1960 and 2005, countries with more than half a million immigrants more than

doubled – from 30 to 64. With 38 million in 2005, the United States has the largest number.

■ *Women migrants to the rich world have been increasing faster than men.* In 2005, women comprised half of all international migrants, up from 47% in 1960. This growth was larger in the developed than developing world, where the proportion remained at 46%.

Most women migrants are employed in services and welfare. They only tend to be among the more skilled professions if migration policies are developed for their specific occupation, like nursing.[6]

■ *The expansion of the EU has begun to encourage the greater movement of people* from Eastern Europe. Previously classed as international migrants, they now have automatic rights of entry to some EU states; other states will open their borders in the next few years.

Net migration to Britain from the eight countries that joined the EU in 2004 totalled up to half a million between May 2004 and September 2006. As many as half may have returned home by the end of that period.[7]

Coming on top of migration from outside Europe, arrivals from poorer states within the EU are creating a British society that is 'super-diverse'.[8]

The growth of short-term migration has been especially important. More people are moving temporarily, remaining for a while and then returning home.

They include a growing number of students who stay on in employment, before returning to their country of origin. Temporary migration by very skilled people has become highly significant.

A study of Polish immigrants in London found that many did not intend to remain permanently, unlike large numbers of Eastern European refugees after the Second World War. Almost a quarter were using their earnings to buy a property in Poland.

Rather than migration being linear (from Poland to London), many were in a circular movement from Poland to London and back again. Poles would come to London, visit home periodically and then return to Poland.

They would tell their friends at home about the opportunities and give them advice. When they settled back in Poland, a friend or relative would take their place.[9]

Among care workers, there is a clear chain of migration. A nanny cares for the child of a rich country's family for two or three years. Back home, her children are looked after by a paid mother, whose own children are cared for by an aunt or the eldest daughter.

A 'globalisation of love' takes place. The rich family has maternal abundance – a full-time nanny, plus the biological mother when she returns from her job.

> 'A globalisation of love is taking place'

Children at the other end of the chain experience maternal deprivation. They don't see their mother for long periods, while family members have to do the extra work.[10]

Similar dynamics occur in other forms of care.

Remittances are now a major component of the global economy. The World Bank has produced astonishing figures. It estimates that migrants sent home officially more than $167 billion to their families in developing countries in 2005, approaching double the amount five years before.

This was more than twice the level of international aid. If you add in remittances through informal channels (such as relatives taking money home in cash), the total could be 50% higher.

Remittances have become the largest source of external capital in 36 developing countries.[11] Some 500 million people – 8% of the entire world population – receive remittances.[12]

Alongside these flows of money are 'social remittances' – 'the ideas, behaviours, identities and social capital that migrants export to their home communities. They may include ideas about democracy, health, gender, equality, human rights and community organisation.'[13]

These social remittances can be a force for democracy and accountability. But they may also lead to greater materialism and individualism, which can undermine social cohesion.

Migrants often live in two interlinked worlds – they have a foot in their host country but another back home. It is not enough to adopt a nation state view and see migrants as people who either leave your country or arrive. Migration should be seen in the context of global connectedness.

Using improved communications, money and information flow constantly between immigrants and their families and friends at home – and so do people: a migrant may return home for Christmas or be visited by her brother.

Having a foot in different worlds helps migrants to see diversity as normal. As nurses, builders or waiters, they learn to provide a service to people who are very different to them.

American-speaking Filipina nurses recruited to Britain's health service in 2002 were subjected to hours of *Coronation Street,* a TV soap, so that they could learn that when a patient said they wanted 'to spend a penny', they were not talking about money.[14]

People in host countries become more used to diversity, too. Subtly, this encourages a 'cosmopolitan' view that we are all part of a worldwide community, in which diversity is OK. Migration draws the world together.

Migration illustrates the tensions between globalisation and nation states. Globalisation involves the increasingly open flow of goods and capital, the ever-expanding movement of people on holiday or doing business, and instant communication between individuals on different sides of the world.

As countries open up their borders, it is natural that more people should want to live and work abroad. Migrants, gangmasters, traffickers, many employers and states exporting migrants (and enjoying their remittances) now have a stake in migration.

On the other side are electorates and some politicians in host countries who want to close borders and make it harder for new arrivals to enter. They are worried about:

- overcrowding;
- threats to national identity;
- fears that local people will lose their jobs.

The clash between these two sets of interests will determine the future course of international migration.

As the desire to limit migration has come head-to-head with the desire of millions to move, unauthorised immigration has thrived.

Between 300,000 and one million illegal migrants enter the United States from Mexico each year. A possible 800,000 enter 'fortress' Europe.[15] In recent years Australia, Denmark and many other host countries have tightened immigration controls to reassure voters.

But as a study of German immigration asked,

'How can one hope to control the approximately 66 million annual visitors, 20 million automobiles and 2 million heavy trucks that cross Bavaria's borders, thoroughly checking everyone's identity papers, without the border traffic coming to a complete standstill? Even forgery-resistant identity cards with biometric data are only a useful means of hindering unauthorised entry if potential fraud can be checked.'[16]

How will tensions over migration be resolved? Will ever more ingenious attempts be made to keep immigrants out? Or will 'managed migration' allow more people to move temporarily, provided they meet an economic need?

1 'World Urbanization Prospects: The 2003 Revision', United Nations Population Division, 2004, **http://www.un.org.**

2 *Trends in Total Migration Stock: The 2005 Revision*, New York: United Nations, 2006, p. 1. These numbers have been boosted by the 27 million or more people in the former Soviet Union who were counted as internal migrants in the 1980s, but became classified as international migrants after the break-up of the USSR.

3 'Global Estimates and Trends', **http://www.iom.int** (downloaded March 2007).

4 *Trends in Total Migration Stock: The 2005 Revision*, New York: United Nations, 2006, p. 4.

5 Figures in this section are taken mainly from *Trends in Total Migration Stock: The 2005 Revision*, New York: United Nations, 2006, pp. 1–3.

6 *World Migration 2005*, Geneva: International Organization for Migration, 2005, p. 15.

7 David G. Blanchflower, Jumana Saleheen & Chris Shadforth, 'The Impact of the Recent Migration from Eastern Europe on the UK Economy', January 2007, pp. 3–11, **http://www.bankofengland.co.uk.**

8 Steven Vertovec, 'The emergence of super-diversity in Britain', *Working Paper No. 25*, Centre on Migration, Policy and Society, University of Oxford, 2006.

9   John Eade, Stephen Drinkwater & Michael P. Garapich, 'Class & Ethnicity – Polish Migrants in London', *Research Report for the ESRC*, Centre for Research on Nationalism, Ethnicity and Multiculturalism, University of Surrey, **http://www.surrey.ac.uk** (accessed 15 March 2007). The study was undertaken in 2005-06.

10 Nicola Yeates, 'Global care chains: a critical introduction', *Global Migration Perspectives*, 44, Global Commission on International Migration, 2005, p. 7.

11 *Global Economic Prospects 2006: Economic Implications of Remittances and Migration*, Washington: World Bank, 2006, pp. 86–89.

11 *Global Economic Prospects 2006: Economic Implications of Remittances and Migration*, Washington: World Bank, 2006, pp. 86–89.

12 Kathleen Newland, 'A New Surge of Interest in Migration and Development', Migration Policy Institute, 1 February 2007, **http://www.migrationinformation.org.**

13 Peggy Levitt & Ninna Nyberg Sorenson, 'The transnational turn in migration studies', *Global Migration Perspectives*, 6, Global Commission on International Migration, 2004, p. 8.

14 Robin Cohen, *Migration and its Enemies*, Aldershot: Ashgate, 2006, p. 192.

15 Philippe Legrain, *Immigrants: Your Country Needs Them*, London: Little, Brown, 2006, pp. 32, 35.

16 Jorg Alt, 'Life in the world of shadows: the problem of illegal migration', *Global Migration Perspectives,* 41, Global Commission on International Migration, 2005, p. 12

WHAT WILL HAPPEN TO GLOBAL MIGRATION? WHAT WILL SHAPE THE NEXT 20 YEARS?

- Global migration will increase significantly
- Globalisation will strengthen the forces behind migration
- Host nations will be under mounting pressure to relax immigration controls
- Sending countries, too, will be more eager to manage than prevent migration
- Humanitarian concerns will push managed migration up the agenda

The UN expects global migration to increase significantly. The total number of migrants is projected to rise from 191 million in 2005 to 294 million in 2050.[1]

The table below gives figures for net migration to the more developed world, the main destination of international migrants. The rate of increase will continue to accelerate up to 2010, as it did during the second half of the twentieth century, but is expected to stabilise at a lower figure thereafter.

This lower plateau for migration seems implausible. Demographics alone point in a different direction. In developing countries 31% of the population is below the age of 14, compared to 18% in high-income countries.

Average annual net number of international migrants to more developed regions per decade, 1950–2050 (actual and projected figures)

1950–1960	3000
1960–1970	556,000
1970–1980	1,088,000
1980–1990	1,530,000
1990–2000	2,493,000
2000–2010	2,902,000
2010–2020	2,268,000
2020–2030	2,269,000
2030–2040	2,272,000
2040–2050	2,272,000

Source: *World Population Prospects. The 2006 Revision,* New York: United Nations, 2007, p. 26.

As these children become young adults, many more people will be in the age group most likely to go abroad.[2]

G1obalisation will strengthen the forces behind migration. More employers will want migrant labour, more people will want to move abroad and moving will be easier.

Globalisation will raise the demand for migrant labour, especially in rich countries. A more open world will continue to increase prosperity, creating jobs in the global North, particularly in the service sector.

Unlike manufacturing, producers of many services have to be near their customers. If labour shortages exist, a care home can't shift its operations abroad: it will have to import labour instead.[3]

The demand will balloon for workers in lower-skilled jobs, such as in catering (think of Chinese restaurants) and various forms of care. In 1996 over half the legal immigrants to the US were women, their median age was 29 and many were employed in care work.[4]

There will also be a growing demand for skilled labour. As baby-boomers retire in the rich world, not enough skills may exist among the smaller cohorts behind. Employers will turn to migrants.[5]

'Just look at Silicon Valley's large supply of successful Indian and Taiwanese computer scientists and venture capitalists. The enhanced appetite for such professionals reflects the shift to a globalised economy in which countries compete for markets by creating and attracting technically skilled talent.'[6]

Globalisation will also boost the supply of migrant labour, not least because of better education. Over half of boys and a third of girls in South Asia are now in high school, and both figures will rise as Asia competes in the global economy.[7]

To keep pace with the growing number of high-schoolers, the boom in university education will continue. Higher education will widen individuals' horizons, increase their confidence and give them the skills to work abroad, including cultural skills: education can act as a bridge between cultures.

An American survey found that over half of migrant nannies had college degrees.[8] More students will study overseas and many will stay on after they graduate. An estimated 70% of newly minted PhD graduates from abroad remain in the United States. Many become citizens.[9]

With few signs that the global widening of inequality will be reversed, the wage gap will encourage people to migrate.

For example, pay in skill-intensive industries such as aircraft production has been going up faster than wages in low-skill industries, such as garments.[10] This trend will persist as developed countries push into higher value production.

> '70% of newly minted PhD graduates from abroad remain in the United States'

The global pay gap will be especially marked for professional and other highly skilled jobs. Professional salaries in poor countries will be depressed by low levels of pay generally, which will limit what these countries can afford. Rich countries, on the other hand, will afford higher salaries as top earnings race ahead.

Teachers, nurses and other skilled workers in the South will seek jobs overseas, at least for a time. For some, this will be a way of insuring against a loss of family income due to illness, old age, unemployment or crop failure on the family farm. Migration can diversify risk.

Moving will be easier as the world gets better connected. Improved telecommunications will support quicker, fuller and more accurate information about potential jobs, reducing dependence on less reliable, informal networks. As now, global media will beam idealised images of northern lifestyles into the poorest villages, increasing the desire to move.

Despite higher energy prices, technology will lower travel costs, continuing a long-term trend – costs are a big constraint on migration. Even more than today, facilitating migration will be a major international business involving travel agents, bankers, lawyers and recruiters.[11] 'Circular migration' from home and back again will become more attractive.

This migration will be self-reinforcing. Immigrants will form communities that welcome newly arriving compatriots, help them to make a home and put them in touch with useful networks. Increased immigration will create more of these communities (often outside the large cities), making it easier for others to migrate.

Migrants returning home will tell relatives and friends about job opportunities and put them in touch with people who can help. People who have migrated once are more likely to do so again.[12]

Host nations will be under mounting pressure to relax immigration controls, despite public concerns. Managed migration – admitting larger numbers in an orderly way – will rise up the policy agenda. This is already happening in some countries, such as Britain.

Temporary migration will benefit their economies. Migrants will fill vacant jobs, which will check wage inflation and take the heat off interest rates.

An upswing in net migration cut Britain's interest rates by an estimated 0.5% in 2006, with the effect likely to grow to 1%.[13] UK Treasury officials reckon that immigration adds almost 0.5% to the country's economic growth.

> 'Immigration adds an estimated 0.5% to Britain's economic growth'

Temporary migration will not be ideal: workers may return home when they are becoming most skilled. But it could ease the transition to an older workforce.

Unlike immigrants who settle permanently, bring in their families, age and depend on younger workers when they retire, temporary migration allows vacancies to be filled by foreign workers who return to their countries of origin and are replaced by others.

Societies will pay a high price for tight controls on migration. The price may be higher than the political costs of letting in more immigrants on a short-stay basis. *Some fears about migration are ill founded,* in particular that immigrants pinch jobs from the locals. Using UK data from the mid 1970s to mid 2000s, a 2006 study found that immigration depressed the earnings of other migrants, but had a negligible effect on the pay of workers born in the host country.

This was because immigrants did 'naff jobs' that local people were unwilling to take, or filled skilled posts for which nationals were not qualified. Immigrants were not in competition with local people.[14]

Indeed, through their own spending and by working in activities that would not be viable without them, immigrants actually create jobs.[15]

The costs of reducing migration will remain high. As mobility increases, the sheer weight of numbers will be against controls. An estimated 1 million-plus immigrants enter Europe and North America illegally each year.[16]

Security measures to keep them out will remain expensive. Germany spends over £1 billion a year on border patrols alone.[17] There will also be high indirect costs. Tight conditions for entry may force immigration underground, with a loss of tax receipts and a boost to the criminal economy.

Illegal migrants who want to settle temporarily will have to stay longer to pay off the extra costs of their illicit entry, defeating the object of immigration controls. *'Let the market rip' will be no alternative,* however. Some argue that immigration should be allowed to find its own level. Migrants will come if the jobs exist, enriching the host country economically and culturally. But once the vacancies are filled, the number of immigrants will drop. The market will regulate migration more effectively than artificial controls.[18]

But this ignores many people's deeply held concerns about overcrowding and identity. No politician will be able to ignore public fears (whether valid or not) of being swamped, of immigrants 'changing our way of life' or of new arrivals taking 'our' jobs, 'our' houses and 'our' welfare benefits.

Governments will be on a hiding to nothing. To counter public anxiety about immigration, politicians will have to take action to stem illegal entry. These measures will heighten the perception that immigration is a problem.

When evidence later emerges – as it surely must – that illegal immigration remains a problem, politicians will have to announce a further set of initiatives. The announcement will reinforce public anxiety ('the problem must be bad'), which will intensify the political pressure the announcement was meant to relieve.

Meanwhile, the Treasury and other parts of government will want to expand immigration because of its economic advantages.

Shifting the debate from 'immigration is a problem' to 'immigration is a benefit' would get politicians off the hook. To bring about that change, managed migration – allowing in temporarily only the people the economy needs – will be a growing priority.

Sending countries, too, will be more eager to manage than prevent migration.[19] This is despite the fact that as now, emigration will impose emotional costs on families who are separated and economic costs on the country of origin.

In the case of high-skilled emigration, the sending country may:

- lose its return on workers trained at public expense;
- have fewer opportunities to get economies of scale in skill-intensive activities;
- pay a higher price for services that experience a skills shortage;
- find it harder in some cases to improve their population's health because health professionals have moved abroad.

Remittances from migrants to their home countries will help to offset these disadvantages. Remittances already represent a large source of income for the countries concerned, as we have noted.

For instance, in Latin America and the Caribbean, which receive more than any other region, remittances reached over $45 billion in 2006. This was more than all the foreign direct investment and official development assistance to the region.[20]

Remittances may come with a price tag: a migrant may live a miserable existence to earn the cash. But the benefits back home can be large:

- Remittances reduce poverty, even though they may not cut inequality – indeed, a new source of inequality may emerge between those who receive remittances and those who don't.
- They provide sums for investment in farms and small-scale business.
- They increase household spending on education and health, which are important for development.
- They can help households cope with shocks at home. After Hurricane Mitch in 1998, the El Salvador government asked the US not for aid, but for permission for Salvadorian immigrants to stay longer in America so that they could send money to their storm-affected relatives.[21]

High-skilled emigration will bring gains apart from remittances. If suitable jobs are not available locally, skilled workers may find employment abroad to match their qualifications. They will gain valuable experience and often extra training, which will benefit their country of origin if they return home – a 'brain gain' rather than 'brain drain'.

Countries may increase their influence through their diasporas.

'Boasting several British Lords, senior justices across post-colonial Africa, the president of Guyana, a dozen Canadian MPs and increasingly high-level federal appointees in America, Indians are poised to capitalise on the diversity of Western democracies.'[22]

Low-skilled emigration can benefit poor workers left behind. Aside from remittances, it can free up jobs for people who would have been unemployed, boosting the incomes of their extended families and acting as a safety valve for the failure to create enough jobs at home. Working abroad will increase migrants' skills, enabling them to earn more when they get home.

For these reasons, countries of origin will put a growing emphasis on managing migrations. They will want policies that maximise these benefits and minimise the disadvantages.

Humanitarian concerns will push managed migration up the global agenda. In 2001 the United Nations Office for Drug Control and Crime Prevention stated that human trafficking – the enforced transportation of people for employment against their will – was the fastest growing form of organised crime.

It was less risky than the drugs or arms trade and produced bigger profits. The US State Department estimates that 600,000 to 800,000 people, mostly women and children, are trafficked across borders each year – today's slave trade.[23]

In addition will be the many more people who choose to be smuggled across borders, and end up heavily in debt to and dependent on those who have arranged the journey.

As now, their vulnerability may lead to passport confiscation, types of work very different to what they were promised, slave-like employment (with wages held back on the pretext of repaying travel costs)[24] and other forms of abuse. Some of these abuses occur even when the travel arrangements are legal.[25]

On top of human trafficking and smuggling will be refugees and asylum seekers who are displaced by armed conflict, natural disasters and political threats within their home countries. They totalled almost 12 million in 2004.[26]

At present, destination countries view asylum seekers and smuggled migrants as a threat – both to security and to their attempts to control immigration. But this view will be increasingly at odds with the human rights agenda.

Might perceptions change as abuses are documented and brought to public attention? Might more people see smuggled migrants as victims, almost on a par with people trafficking, rather than a danger?

Support could grow for NGOs and international agencies that champion the cause of migrants who are displaced or abused. Current forms of control are likely to be increasingly criticised.

Not only does evading controls drive migrants into the hands of criminals, but if they are caught – as noted in chapter 11 – 'illegals' may be subject to further abuse.

How far will pressure mount for ways of managing migration that better protect human rights?[27]

1 *Trends in Total Migration Stock: The 2005 Revision, New York*: United Nations, 2006, p. 1, and World Population Prospects. The 2006 Revision, New York: United Nations, 2007, p. x.

2 *Global Economic Prospects 2006: Economic Implications of Remittances and Migration*, Washington: World Bank, 2006, p. 28.

3 Robin Cohen, *Migration and its Enemies*, Aldershot: Ashgate, 2006, p. 134.

4 Arlie Russell Hochschild, 'Global Care Chains and Emotional Surplus Value' in Will Hutton & Anthony Giddens (eds.), *On The Edge*, London: Vintage, 2001, pp. 130–146.

5 For example, it is estimated that about 13.5 million job openings will be created in Britain between 2002 and 2012, of which almost 12.2 million will be replacements for existing workers. The number of new jobs will be just over 1.3 million. Warwick Institute for Employment Research, *Bulletin No. 73*, 2004.

6 Jagdish Bhagwati, *In Defense of Globalisation*, New York: OUP, 2004, p. 213.

7 Jerome C. Glenn & Theodore J. Gordon, *2004 State of the Future*, Washington: American Council for the United Nations University, 2004, p. 33.

8 Arlie Russell Hochschild, 'Global Care Chains and Emotional Surplus Value' in Will Hutton & Anthony Giddens (eds.), *On The Edge*, London: Vintage, 2001, p. 138.

9   Jagdish Bhagwati, *In Defense of Globalization*, New York: OUP, 2004, p. 214–216.

10 David Dollar, 'Globalization, Poverty, and Inequality since 1980', *World Bank Policy Research Working Paper No. 3333*, June 2004, p. 16, **http://www.econ.worldbank.org.**

11 United Nations High Commissioner for Refugees, *The State of the World's Refugees 2006: Human displacement in the New Millennium*, Oxford: OUP, 2006, p. 13.

12 Robin Cohen, *Migration and its Enemies*, Aldershot: Ashgate, 2006, p. 131.

13 Ernst & Young Item Club, quoted by David Smith, 'Migrants "have kept interest rates down"', *The Sunday Times*, 23 April 2006.

14 Marco Manacorda, Alan Manning & Jonathan Wadsworth, 'The Impact of Immigration on the Structure of Male Wages: Theory and Evidence from Britain', *CEP Discussion Paper No. 754*, London: LSE Centre for Economic Performance, October 2006.

15 In Israel, for example, over 710,000 Russian immigrants, 15% of Israel's working-age population, arrived between 1990 and 1997. Far from causing unemployment, they sparked an investment boom which increased employment. Sarit Cohen Goldnet & Chang-Tai Hsieh, 'Macroeconomic and Labor Market Impact of Russian Immigration to Israel', April 2000, **http://www.hiebs.hku.hk.**

16 Philippe Legrain, *Immigrants: Your Country Needs Them*, London: Little, Brown, 2006, pp. 324–325

17 Jorg Alt, 'Life in the world of shadows: the problem of illegal migration', *Global Migration Perspectives*, 41, Global Commission on International Migration, 2005, p. 13.

18 Philippe Legrain, *Immigrants: Your Country Needs Them*, London: Little, Brown, 2006.

19 Except where stated, this section is based on *Global Economic Prospects 2006: Economic Implications of Remittances and Migration*, Washington: World Bank, 2006, ch. 3 & 5.

20 Kathleen Newland, 'A New Surge of Interest in Migration and Development', Migration Policy Institute, 1 February 2007, **http://www.migrationinformation.org.**

21 Kathleen Newland, 'A New Surge of Interest in Migration and Development', Migration Policy Institute, 1 February 2007, **http://www.migrationinformation.org.**

22 Parag Khanna, 'Bollystan: India's Diasporic Diplomacy' in Prasenjit K. Basu et al., *India as a New Global Leader*, London: Foreign Policy Centre, 2005, p. 18

23 Silvia Scarpa, 'Child trafficking: the worst face of the world', *Global Migration Perspectives*, 40, Global Commission on International Migration, 2005, pp. 2–3.

24 Mean costs for smuggling and trafficking between Asia and the Americas may exceed 26,000. On other routes the figures tend to be less. Melanie Petros, 'The costs of human smuggling and trafficking', *Global Migration Perspectives*, 31, Global Commission on International Migration, 2005, pp. 4–5.

25 Jacqueline Bhabba, 'Trafficking, Smuggling & Human Rights', *Migration Information Source*. March 2005, **http://www.migrationinformation.org.**

26 US Committee for Refugees, 'Key Statistics', World Refugee Survey 2004, **http://www.refugees.org.**

27 Paper No. 3333, June 2004, p. 16, **http://www.econ.worldbank.org.**

WHAT WILL HAPPEN TO GLOBAL MIGRATION? WHAT MIGHT BE THE IMPLICATIONS?

- A slow shift from restricting to managing migration is likely
- 'Who are we?' will become a more pressing question

A slow shift from restricting to managing migration is likely. This will come about because of:

- individuals' strong desire to move;
- the benefits to receiving and sending nations;
- difficulties in limiting the movement of people;
- humanitarian concerns.

Though this shift has already begun in the immigration policies of countries like Britain, it will be a major departure from the 'keep them out' approach widespread today.

Gradually switching to 'let them in' (temporarily and if they meet an economic need) will be far from easy. It will run up against deep-rooted public anxieties, especially in host countries.

Seeing immigrant numbers grow, people will wonder if their national identities are at risk. Their fears may be assuaged if migrants stay for short periods, but there will still be claims that too many are staying on, that legal entrants are the tip of an illegal iceberg and that national cultures are under threat.

So relaxing restrictions will be hard, but probably inevitable.

Encouraging temporary rather than long-term migration will be one element of a managed approach. This will work with the grain of today's circular movement of migration. Policies may include:

- issuing temporary work permits;
- promoting competition within the 'migration business' to make the process cheaper — migrants would be able to recover their costs and return home more quickly;
- providing jobs and other incentives for migrants to settle back home;
- further restricting the entry of dependants, possibly. If immigrants cannot be joined by close relatives, they will have stronger incentive to return home.

One suggested policy-mix would include a market-driven system of bidding for immigration visas. Visas would go to the highest bids, making sure that only immigrants who made the greatest economic contribution were allowed in.

Proceeds from the bids could be used to expand schooling and other provisions in areas where most new arrivals settled.

Temporary immigrants could only stay on if they had acquired language skills and other tools of social integration. Migrants would not be entitled to welfare benefits for a period, to reduce some of the opposition to immigration.[1]

Tightening controls on illegal entrants and 'over-stayers' will be a second element. In countries like Britain, technology may allow a shift from border controls (which are largely ineffective) to controls based on identification.

To improve security, biometric technologies will be used increasingly for credit cards, to gain access to buildings (iris scanning is starting to be used) and for other everyday purposes, such as driving your car (making it harder to steal).

Identity cards with effective authentication (using several biometric technologies) will one day seem natural as we continue to move – with public acquiescence – towards this surveillance world. Though fraud will remain possible, life will be tougher for illegal migrants.

Eventually, more effective controls are likely to enhance public confidence in the immigration system. Governments will find it easier to expand temporary migration in response to labour-market demands.

Managed migration based on creating trust in the system will be difficult, but will be a plausible response to the mounting pressures for people to move.

Greater international cooperation to secure these goals will be the third element. This will include bilateral agreements between states, regional collaboration (will the widespread 'regional consultative processes' on migration become more formal?) and global arrangements.[2]

Of all flows, global migration has the weakest international regime. Trade has the World Trade Organization, finance has the World Bank and other institutions, dangerous diseases have the World Health Organization and so on. But migration has no equivalent.

Though global initiatives on migration are still in their infancy, this is likely to change. The global North and South will seek to harness the economic benefits of migration, while NGOs and others will press for the stronger protection of human rights.

Will new global institutions augment initiatives at national and regional levels? Like trade, the environment, the Internet and many other aspects of modern life, will managing migration go global too?

'Who are we?' will become an even more pressing question than it is today. If, as seems likely, managing migration allows larger movements of people, the issue of identity will grow even more acute.

More people leaving their societies behind will ask themselves what it means, in their new context, to be a Kenyan, an authentic Muslim or a lawyer (if they get a job that makes very different demands from those expected at home). Identity becomes an issue when you rub shoulders with other people.

Host nations may be forced to redefine their identities. Some may add diversity to their understanding of themselves, as is currently the case with parts of Canada. For many, being Canadian includes welcoming different cultures: the City of Toronto translates all official documents into a dozen languages.[3] An elastic identity helps others to fit in.

> 'An elastic national identity will help others to fit in'

Other nationalities may define themselves in terms of how they are different to their migrants – 'We are us and you are you. If you stay you must become like us, but visitors can be different provided they stick to the rules.'

Countries will be faced with an ethical choice: 'What sort of people do we want to be?'

---

1 Irwin Stelzer, 'More economists or grief-counsellors? My answer to the immigrant dilemma', *The Times*, 24 October, 2006. Irwin Stelzer is director of economic policy studies at the Hudson Institute.

2 *World Migration 2005*, Geneva: International Organization for Migration, 2005, ch. 22.

3 Philippe Legrain, *Immigrants: Your Country Needs Them*, London: Little, Brown, 2006, p. 285.

CHAPTER 7

HOW WILL GLOBAL COMMUNICATIONS AFFECT PEOPLE'S LIVES?

THE STORY SO FAR

> ■ The world's rich increasingly live in a media cocoon
> ■ The physical economy is being supplemented by an online economy
> ■ The information economy is being transformed into a social economy
> ■ Mass media is evolving into personalised media
> ■ Offline concentrations of power are being replicated online

The world's rich increasingly live in a media cocoon. An English student returning from China commented,

> 'Where I was in China, people lived their lives through the family. The family was always the focus of conversation. The first question they would ask me was, "What does your family think of you coming to China?"
>
> 'Returning to England, I was struck by how we live our lives through the media. Our conversations centre on the films we've seen, what happened in the soap last night and stories on the news. We are constantly talking online and by mobile phone.'

The spread of communication technologies is bringing more and more people into this cocoon, which is becoming increasingly global in nature.

The Internet in particular is global in design – it jumps territorial boundaries. It is creating an e-world of e-commerce, e-friendship, e-government and e-mail.[1]

'To imagine that the *world* is coming together would be a clear exaggeration'

Internet users leapt from nearly half a billion to slightly over a billion between 2001 and 2005. In 2004, 38% of all Internet subscribers worldwide had access to broadband.[2]

Falling costs allow more and more people across the planet to stay closer in touch by phone. Mobile phone subscribers more than doubled from just under a billion in 2001 to 2.1 billion in 2005.

Yet when two-thirds of the world's 6 billion people do not have a phone and five-sixths don't use the Internet, to imagine that the *world* is coming together would be a clear exaggeration.[3]

How are communication technologies, especially those using the Internet, affecting the lives of the minority who have access to them? We give some examples, recognising that experiences will differ from one part of the world to another.

The physical economy is being supplemented by an online economy. The Internet allows many business activities to be done more efficiently – from sharing and editing documents collectively to outsourcing and offshoring. In 2005, services worth an estimated $30 billion had been offshored, with potential growth to $300 billion.[4]

The United States leads the way in using the Net for customer services: online sales in manufacturing, wholesale, retail and selected services accounted for nearly 10% of these sectors' total revenue in 2004. Online sales were most important in manufacturing (approaching 25%), followed by wholesaling (nearly 15%).[5] UK online sales are expected to double from 10% of all retailing in 2007 to 20% by 2010.[6]

Communication technologies have made possible an army of new products – from data warehousing, to Web hosting, to the music-download business, to multi-player computer games. This multiplication of new products is only just beginning.

The information economy is being transformed into a social economy. Many have predicted that we would live in an economy where information is at the heart of what is bought and sold. Instead, rich nations seem to be entering a social economy, in which interactions and relationships are central. Exchanging information helps build those relationships.

Passivity is giving way to participation. Radio and TV audiences increasingly interact with programmes, voting and e-mailing comments. For many, time spent on the computer reduces the time spent passively in front of television.[7]

YouTube, Newgrounds and many other sites are expanding the opportunity for creative expression. Users (mainly young people) are creating new forms of communication by combining content from a third source with their own material (in mashups).

Are we witnessing a change in our concept of literacy as multimedia messages begin to overtake text?

New technologies are being used in social ways. UK research shows that the iPod, for example, does not isolate individuals. The ability to carry their music collection with them enables listeners to play new tracks to their friends.

> 'Will multimedia messages change our concept of literacy?'

Many iPod users compile special collections of tunes, or playlists, for family listening in the car. Family members negotiate the playlist, so that Disney tunes end up juxtaposed with Jazz or the latest number one.[8]

Within urban Chinese families, far from being a substitute for conversation, communication technologies are often the topic of conversation.[9]

The social side of online communities is growing in importance. Traditional communities on the Internet were built around interests. Friendships formed as people spent time with others who were interested in the same thing.

On MySpace and other social network sites, however, the starting point is different. It's 'me' (a representation of myself to others) and my network of connections. The social dimension – 'find out about me' – is stronger.

A 2007 study found that Facebook's British members spend an average of 143 minutes a month on the site, checking on their friends, looking up former partners and updating their profile.[10]

Danah Boyd of the University of California has studied how young Americans use MySpace to meet friends or form new relationships.

> 'It's about identity formation – how I fit into society, who am I ... It's a new forum for hanging out that creates new publics. The burger joints where kids used to meet are gone and malls are now banning teenagers who are not with adults. This is the sort of place where they are going instead.'[11]

Family and friendship ties are being reinforced. Some people are afraid that the more time individuals spend online the less time they will have for other people. But from its early days the Internet has strengthened social and kinship ties.

In a Pew Research Centre poll in 2000, users reported that the Net had improved their links with family and friends. The longer they had used the Internet, the more likely they were to say this.[12]

Mobile phones allow users to be continually present to friends and family. 'What is new is the emerging feeling that one should be accessible everywhere and at all times.'[13]

Relationships within society are being strengthened more than damaged. Again, fears – that communication technologies would encourage the fragmentation of society – have not been borne out.

In the 'Netville' experiment near Toronto, those who were given free Internet access in the late 1990s talked with twice as many neighbours as those who weren't. They used the Internet to talk about small things, like finding a plumber.

They were invited into the homes of an average of four neighbours compared to 2.5 for the unwired. One resident commented:

> 'I have noticed neighbours talking to each other like they have been friends for a long time. I have noticed a closeness that you don't see in many communities.'[14]

When an issue emerges that grabs the attention of different groups online, the speed of Internet communication allows information to spread like wildfire.

On Monday 27 March 2006, after a weekend of immigration protests, tens of thousands of American teenagers walked out of class for their own protest. Many did so in response to messages on MySpace.[15]

The new media create significant opportunities for building social capital.

Mass media is evolving into personalised media. Personal video recorders (PVRs) allow users to record more than one programme at a time, or record one programme while playing back another, or to pause and rewind a live programme.

Recorders can learn their users' preferences and record programmes accordingly. Together with television over the Internet (which could be widespread within a few years), they make video-on-demand possible.

'Personalised scale' is the essence of the Internet. The more people who use the Net, the more each person can find exactly what they want on it.

New media enable individuals to personalise aspects of their everyday lives. 'Aproximeeting', for example, is becoming commonplace. Instead of making firms plans about time and place to meet, individuals are finalising details by mobile phone while they are out and about.[16]

'Mobiles are great', one person commented. 'In the past you had to arrive when you said. Now you can call or text that you will be 10 minutes late.' Individuals are personalising arrangements to fit their circumstances at the time.

Are individuals 'customising' their identities – changing who they are to fit different audiences? To an extent, people have always done this, but it has been claimed that the Net allows users to play with their identities more radically. Men can masquerade as women, disabled people as able-bodied, someone with a coloured skin as white.

Yet this is far from typical. Role playing in computer games is not very different in principle to role playing in real life games or on the stage.

Blogging and personal Web pages enable individuals to bring together various aspects of themselves, which they present to an online audience. This may actually strengthen their core identities.[17]

Offline concentrations of power are being replicated online. This is despite the fact that communications technologies are empowering individuals in all sorts of new ways. Global campaigns, such as the 2005 'Make poverty history', can be organised and amplified using the new media.

> 'The Internet may strengthen people's identities'

Bloggers can emerge from obscurity and acquire a worldwide following. Entrepreneurial journalists can create their own websites, sell adverts and make a living writing stories.

But the hopes of some that the Net would become a haven of untrammelled equality and freedom have been dashed. Inequalities and forms of control that are typical offline are to be found online.

- Hierarchies have been recreated in online communities.
- Businesses routinely pay extra for fast, secure 'tunnels' through the network, giving their traffic priority over 'ordinary' users. Companies like Google secure dominant positions on the Internet.
- Commercial interests cash in on talent discovered online, enabling hierarchies of skill to emerge – in some 'open source' communities, the best talent gets rewarded.
- The Chinese government controls what users can see on the Internet.
- Communication technologies allow greater social control through workplace surveillance (such as the counting of key strokes) and consumer surveillance. This is not always a bad thing. A programme called 'Turnitin' is being used to detect plagiarism among American students.
- Geodemographic data allows companies to profile their customers – where they live, their likely income and lifestyle – so that they can target their sales messages to people most likely to respond.[19]
- Google hopes to monitor the sites its users visit and the queries they ask to build ultra-precise portraits of them. It aims to become the supreme life coach, able to offer tailor-made advice on anything – from careers to what to do on the weekend – because it knows individuals so well.[20]

1 Jan Aart Scholte, *Globalization: A Critical Introduction*, Basingstoke: Palgrave, 2005, p. 68.
2 UNCTAD, *The Information Economy Report 2006. The Development Perspective*, New York: 2006, pp. 3–10.
3 Colin Sparks, 'Media and the Global Public Sphere: An Evaluative Approach' in Wilma de Jong, Martin Shaw & Neil Stammers (eds.), *Global Activism, Global Media*, London: Pluto, 2005, pp. 43–44.
4 UNCTAD, *The Information Economy Report 2006. The Development Perspective*, New York: 2006, p. 26.
5 UNCTAD, *The Information Economy Report 2006. The Development Perspective*, New York: 2006, pp.16–17.
6 IMRG, 'Annual Statement 2007', 29 April 2007.
7 Ronald E. Rice & Caroline Haythornthwaite, 'Perspectives on Internet Use: Access, involvement and interaction' in Leah A. Lievrouw & Sonia Livingstone (eds.), *The Handbook of New Media*, London: Sage, 2006, p. 104.
8 Research by Dr Michael Bull (University of Sussex), cited by Tom Standage (ed.), *The Future of Technology*, London: The Economist, 2005, pp. 220–221.
9 Sun Sun Lim, 'From cultural to information revolution. ICT domestication by middle-class Chinese families' in Thomas Berker, et al., *Domestication of Media and Technology*, Maidenhead: Open University Press, 2006, pp. 192–194.
10 Quoted by *The Times* on 28 July 2007.
11 Quoted in *The Times*, 21 February 2006.
12 Ronald E. Rice & Caroline Haythornthwaite, 'Perspectives on Internet Use: Access, involvement and interaction' in Leah A. Lievrouw & Sonia Livingstone (eds.), *The Handbook of New Media*, London: Sage, 2006, p. 102.
13 Knut H. Sorensen, 'Domestication: the enactment of technology' in Thomas Berker et al., *Domestication of Media and Technology*, Maidenhead: Open University Press, 2006, p. 55.
14 Barry Wellman, 'Connecting Community: On and Offline', 2005, **http://www.chass.utoronto.ca.**
15 Danah Boyd, 'Friends, Friendsters, and Top 8: Writing community into being on social network sites', *First Monday*, December 2006, **http://www.firstmonday.org.**
16 'The phone of the future', *The Economist Technology Quarterly*, 2 December 2006.
17 Nancy K. Baym, 'Interpersonal Life Online' in Leah A. Lievrouw & Sonia Livingstone (eds.), *The Handbook of New Media*, London: Sage, 2006, pp. 40–43.
18 *The Economist*, 11 March 2006.
19 Jennifer Daryl Slack & J. Maggregor Wise, 'Cultural Studies and Communication Technology' in Leah A. Lievrouw & Sonia Livingstone (eds.), *The Handbook of New Media*, London: Sage, 2006, pp. 153, 156.
20 Rhys Blakely, 'They know everything about you and didn't even have to ask', *The Times*, 26 May 2007.

HOW WILL GLOBAL COMMUNICATIONS AFFECT PEOPLE'S LIVES?
WHAT WILL SHAPE THE NEXT 20 YEARS?

- The capacity of communication technologies will leap ahead
- Communication technologies will continue to spread
- Commercial interests will influence the impact of communication technologies
- Social contexts will influence how media technologies are employed

The capacity of communication technologies will leap ahead as four 'BANG' technologies converge.[1]

Bits – information technology, which will continue to power ahead.

Atoms – nanotechnology, which offers the potential to create new materials and products 'bottom up', through the manipulation of molecular and atomic particles.

Neurons – brain sciences, which will feed breakthroughs in artificial intelligence.

Genes – biotechnology, such as biomimicry, which takes advantage of organic models. Algorithms based on natural selection can be used to 'evolve' new software and hardware.

Media technologies will be cheaper, easier, smarter and everywhere.

They will be cheaper in many cases. For example, Voice Over Internet Protocol allows phone calls to be made over the Internet at minimal cost.

In time, symbiotic networks may take advantage of the inbuilt wireless capability of mobile handsets and other devices. Data traffic would reach its destination via short hops from one device to another.

With plenty of such devices in a town centre, people on the move would access broadband and communicate across the network free of charge.[2]

> 'You'll boot up a computer as quickly as switching on an electric light'

Technologies will be easier to use. Wireless technologies will provide convenient computing that is always with you, for example, with broadband speeds much faster than today.[3] Eventually, you'll be able to boot up your computer as quickly as you switch on an electric light.

As technologies converge, hand-held devices will double-up as phones, portable TVs, cameras,

MP3 players, game boys, 'sat navs', house keys and credit cards – 'the remote for life'.

Swipe the mobile over the waiter's matching device and the bill will be paid. Next morning you'll receive a statement of what's left in your bank account.[4]

Technologies will also be smarter. Improved techniques of data mining – the process of analysing large volumes of data to identify patterns or relationships – will vastly enhance our ability to research human behaviour.

Applications will range from crime control to target setting: by tracking what workers do, it should be possible to replace crude output targets with feedback based on desired processes.

The Intelligent Software Agents Lab at Carnegie Mellon University, Pittsburgh, envisages a world in which autonomous, intelligent software agents perform increasingly sophisticated Web searches and many other tasks now undertaken by human users of the Web – 'find the cheapest apartment for six in Naples, Florida in August, and tell me if there are any special flight deals.'[5]

Rapid developments are occurring in virtual reality, including simulated environments that you interact with (as in video games), simulated environments that you feel immersed in (such as a flight simulator) and 3-D video-conferencing in which you can almost feel as if you are in the same room as the other person.

DreamWorks will produce all its animated films in 3-D from 2009. Movie-goers will enter the cinema with a ticket in one hand and glasses in the other – expect 3-D glasses to become fashion items.

Perhaps most significant, technologies will be everywhere. In the age of 'pervasive computing', smart chips only a fraction of a millimetre in size will make possible:

- 'smart dust' – tiny wireless microelectro-mechanical sensors that can do anything from tracking human movements to sensing minute vibrations;
- sensor packages that survive the slow-motion crush of glaciers;
- radio frequency identification (RFID) tags that monitor anything from oil pipelines to supermarket merchandise as it travels along the supply line. It is becoming possible to measure the carbon footprint of supermarket products;
- wearable computers such as 'love badges', which heat up when you meet someone at a party who's available for a date.

We shall be immersed in an 'Internet of things'.[6] Many of the applications we can scarcely imagine, but already they range from light bulbs that switch off automatically when you leave the room to educational games.

For example, the ListenReader system is based on electronically augmented paper books. It enhances reading by enabling readers to discover ambient sounds related to the story. Readers move their hands above a sensor-embedded book while sitting in a special 'reading chair'.[7]

Communication technologies will continue to spread– but how quickly and how widely?

Rapid dissemination will be helped by— for example:

- *The growth of the world economy.* As the global middle class expands by more than the size of today's EU, so will the market for new technologies.
- *The falling cost of technology.* Contrary to Moore's law (which in one formulation predicts that the cost of computing halves every 18 months), the price of PCs halved every 50 months between 1976 and 1989, every 28 months in the early 1990s and every 24 months in the late 1990s. Innovation will continue to cut costs, but will they keep falling at a faster rate?[8]
- *The emergence of new business models.* Web 2.0 is revolutionising Internet business. Websites are being turned into computer platforms serving Web applications and harnessing collective intelligence – through open source approaches, for instance. New business models in the next 20 years will further expand commercial opportunities online, making communication technologies even more attractive.

However, the spread of new technologies will run up against barriers, such as:

- *The dominance of corporate giants.* Size brings tremendous benefits – the more subscribers to a phone network, the lower the unit costs. But large companies also face less competition, which makes them more cautious and slows innovation. They can use their market power to force out innovative competitors.
- *Slow user take-up.* As now, consumers will be reluctant to buy the latest technology while they are paying off the cost of its predecessor. Or they may delay making a purchase in the expectation that a better or cheaper version will appear.
- *Lack of common standards.* Sales growth may stall after a successful launch because the new product is not compatible with others.

A variety of 'digital divides' will persist – see box below.

DIGITAL DIVIDES

Divides of access. Most of the world's population will still not have the Internet in their homes by 2030. In rich countries, people not using the Internet risk becoming technological 'misfits' who don't fit in with the network society.[9]

Divides of quality. For those with access, there will be differences between individuals who can afford the best technologies and those who make do with second rate, and between those who can afford the best support and those who can't.

Divides of ability. Even when people have access to the Internet and some basic skills in using it, they often have a limited view of its usefulness for their lives. Some users will have greater imagination and aptitude than others.

Commercial interests will strongly influence the impact of communication technologies. As now, these interests will dominate the new media because they will have the most money. Business models will continue to rely heavily on advertising, and advertisers will constantly seek new ways to reach their audiences.

Commercial interests will increasingly colonise public space. Flat TV screens, for instance, have begun to appear in supermarkets and elsewhere. As they get larger and cheaper, they will become more widespread, and their entertainment quality will improve with experience. These developments will be paid for largely by advertising, which will be even more present in everyday life.

Commercial values threaten to become more dominant over civic values. In rich countries commercial values, which are reflected in the pursuit of personal goals through buying products, seem to have gained the upper hand over civic values, which are about taking part in shared civic life.

As advertising becomes more sophisticated and pervasive within the new media, values to do with buying and selling will become even more entrenched.

In particular, advertising will continue to foster a cynical, 'buyer beware' view of the world. Knowing that advertisers have an ulterior motive, media-savvy consumers will assume even more strongly than now that politicians, religious leaders and other public figures are the same.[10]

Commercial interests are likely to jeopardise equality of access. There are fears that commercial interests will successfully push for a two-tier Internet – so-called 'Net neutrality'.

On the grounds that the Internet could be swamped with traffic, pressure is mounting to charge ordinary consumers a premium for the high-speed transfer of data. Some Internet sites may be available only to users who pay more. Both developments would undermine the ideal of universal access.[11]

Users' social contexts will massively influence how media technologies are employed. One model, for instance, identifies six moments in the process by which media are integrated into a home:

- production of the media product;
- imagination, where advertising fuels the desire for the product;
- purchase of the product;
- fitting the product into its surroundings ('the new PC will go in the study upstairs');
- fitting the product into the household's rules ('my PC is for work, and only I can use it');
- using the product to make a statement about the values of the home ('I'll access the Internet for leisure downstairs to keep "home" separate from work, which is upstairs').[12]

We have suggested that ten consumer values will influence how new technologies are used – they are discussed more fully in our GLIMPSES database of emerging trends.[13] Our 'top 10' are:

Identity. Consumers will use communication technologies to identify and fit in with people who matter to them.

Connectedness. 'Always on' people will welcome richer and more varied means to stay in touch with each other, such as personally owned virtual-reality spaces – 'meet me on my island at 6.30'.

Entertainment. The demand will persist for:

- extreme events (a virtual-reality bungee jump) alongside tranquillity (a virtual monastery with calm surroundings, soothing chants and perhaps restful physical sensations);
- small-sized entertainment (café tables with embedded screens that allow

friends to play computer games) alongside big events (large screens in public places that bring people together for major happenings);

■ participation (voting in reality shows) alongside passivity (opportunities to chill out after a busy week).

Self-improvement. The demand for online coaching and counselling is likely to grow. Even more than today, holidays will combine fun with ways to improve your knowledge. In major cities, an expanding range of tours with automated themed commentaries will become available. You'll download them onto your iPod before you leave.

Health and well-being. As the global health economy booms, health and well-being will shape the demand for food, cosmetics, fashion items, building materials and many other products. Barcodes on food purchases will enable you to check the item's vitamin content and whether it has been sourced from organic products.

Security. When life feels like a laboratory with no one in charge, it is natural that people should be anxious. As now, mounting concerns about personal security will reflect widespread social angst in the richer parts of the world. Cars, laptops, iPods and phones will increasingly come with tags that link to the Global Positioning System (GPS), to help trace stolen goods.

Simplicity. As lives become more complicated and people pack more into the day, the demand will grow further for help in simplifying life. This is a key force behind the convergence of technologies, now happening so fast, and will encourage other innovations that make communication technologies easier to us.

> 'Life feels like a laboratory with no one in charge'

Control. Users want to feel in control, but the 'Internet of things' risks putting the product or system in control. Effort will keep being put into developments that allow life to be more automated without the user feeling powerless.

Personalisation. The demand will grow for media technologies that mould themselves round the individual, such as hardware that senses whether you want to scroll quickly or slowly.

Cost. As now, consumers will be price sensitive, despite greater affluence. Intelligent search engines that seek out the cheapest product will make people even more price alert.

---

1 Eamonn Kelly, *Powerful Times*, New Jersey: Wharton School Publishing, 2006, p. 91.

2 Ian Pearson & Michael Lyons, *Business 2010. Mapping the new commercial landscape*, London: Spiro, 2003, p. 16.

3   Seoul in South Korea, for example, has been covered with high-speed wireless access, 20 times faster than broadband in the UK. Korean telecom manufacturers are working with BT to bring the technology to Britain. **http://www.vnunet.com** (posted 16 January 2006).

4   In 2006-07, 200 season-ticket holders at Manchester City football club were trialling a system through which they 'showed' their Nokia 3320 handset to an automatic reader to get into a game, instead of handing a card into a gate attendant. In December 2006, Barclay's announced that it would trial a combination of its credit card with London's Oyster card. Users would swipe the card to get on to London's transport or to pay for transactions worth less than £10 in selected shops.

5   **http://www.cs.cmu.edu.**

6   International Telecommunication Unit, *ITU Internet Reports 2005: The Internet of Things*, New York: ITU, 2005.

7   Cited by Yvonne Rogers & Henk Muller, 'A framework for designing sensor-based interactions to promote exploration and reflection in play', **http://www.infomatics.sussex.ac.uk** (accessed 29 June 2007).

8   Ilkka Tuomi, 'The Lives and Death of Moore's Law', *First Monday*, 2002, **http://www.firstmonday.org.**

9   Jan A. G. M. van Dijk, *The Network Society: Social Aspects of New Media*, London: Sage, 2006, p. 3.

10 David Croteau & William Hoynes, *The Business of Media: Corporate Media and the Public Interest*, London: Pine Forge Press, 2006, p. 205.

11 David Croteau & William Hoynes, *The Business of Media: Corporate Media and the Public Interest*, London: Pine Forge Press, 2006, p. 242.

12 Katie Ward, 'The bald guy just ate an orange. Domestication, work and home' in Thomas Berker et al., *Domestication of Media and Technology*, Maidenhead: Open University Press, 2006, p. 151.

13 **http://www.tomorrowproject.net.**

HOW WILL GLOBAL COMMUNICATIONS AFFECT PEOPLE'S LIVES? WHAT MIGHT BE THE IMPLICATIONS?

- Communication technologies will propel us into the virtual economy
- Communication technologies will continue to increase sociability
- Will communication technologies change the nature of family and friendship ties?
- Communication technologies could help to change what it means to be human

Communication technologies will propel us into the virtual economy. Rich countries have shifted from agriculture to manufacturing to services. Will virtuality be the next phase? Just as manufacturing did not replace agriculture, virtuality would be a new layer on top of these other sectors.

The virtual economy will comprise paid-for products that are created purely online — goods, services and other activities. It will include aspects of online commerce, which is growing apace. As we've noted, online sales in the US accounted for nearly 25% of manufacturing revenue in 2004 and an average of 10% of retailing and selected services.

This represented an astonishing growth in just one decade that the Internet had been open for business. Over the next 20 years will cheaper, easier-to-use and always-on technologies allow virtuality to become even bigger than services?

Virtual reality will be a growing dimension of the virtual economy, as discussed in chapter 1. Parallel economies like *Second Life* could become a major source of income.

Even now, a growing number of companies are establishing a presence in *Second Life*. Some people who spend a lot of time there list it as their address, or say that this is where they would prefer to live rather than the real world.[1] A Chinese version of *Second Life* has been launched, and is expected to cater for a large demand.

As almost anything in real life becomes easier to do in these virtual worlds, inhabitants of these economies will have enormous opportunities for making money.

Some people will have their main jobs in these parallel economies. How many others will have two jobs – one in the real world and another in a virtual one, doubling up as leisure?

'Some people list *Second Life* as their address'

Virtual reality will not substitute for physical reality – people will want to live in both spheres. But it may fuse with the physical world and influence how people look at their natural surroundings.

Tourists will hire glasses that augment reality, for example. Lining them up in the right direction, they will see perhaps a film of how the landscape evolved through the centuries, superimposed on the view before them. Elsewhere, they might see how the view will alter after 100 years of climate change. In another venue, famous historical events may be re-enacted 'on' the landscape.

Always-on media with always-on performances will encourage people to be constantly amused. So when individuals look at a landscape, it will no longer be enough to see a view: they will expect it to entertain them. The world will literally become a stage – to be commercially exploited in new ways.

Communication technologies will continue to increase sociability. Other current trends, like the personalisation of media, will keep going too. But for those who can afford the new media, the increase in sociability will be especially important.

One Norwegian psychologist has claimed that young Europeans are now so reliant on digital communications that taking a mobile phone away from a teenage girl is equivalent to child abuse (in their eyes).[2]

People will spend more time interacting with each other at work and in their leisure.[3] Always-on communications will bring more varied ways for individuals to be constantly in touch with each other – text, e-mail, mashups, voice messages, video messages, phone conversations, video conferences, virtual reality and face-to-face.

> 'Taking a mobile phone from a teenager is equivalent to child abuse (in their eyes)'

Using technologies that are here already, friends might be together throughout the day, even though they are in different parts of the world. Their icons might bob away at the bottom of the screen on their hand-held devices. Perhaps they text each other in the morning, 'Hi, how r u?'

One person has a question, which leads to an exchange of e-mails. Two friends phone each other about it, and suggest that they all meet in their virtual reality space at the end of the day. Meanwhile, Mary leaves a picture message containing a video ad about their hoped-for holiday, which will enable them to meet face-to-face.

Managing many different relationships will continue to be a priority in the workplace and a preoccupation for people when not at work – life will feel even more hectic than it does today. Rules governing the appropriateness of different forms of communication will emerge, and will vary from one social group to another.

Will communication technologies change the nature of family and friendship ties? There is some evidence that the Internet is helping to expand the number of people individuals consider as friends.

A 2006 Microsoft survey of over 1000 British people found that each person had an average of 54 friends – an astonishing increase of 64% since 2003. Nearly a third of the sample had made friends online.[4]

An American study, on the other hand, found that the average circle of *close* friends or confidants had shrunk between 1985 and 2004.

It found that the mean number of people with whom adult Americans could discuss matters important to them had dropped by nearly a third, from 2.95 people to 2.08. The number of respondents who said they had no one to discuss such matters with more than doubled, to nearly 25%.

The largest loss of discussion partners was from outside the family. Within families, siblings, parents and children were less significant, but spouses had become more so – up from 30.2% of respondents to 38.1%. People seemed to be turning from close friends to partners.[5]

Could it be that the increase in friends and the smaller number of confidants are linked? As people spend more time at work and travelling to work, they have less time to make close friends, so that family becomes more important.

The Internet helps to compensate for this by allowing individuals to expand their overall circle of friends. But as they keep in touch with all their contacts on line, they have less time to cultivate close friendships. This reinforces the significance of their partners, which in turn encourages the collection of numerous scattered friends to help them feel connected.

Might this become a long-term trend – a polarisation between one or two very close relationships and a growing number of weak ones? The results could be a mixed blessing.

Close relationships are really good for emotional support. So fewer close ties – and the increase in loneliness implied by the US survey – could leave people feeling more fragile.

On the other hand, individuals are exposed to a wider range of information when they have lots of weak ties rather than a few close ones. Might the extension of weak ties be good for building forms of social capital that 'bridge' different people?

Communication technologies could help to change what it means to be human. Transhumanists argue that 'BANG' technologies will enhance human capabilities to such a degree that the very nature of being human will be transformed.

> 'Fast, broadband interfaces direct between the human brain and machines will transform work in factories, control automobiles, ensure military superiority, and enable new sports, art forms and modes of interaction between people.'[6]

Computer chips may be inserted to repair the brain or improve its functioning.

Transhumanists believe that the human species in its current form represents a comparatively early phase of development. Human enhancement will follow an exponential curve till ultimately humans merge with technology.

Ray Kurzweil, one exponent, believes that by the mid 2040s the non-biological portion of our intelligence will be billions of times more capable than the biological portion. These and other developments will revolutionise what it means to be human.[7]

Many of these claims have been greeted with scepticism. Other people are worried that they may actually be true.[8] Might these claims provide a long-term perspective on developments over the next 20 years? Could it be that upcoming advances in communication technologies will lay foundations for a dramatic redesign of the human race?

---

1 We are grateful to Professor Christine Ogan at Indiana University for drawing our attention to this.

2 Quoted by Microsoft Senior Design Anthropologist, Anne Kirah, at a conference in Sydney on 23 August 2006, **http://www.apcstart.com.**

3 Michael Moynagh & Richard Worsley, *Working in the Twenty-First Century*, Leeds: ESRC Future of Work Programme, 2005, p. 30.

4 'Britons Make More Time for Friendship than Ever Before', November 2006, **http://www.microsoft.com.**

5 Miller McPherson, Lynn Smith-Lovin & Matthew E. Brashears, 'Social Isolation in America: Changes in Core Discussion Networks over Two Decades', *American Sociological Review*, 71, 2006, pp. 353–375.

6 Mihail C. Roco & Williams Sims Bainbridge (eds.), *Converging Technologies for Improving Human Performance*, Washington: National Science Foundation & Dept. of Commerce, 2002, p. 4.

7 For more on this, see Ray Kurzweil, *The Singularity is Near: When humans transcend biology*, New York: Viking, 2005.

8 Some of these issues are discussed in Paul Miller & James Wilsdon (eds.), *Better Humans? The politics of human enhancement and life extensions*, London: Demos, 2006.

CHAPTER 8
HOW WILL THE WORLD BE GOVERNED?
THE STORY SO FAR

- Global governance has never been more important
- Global governance is now based on multiple centres
- Ad hoc innovation has made global governance highly complex
- Accountability remains a big issue
- US dominance threatens the legitimacy of global institutions
- Can today's system of global governance cope?

Global governance has never been more important. Today's plethora of international bodies and meetings may feel remote to all but a fraction of the world's population, but never before have they had such an impact on everyday life.

An agreement in the World Trade Organization (WTO) may put thousands out of work in one country but create jobs elsewhere. Decisions by the G8 – meetings of heads of government from eight of the world's largest economies – can stall or release momentum to tackle climate change, which is changing weather patterns all over the world.

The work of the Internet Activities Board helps to shape how users experience the Internet. Global governance impinges on daily life without people noticing.

Global governance has been understood in lots of ways. One view is to see it not as government, but as a minimum set of rules necessary to tackle global problems. The rules are guaranteed by global institutions and national governments.[1]

Global governance is no longer based on the nation state, but on multiple centres. This contrasts with the situation 50 years ago, when national governments were at the heart of arrangements to oversee the globe.

Relationships between states were the linchpin of international affairs. Humanity was governed largely by bureaucratic states, which exercised sovereign power over defined territories.

'Ten years ago, if you had told me I would spend a significant part of my premiership on foreign policy, I would have been surprised, a little shocked ...'
Tony Blair, *The Economist*, 2 June 2007

The position now could be scarcely more different. National governments remain immensely important, but they are part of a complex web of governance involving thousands of actors.[2]

Governance is multi-tiered, taking place at global, regional (such as the EU), national and local levels. Developments at one level may strengthen another.

The EU's Committee of the Regions, for example, requires all members to send regional representatives. Particularly in the UK, this has strengthened the tier below national government.

Governance involves many actors – including:

- international bodies set up by nation states, such as the United Nations (UN) and the International Criminal Court;
- looser groupings of governments, such as Cities for Climate Protection, involving 675 local authorities across the world;[3]
- non-governmental organisations (NGOs) such as Greenpeace;
- multinational corporations, who set international product standards, for instance;
- expert advisers, such as the Intergovernmental Panel on Climate Change;
- a host of informal networks.

Governance takes a wide variety of forms – from the one-member-one vote constitution of the World Trade Organization, to weighted voting in the International Monetary Fund (the more a country invests in the Fund's reserves, the more votes it gets), to the passing of resolutions by the UN General Assembly, to a complete absence of agreed statements from the World Social Forum (which provides a context for NGOs and others to network).

Ad hoc innovation partly explains why global governance has become so complex. After the Second World War, a relatively simple architecture for global governance was set up. It was based largely on:

- the United Nations;
- the International Monetary Fund (IMF), whose task was to correct imbalances in international monetary flows;
- what came to be known as the World Bank, which initially was to finance post-war reconstruction;
- the General Agreement on Tariffs and Trade (GATT), which provided a framework for lowering trade barriers.

These instruments have themselves evolved over the past 60 years, acquiring more participants and widening their remits. Yet despite this, they have been inadequate to tackle the multiplicity of problems now facing the world.

For example, the global environmental regime is anchored in the UN Environment Programme (UNEP), set up in 1972. But UNEP has been hampered by a narrow mandate, modest budget and limited political support.

To fill gaps in its work, a dozen other UN bodies – such as the Commission on Sustainable Development – have occupied parts of its terrain. Independent secretariats have been established under numerous treaties, like the Montreal Protocol to protect the ozone layer. The result is high fragmentation in a sphere where many problems overlap.[4]

New issues have also spawned more informal ways of collaborating. Coalitions to fight the second Iraq war and deal with other conflicts is just one recent example. 'We "ad hoc" our way through coalitions of the willing. That's the future,' predicted one US State Department official in January 2006.[5]

Sometimes collaboration between some countries has encouraged nations favouring a different approach to set up alternative arrangements.

In 2005, for instance, the United States and Australia, who both refused to sign the Kyoto agreement on climate change, joined China, India, Japan and South Korea to establish the 'AP6' (the Asia-Pacific Partnership on Clean Development and Climate). The aim is to develop sustainable solutions to global warming 'through bottom-up practical action', such as cooperation on research.[6] The US and Australia see this as an alternative to Kyoto.

In Europe, 'variable geometry' refers to the freedom for some countries to integrate faster (or more fully) than others.

Accountability remains a big issue. More and more, the institutions of global governance reach outwards to draw others in.

National governments and intergovernmental organisations (IGOs) increasingly expect the business community to couple its new global reach with greater responsibility. Corporations have set standards for human rights and environmental protection by adopting voluntary codes of conduct in lieu of public regulation.

'They have extended their regulatory reach to suppliers as well as their own subsidiaries on a transnational scale that is beyond the capacity of most governments or IGOs.'[7]

NGOs are now engaged throughout the policy cycle. They are involved in advocacy, rule making and standard setting; in promoting, monitoring and evaluating treaty obligations; and in delivering a variety of services round the world.

Over the last quarter of a century they have changed the landscape of global governance by representing a wider range of interests and bringing in fresh expertise.

Yet despite this broadening out, 'technocracy has won over democracy in the governance of globalisation to date. Regulation of global affairs has mostly rested with the bureaucracies that are largely insulated from public inputs and public controls.'[8]

'Democratic deficits' exist in:

- the lack of influence exercised by poor countries compared to richer ones;
- the general failure to hold decision-makers to account – scrutiny by national parliaments is largely inadequate, for example;
- the widespread absence of transparency;
- the democratic shortcomings of some NGOs.

These weaknesses have prompted a clamour for reform to make global governance more accountable.[9]

US dominance is raising questions about fairness. The US has dominated global institutions, particularly since the collapse of the former Soviet Union. Economic and military power has given America immense influence.

This is true even in organisations like the WTO, where one-member-one-vote theoretically exists. Countries that rely on the US for aid and other support can be forced to toe the American line. Or the US can exert pressure by threatening to withdraw from the discussions.

US corporations tend to dominate bodies that set standards for global industries. 'For years some of Australia's air safety standards have been written by the Boeing Corporation in Seattle, or if not by that corporation, by the US Federal Aviation Administration in Washington.'[10] American influence also flows through its NGOs, of which it has more than any other country.

Though it doesn't rule the world, the United States has used the instruments of global governance to shape globalisation to its ends, often supported by other rich countries.

Critics claim, for example, that the world's intellectual property regime favours American and European companies: when a new product has been developed, consumers have to wait an unreasonable time before being able to buy a cheaper version from an alternative source.[11]

Fears that the US is using its power at the expense of others is undermining the legitimacy of global governance. 'Is it fair?' has become a pressing question.

> '"Is it fair?" has become a pressing question'

Can today's system of global governance cope? Alongside accountability and fairness is perhaps an even more urgent question about capability. As global problems – from Internet crime to failed states to food shortages – become more numerous and pressing, will global governance be up to the job?

Serious weaknesses have been identified:

- *Coordination.* Global institutions are specialised – in health, finance and so on. But issues are increasingly linked.

   The World Health Organization (WHO) focuses mainly on disease eradication, for instance, but has scarce resources for strengthening public health systems, a priority for tackling global poverty.

   The Millennium Development Goals in areas of poverty, gender equality, universal education, mortality, disease eradication, the environment and international cooperation assume that development is multi-dimensional. But who on the world stage coordinates these dimensions?

■ *Prioritisation.* Priorities among such areas as finance, health, gender equality, trade, economic growth and the environment are becoming the stuff of global politics (just as they are at national level). What should be the trade-off between tackling climate change and growing the world economy?

When investing in sub-Saharan Africa, what balance should the World Bank strike between health and education? Health ministers can't make these decisions, but heads of state can. Yet no mechanism exists for them to do so.[12]

Will global governance adapt so that it delivers the right decisions, quickly enough, and ensures they are implemented?

1 Definition cited by Martin Albrow in Tomorrow Project/ESRC lecture, 'The future of globalisation', 12 March 2007.

2 Klaus Dingwerth & Philipp Pattberg, 'Global Governance as a Perspective on World Politics', *Global Governance*, 12, 2006, pp. 185–203.

3 Michelle M. Betsill & Harriet Bulkeley, 'Cities and the Multilevel Governance of Global Climate Change', *Global Governance*, 12, 2006, p. 143.

4 Daniel C. Esty, 'Global Environmental Governance' in Colin L. Bradford Jr. & Johannes F. Linn (eds.), *Global Governance Reform*, Washington: Brookings, 2007, pp.109–110.

5 *Financial Times*, 4 January 2006.

6 **http: //www.dfat.gov.au** (accessed 20 February 2006).

7 Shepard Forman & Derk Segaar, 'New Coalitions for Global Governance: The Changing Dynamics of Multilateralism', *Global Governance*, 12, 2006, p. 218.

8 Jan Aart Scholte, *Globalization: A critical introduction*, Basingstoke: Palgrave, 2005, p. 370.

9 For a review of proposals for reform, see Heikki Patomaki & Teivo Teivainen, *A Possible World. Democratic Transformation of Global Institutions*, London: Zed, 2004.

10 John Braithwaite & Peter Drahos, *Global Business Regulation*, Cambridge: CUP, 2000, p. 3.

11 Joseph Stiglitz, *Making Globalization Work*, London: Allen Lane, 2006, pp. 103–106.

12 Colin L. Bradford Jr. & Johannes F. Linn, 'Global Governance Reform: Conclusions and Implications' in Colin L. Bradford Jr. & Johannes F. Linn (eds.), *Global Governance Reform*, Washington: Brookings, 2007, p. 128.

HOW WILL THE WORLD BE GOVERNED?
WHAT WILL SHAPE THE NEXT 20 YEARS?

- Global governance will evolve in response to urgent challenges
- The nation state will limit the amount of economic integration
- New powers will challenge American dominance
- Moving towards a multipolar world will impact global governance
- Civil society will bring new voices into global governance
- Far-reaching reform of global governance will remain extremely difficult

Global governance will evolve in response to urgent challenges facing the world. These will include the challenge of integration (how do we manage the effects of economic globalisation?), inclusion (how can we reduce the numbers being left behind by globalisation?) and insecurity (how can we tackle the globalised threats to security?).

New issues will spawn new networks and perhaps new institutions.

The nation state will limit the amount of economic integration. Dani Rodrik, from Harvard University, has argued that the nation-state system, deep economic integration and democracy create an impossible tension: you can't have all three.[1] *Much more global integration would weaken the nation state, or democracy or both.* Stronger economic integration, for example, would require greater tax harmonisation, to prevent governments giving their companies an unfair tax advantage. National governments would have less discretion over tax.

As vital decisions shifted from the national to global level, where democracy is virtually non-existent, decision-makers would be less accountable to ordinary people. Global integration would erode both the nation state and democracy.

Or, if mass politics became possible on a planet-wide scale, democracy would move 'upwards', further weakening the nation state. Global institutions would get a popular mandate, increasing their influence over national governments – 'We speak for the world. Who do you speak for?'

Yet a big shift away from the nation state is hard to envisage. Markets are embedded in a variety of cultures. The West favours private property rights, whereas China seeks to combine the benefits of private property with communal forms of ownership, such as the Household Responsibility System. Countries have different approaches to social security, regulation and other matters.

These differences reflect deep-seated values that are extraordinarily hard to give up. True, national values are changing as the world draws together, but people will accept only so much change.

They especially resist the idea that their governments are no longer in control. As now, politicians will be expected to protect their citizens' 'way of life', guaranteeing a substantial role for the state.

So only relatively thin economic integration will be possible at a global level, which will require comparatively thin political integration to oversee it. The number of issues tackled in international gatherings will increase as the world gets more interdependent and complex. But they will be approached in ways that guarantee a major role for the state.

National governments will keep their pivotal place in world deliberations. This could mean:

- slowing down global decision-making in some areas, such as trade liberalisation, to protect national interests;
- using framework agreements more often. Countries can apply these agreements in different ways;
- states retaining their key role in certain aspects of domestic policy, such as equipping their people to compete in the global economy;
- the further spread of 'symbolic' politics, in which national governments promote and defend symbols of national identity in the face of globalising trends ('this is what *we* stand for in the world'). The Beijing Olympics might be an example.

Global governance will be thin in that it will stretch over more issues, but leave the nation state with lots to do and it will play a lead part on the world stage. *National governments will also dominate regional groupings,* which will be increasingly important. During the 1990s, 93 regional trade agreements were concluded worldwide.'² As now, regional blocs will include the EU, the ASEAN (Association of Southeast Asian Nations) group of 10 nations in Southeast Asia and the African Union.

The African Union, for example, was established in 2001 with an executive Commission and a Pan-African parliament, selected from 'deliberative organs' of member states. It aims eventually to have a single currency and an integrated defence force.

As China, India, the United States and regional groups like the EU shape global discussions and dominate their regions, smaller nations will strengthen their regional ties as counterweights.

Yet for the same reasons that the nation state will be central in global governance, it will remain key in regional blocs.

Is it significant that the pace of economic integration has slowed in the EU, while at the same time integration is advancing in other areas, such as developing ties with non-European countries? Might this be a pointer to the future?

Global governance will embrace more and more issues, but there will be limits to the amount of integration in each sphere – more breadth but limited depth.

> 'Global governance will have more breadth but limited depth'

New powers, especially China and India, will challenge American dominance. Assuming their economies stay on track, China could be the world's second largest economy by 2016 and India the third largest by 2032. Russia and Brazil could emerge as leading second rank economies, alongside Japan, by the mid 2030s.[3]

Clearly, these long-term trends could be hijacked by resource constraints and internal tensions, such as a clash between economic and traditional values. China and India could break up under the strains of uneven economic growth over the next 20 years – regions left behind may pull the countries apart.

Yet more likely is that today's trajectory of change will continue.[4] The US will maintain its global leadership till at least 2020. After that, a multipolar world will emerge. China and India (and perhaps Russia) will challenge US dominance in global institutions and in certain regions. The effects will be felt even before 2020, as American supremacy is slowly eroded.

For example, increasingly the EU and China have been working together. They have shared space technologies, with China's participation in Europe's GALILEO satellite navigation programme. European technology has contributed to China's advances in space.

This has stoked Washington fears of Chinese competition. Washington has also been angered by EU proposals to lift its embargo on arms sales to China. Though US pressure has blocked the latter for now, relaxing the embargo is widely seen as a matter of time.[5]

Will the transition to a multipolar world be peaceful? Fears exist that a military clash between the United States and China could be sparked by:

- competition over natural resources;
- US resistance to growing Chinese influence in Southeast Asia;
- Chinese invasion of Taiwan to satisfy nationalist feelings at home.

Yet though a miscalculation is possible, military conflict seems unlikely.[6] In early 2001–02, some of Beijing's top US experts worked on what they called a ratio of relative interdependence with the United States. A 50:50 ratio would denote an equal degree of mutual dependence between the two countries.

They thought the figure was about 70:30 in the mid 1990s, meaning that China needed the US much more than the US needed China. With large American companies like Boeing becoming heavily reliant on the Chinese market, the ratio had moved closer to 60:40 by the early 2000s. It would reach 50:50 in the foreseeable future.[7]

As both economies depend more on each other, military confrontation will be in neither's interest.

Moving towards a multipolar world will impact global governance over the next 20 years – inevitably.

International bodies will change how they do things to reflect the emerging balance of power. Decisions in the World Bank, for instance, will give greater weight to China and India. India and perhaps Brazil will become permanent members of the UN Security Council.

Large emerging economies will have greater influence as:

- their legal presence in global institutions grows;
- their governments exert pressure on the growing number of countries dependent upon them;
- their NGOs become more numerous and globally active;
- they produce more large corporations of their own, which will help to shape the rules of international business.

The UN may become more influential. The IMF, World Bank and WTO have generally had more impact on globalisation than the UN, whose authority in social and economic areas has been depleted.

This largely reflects the market model of globalisation championed by the US and carried forward by these three institutions.

The emerging new powers may well champion the UN and its agencies instead. UN agencies tend to highlight social needs, give more weight to the development of poorer countries and seem less dominated by the rich world.[8] New concepts of development could win out.

Global decisions will increasingly favour the South. There have been signs of this already in world trade negotiations: China, India and Brazil have joined other countries from the South in pressing the US and EU to open their agricultural markets.

China's former leader, Deng Xiaoping, emphasised that socialist China belongs to the third world and will always stand by it. This is likely to remain a guiding principle of Chinese foreign policy.[9] India may come to see its role as a bridge between developed and least-developed countries.[10]

Will the South reshape today's concepts of development? The 'Beijing Consensus', discussed in chapter 3, may point in that direction.

But the South is unlikely to gang up on the North. The interests of China and India will often coincide with those of the United States and Europe. All of them will want stable energy supplies, for example.

China's and India's interests may also collide periodically with the poorest nations. Poor countries may want to protect their new and fragile industries, and resist demands that they open their markets to exports from China and elsewhere.

Shifting alliances, as countries try to exploit differences between the dominant powers, will make global governance even more complex than it is now.

Civil society will bring new voices into global governance. Many officials in international institutions, which are supposed to be 'above' national politics, welcome the chance to consult representatives of civil society. This fits the ethos of their work.

As civil society grows, international NGOs will become increasingly influential. They will score over national politicians by articulating concerns and values that jump territorial boundaries.

Expansion of higher education will swell the size of global civil society. In 2005 China had 23 million students in higher education, nearly five times more than in 1998, with numbers growing at 5% a year.[11] India was churning out 3.1 million college graduates annually in the early 2000s, 50% more than the United States.[12]

With better education, millions more people will be aware of global issues, feel more confident in addressing them and be more able to organise behind global campaigns. The number of NGOs from the South will proliferate and become more influential in global politics.

At the same time, the continued spread and improvement of global communications will create new opportunities for NGOs to acquire relevant knowledge and mobilise support.

Cory Doctorow, an activist seeking reform of the World Intellectual Property Organization (WIPO), has described how he used new communication technologies to raise a voice in international treaty negotiations.

Using WiFi networks, two or three people would take notes of the meetings as they occurred, publishing them online twice a day.

> 'The delegations there were accustomed to the old WIPO regime, where the notes would be taken by the secretariat, sent out for approval by the delegates, sanitised – all the bodies would be buried – and then published six months later.
>
> But what happened once we started working together like this is that delegates would get calls on their lunch breaks about things they'd said that morning.
>
> Suddenly, they were immediately accountable for their words, which changed the character of the negotiations.'[13]

Using new technology, might NGOs begin to represent not just interest groups, but 'tribes' – individuals who identify less with a nation and more with a global group of people? Some tribes might be based on a shared interest, but others might have ethnicity or place of birth in common.

Far-reaching reform of global governance will remain extremely difficult. There have been calls to make global governance:

- *more effective.* Bodies like the UN are weakened when they are bypassed by the US and other large countries;
- *more joined-up.* As we've noted, global institutions are highly fragmented. Yet with any one issue having implications for others, coordination is becoming increasingly urgent;
- *more accountable.* Elites who staff, lobby or hang around global institutions often seem detached from the rest of the world. Many decisions still lack transparency;
- *more representative* of the world as a whole. Despite being a minority of the world's population, the rich nations dominate global governance;
- *more democratic.* The world's population has little effective say in decisions made at a global level. Where representatives are accountable to national parliaments, parliamentary scrutiny – at best – tends to be weak.

But the current system has huge inertia. Each international body has its own governance and its own interests to defend. Reform within a single institution is extraordinarily difficult because 'there are too many conflicting forces, contradictions and complexities to permit decisive action.'[14]

Might the way forward be for leaders of the major powers, including those in the South, to break the logjam by agreeing a framework for global governance reform? Trade-offs could be made within this framework – 'We'll give ground on the UN Security Council if you compromise on the World Bank.'

America and Europe are reluctant to surrender power. Yet this will be necessary to meet the South's demands for a bigger say in institutions like the IMF. Can a solution be found?

If rich countries refuse to permit emerging nations a louder voice, Asia and other regional groupings may set up their own institutions instead. Existing international bodies would have a smaller global reach, reducing the rich world's influence.

Sharing power within the current institutions could be a better bet for the global North.

Increasing the role of civil society is far from straightforward. As a step towards more radical reform, some have called for stronger NGO representation in bodies like the UN and the World Trade Organization, to counter the weight given to governments and business. An 'NGO forum', sitting alongside the UN and informing its decisions, has been proposed.

Yet these and other ideas would run into problems of:

- *Selection.* Which NGOs should be most involved? Those with most members? An 'NGO forum' would be dominated by cancer research trusts and animal welfare groups![15]
- *Numbers.* As NGOs multiply, individual voices may be drowned in a cacophony. Increasing the number of representatives risks diluting the contribution of any one. Sub-groups could help each NGO be more involved, but accountability might then be lost in a bewildering hierarchy of committees and sub-committees;
- *Power.* How much influence will existing interests – national governments and business in particular – be willing to cede to NGOs? Critics accuse NGOs of representing narrow interests and often being unaccountable. They claim the moral case for NGOs having more weight is far from proved;
- *Effectiveness.* If NGOs had a bigger say, would decisions take even longer?

1 Dani Rodrik, 'Feasible Globalizations', *Centre for Economic Policy Research Discussion Paper 3524*, 2002.

2 Jan Aart Scholte, *Globalization: A Critical Introduction*, Basingstoke: Palgrave, 2005, p. 206.

3 Dominic Wilson & Roopa Purushothaman, 'Dreaming with the BRICs: The Path to 2050', *Goldman Sachs Global Economics Paper*, 99, 2003, pp. 3, 10.

4 India has a long track record now of holding together despite internal stresses, while the Chinese government's step-by-step approach to change – coupled with strong decentralisation – looks capable of weathering the tensions ahead.

5 Nicola Casarini, 'China and the EU', paper presented to *Goodenough/ESRC 'China and Globalisation' conference*, Goodenough College, London, 11 May 2007.

6 For an example of the debate over this, see Zbigniew Brzezinski & John J. Mearsheimer, 'Clash of the Titans', January/February 2005, **http://www.foreignpolicy.com.**

7 Willy Wo-Lap Lam, 'Dynamics of Sino-US Relations: The Perspective from Beijing', Spring 2002, **http://www.asiaquarterly.com.**

8 Martin Kohr, *Globalization and the South. Some Critical Issues*, Penang: Third World Network, 2000, pp. 8–9.

9 'Liu Huaqiu on China's Foreign Policy', **http://www.china-embassy.org** (downloaded 2 February 2007).

10 Sunil Khilnani, 'India as a Bridging Power' in Prasenjit K. Basu et al., *India as a New Global Leader*, London: Foreign Policy Centre, 2005, pp. 1–15.

11 'China's colleges: more students in 2007', 29 January 2007, **http://www.chinaeconomicreview.com.**

12 Prasenjit K. Basu, 'India and the Knowledge Economy: The "Stealth Miracle" is Sustainable' in Prasenjit K. Basu et al., *India as a New Global Leader*, London: Foreign Policy Centre, 2005, pp. 59–60.

13 *'World Changing Interview. Cory Doctorow'*, 14 August 2005, **http://www.smartmobs.com.**

14 Colin L. Bradford Jr. & Johannes F. Linn, 'Introduction and overview' in Colin L. Bradford Jr. & Johannes F. Linn (eds.), *Global Governance Reform*, Washington: Brookings, 2007, p. 3.

15 George Monbiot, *The Age of Consent: A Manifesto for a New World Order*, London: Harper, 2003, p. 81. Monbiot makes this point in the context of a trenchant argument for global democracy.

HOW WILL THE WORLD BE GOVERNED?
WHAT MIGHT BE THE IMPLICATIONS?

- Accountability will remain near the top of the agenda
- An expanded G8 could form a new apex of global governance
- Will global governance be reformed more radically?

Accountability will remain near the top of the agenda: 'What right do you have to make these decisions? Who do you speak for?' Building on some emerging trends, which we also discuss in chapter 9 (on organisations), we are likely to see:

- *greater transparency* in decision making;
- *more independent scrutiny* of decision-making processes ('the World Health Organization really did consult widely').
- *codes of practice* for NGOs and business, to ensure they properly represent interests they claim to speak for.

In time, an expanded G8 is likely to form a new apex of global governance. The current annual G8 meetings of heads of states are dominated by the United States and Europe.

A larger and more representative grouping, it has been suggested, could oversee, coordinate and give direction to today's multiplicity of global institutions. It could prioritise global challenges and provide leadership in meeting them.

Building on the G8 could be more attractive to the US than developing the UN, which has yet to inspire American confidence.

A likely development is the eventual full inclusion of Brazil, China, India, Mexico and South Africa – the 'plus 5' who already meet informally with the G8. They would form a G13 – a meeting of 13 global leaders. Six to eight other countries (or regional blocs like the African Union) might attend on a rotating basis, depending on the issue under discussion.

Alternatively, the G20 finance ministers group, which consists of 10 industrial and 10 big emerging economies, might be ratcheted up into a G20 heads of state.

At present, one barrier to these kinds of development is China. To join the G8, China would have to assume the full obligations of membership, including cooperating with other countries in managing exchange rates. China is reluctant to face the extra pressure this would bring to revalue its currency. But as circumstances change, might barriers like this begin to fall?

Extending the balcony from which global leaders orchestrate the world would need a 'grand bargain' between the present G8 and members that would join. If the summit was to provide leadership to the IMF, World Bank and other institutions, the global South would demand that their views be given greater weight.

The time is likely to come when the United States and Europe consider this a price worth paying. Not least, it would avoid the formation of alternative regional blocs and institutions, in which the West had less influence.[1]

Will global governance be reformed more radically? Greater accountability and a more effective summit would be highly significant. But might further changes come into the frame?

Europe has created a new model of interstate cooperation, for example – neither a federal entity, nor a loose association of states, but something novel in between.

The Council of Ministers allows governments to collaborate yet, unlike other international groupings, the people have direct scrutiny of inter-governmental decisions through the elected European Parliament.

As a small but strong central bureaucracy, the European Commission provides an integrating force to counter the sectional interests of individual states.

Could a modified version of this model one day inspire reform of global institutions? Popular elections to bodies like the UN are hard to envisage, but the UN's Economic and Social Council, for instance, has given 'consultative status' to 1500 NGOs.

Might an 'NGO forum' eventually sit alongside the UN General Assembly and Security Council – not a parliament, but a civil society voice that could act as a countervailing force to national governments and the UN bureaucracy? Might other bodies do something similar?

Change might also be driven by the urgency of specific issues. One of the world's leading economists, Jeffrey Sachs, has suggested that global panels of experts should report to the world on progress being made to address agreed international priorities, such as the Millennium Development Goals, and propose solutions.

This would build on the successful experience of the Inter-governmental Panel on Climate Change and other similar groupings. These panels would brief global leaders, and their reports would be a way of holding these leaders to account and mobilising world opinion.[2]

This is similar to the ideas of J. F. Rischard. Drawing on his World Bank experience, Rischard has suggested that 'global issues networks' (GINs) should tackle each of the major problems confronting the globe.

Each network would involve representatives of national governments, international civil society, the appropriate global bodies and corporations with relevant expertise.

The network would seek a 'rough consensus' on action that should be taken, electronically consulting people with an interest in the subject from around the world – a form of open-source global cooperation.

The network would rate governments and other bodies on the steps they were taking to implement its proposals, using reputation as a drive to action. NGOs might refuse to collaborate on development projects in a country with a low reputation, for example, or consumers might be encouraged to boycott a country's exports.[3]

World élites already meet outside the formal structures of global governance – for example:

- at Davos, an annual meeting of business and political leaders;
- within the Aspen Institute (which organises seminars, conferences and programmes to encourage 'enlightened' leadership);
- under the auspices of the Tallberg Foundation (which brings international leaders together to deepen their understanding of global issues).

Could GINs evolve from gatherings like these? In time, might new networks of global governance emerge, overseen by a global summit of heads of state?

---

1 This section is based on Colin L. Bradford Jr. & Johannes F. Linn (eds.), *Global Governance Reform*, Washington: Brookings, 2007, particularly the 'Introduction and Overview' and ch. 9.

2 Jeffrey Sachs, Reith Lectures 2007, lecture 5.

3 J. F. Rischard, *High Noon*, Oxford: Perseus, 2002, pp. 171–192.

CHAPTER 9

WHAT WILL SUCCESSFUL ORGANISATIONS BE LIKE? THE STORY SO FAR

- People's lives have been getting more and more organised
- An 'ABC' of recent changes would start with automation
- A blurring of boundaries has occurred within organisations
- Collaborative networks have become commonplace
- The dis-aggregation and re-aggregation of organisations has proceeded apace
- The elimination of management layers may be approaching a limit
- Flexibility is increasingly prized by organisations

People's lives have been getting more and more organised. The number of organisations has leapt dramatically, whether it is NGOs in Uganda (3,500 registered in 2000 alone) or registered companies in California (which expanded five-fold between 1960 and 2001).

Organisations are reaching into the informal parts of everyday life, like childcare: in many parts of the West, pre-school children are more likely to attend a nursery than be looked after by their parents.[1] The voluntary sector is less informal.

Organisations themselves feel more organised – more regulations, more targets and more accountability.

All this organising reflects a number of worldwide developments.[2]

- *The emergence of empowered individuals.* Instead of being bound by family and community ('this is what the community says so there is nothing we can do about it'), increasingly, well-educated people assume that they can change things, shape their destinies and bring benefits to others. So they organise.

  As more aspects of life become organised, being organised is seen as *the* way to achieve things. Organising spreads to the voluntary sector and other dimensions of social life.

- *The spread of good practice.* Tradition ('this is how our sort of people do it') has given way to good practice ('this is *the* way to do it'). Authority figures who guarded old traditions have been replaced by experts who advise on new traditions – the best ways of doing things.

Organisations become more organising as they seek to extend good practice to a larger number of their activities – 'You can't just advertise for a replacement, you must do it like this'.

■ *The growing need for monitoring and evaluation.* As social life becomes increasingly organised, the demand mounts for accountability and efficiency. 'Are they acting responsibly?' 'Are they using our resources in the best way?'

This adds new layers of organisation – new processes of monitoring and evaluation, and new audit committees and the like to scrutinise performance. Organisations feel more bureaucratic.

As a result, the idea of organising has become part of globalisation itself. The world over, organisations are surrounded by a set of values and meanings that make them the most natural way to do almost everything. These assumptions form a set of global values that are exerting an ever-stronger influence.

Paradoxically, as society becomes more organised, other parts of life feel increasingly disorganised. This is partly because when the rest of life is highly structured, people value space where things are unorganised. They enjoy the greater fluidity of personal life – 'We'll decide whether to go to the party at the last minute'.

In the years ahead, might successful organisations learn how to remain organised, but in ways that feel as if they are not organised?

Life may also feel disorganised because the things you want done slip between organisations, or because organisations keep changing – rapidly. In 1992 about 20% of the top 50 UK companies were engaged in large-scale reorganisation each year. This had jumped to 30% by the end of the decade[3], and the pace shows no signs of slowing.

Just as you think you understand an organisation, it looks different!

An 'ABC' of recent changes would start with automation, which has re-engineered processes and increased customisation: cars may roll off the assembly line with the name of their future owners attached. Automating the movement as well as the production of watches has revolutionised the Swiss watch industry.

Retail banking has been transformed by cash machines and online facilities. Secretarial jobs look very different thanks to the PC and e-mail. Automation means that job after job is not what it used to be.

A blurring of boundaries has occurred within organisations. Bridges have been built between processes and departments that previously had little to do with each other. Traditionally, for example, marketing had few links with R & D. Today that would be almost unthinkable.

These new links have led to more advanced forms of customisation and cut the cycle time from ideas to 'product on the shelves' often dramatically, contributing to a 'faster, faster' world.

Geographical boundaries in many companies have diminished. Only the most basic industries, such as building materials, are still organised by geographical division. In financial services, not one major company is organised on a geographical basis. Foreign exchange dealers trade with each other across the world, scarcely knowing the bonds dealers working one floor below.

Walls between industries have been tumbling down. Sainsbury's and Marks and Spencer are just two UK retailers that have moved into financial services.

Collaborative networks have become commonplace. They range from ad hoc teams within a department, to cross-departmental teams, to company-wide teams spanning the globe, to professional and other networks that jump organisations, to international supply chains, to collaborative ventures.

A 2004 survey found that teamworking among core employees existed in 72% of British workplaces. In 83% of cases, teams were given responsibility for specific products or services. Team members jointly decided how the work was to be done in 61%.[4]

But were these just the tip of an iceberg? Numerous informal networks also exist. Organisations have become networks of networks.

The dis-aggregation and re-aggregation of organisations has proceeded apace. Companies have outsourced like never before.

More than nine in 10 of 2000 UK workplaces surveyed in 2002 had outsourced at least one type of activity, and one half had outsourced four or more. Having started with low-skilled activities, a growing number were outsourcing higher-skilled services such as training (43%) and ICT (26%).

BP is one blue-chip employer that outsourced much of its Human Resource Management as it concentrated on its core competences.[5]

'Just 6% of Britain's call-centre jobs had gone abroad by 2004'

Offshoring has become an important dimension of outsourcing as organisations go global. By 2004, 6% of the UK's call-centre jobs had gone abroad, rather lower than media comment might suggest, but a significant trend even so.[6]

Interviews with senior executives in the early 2000s revealed that the rationale for offshoring was changing. Companies were going beyond mere cost savings and moving towards more radical business transformations, such as creating global supply chains.[7] Offshoring is becoming a means of accessing distinctive skills.

A growing number of 'multinationals' have moved from being international – operating outside their home country – to being global: they integrate their operations across the world.

> 'Multinationals are moving from being international to being global'

Rather than treating each region or country on a stand-alone basis, they view their operations as an integrated whole. 'What is this country uniquely good at? Let's locate the rest elsewhere.'[8] As giant corporations span the globe, smaller ones get drawn into their supply chains.

The elimination of management layers may be approaching a limit. As global competition intensified in the 1980s and 90s, many companies de-layered to cut costs and public-sector organisations followed suit.

But you can't keep flattening hierarchies for ever. As organisations move into more complex activities – often IT based – they seem to need more managers.[9] Likewise, the price of decentralisation may be an increase in managerial support, such as coaching for staff.

In a 2002 survey, 22% of managers in British workplaces said that the proportion of managerial and professional staff had risen in the previous three years, against 8% who thought there had been a decline and 69% who reported little change.[10]

Twice as many workplaces were increasing the number of grades than were decreasing. 'It seems that the move towards flatter organisations and broader grades, which was evident in the late 1980s and early 1990s, has been short-lived.'[11]

Flexibility is increasingly prized by organisations. Supply chains are more responsive to changes in consumer demand, switching quickly from one line to another as demand fluctuates. Agile organisations copy best practice within days of an innovation.

In 2001, from its base in Galicia, Spanish retailer Zara could make an entirely new clothing line from start to finish within three weeks, slashing the industry average of nine months.[12] After 9/11, the Hong Kong-based textile corporation, Li & Fung, took less than a month to shift its time-sensitive operations out of Pakistan, whose political stability seemed at risk.[13]

The standard view is that the trends just described will continue and that organisations will become more adaptive, creative and knowledge based. Organisations will face many influences. In the next section, we highlight three that will have a particular impact and will be global in nature, in the sense of being common round the world.

1 Gili S. Drori, John W. Meyer & Hokyu Hwang, 'Introduction' in Gili S. Drori, John W. Meyer & Hokyu Hwang (eds.), *Globalization and Organization*, Oxford: OUP, 2006, pp. 2–7.
2 This section summarises some of the themes in John W. Meyer, Gili S. Drori & Hokyu Hwang, 'World Society and the Proliferation of Formal Organization' in Gili S. Drori, John W. Meyer & Hokyu Hwang (eds.), *Globalization and Organization*, OUP, 2006, pp. 25–49.
3 Richard Wittington & Michael Mayer, *Organising for Success in the Twenty-First Century*, London: CIPD, 2002, pp. 2–3.
4 Barbara Kersley et al., *Inside the Workplace: Findings from the 2004 Workplace Employment Relations Survey*, London: Routledge, 2006, pp. 89–91.
5 Michael White et al., *Managing to Change?*, Basingstoke: Palgrave, 2004, pp. 25–26.
6 Based on Datamonitor figures provided by CM Insight Ltd.
7 Chris Odino, Stephen Diacon & Christine Ennew, *Outsourcing in the UK Financial Services Industry: The Asian Offshore Market*, Nottingham: Nottingham University Business School Financial Services Research Forum, 2004, p. 19.
8 George S. Yip, *Total Global Strategy II*, New Jersey: Pearson, 2003, pp. 4–9.
9 In the 2002 survey of UK workplaces, workplaces that were extending IT were associated with proportionately more managers. Michael White et al., *Managing to Change?* Basingstoke: Palgrave, 2004, p. 64.
10 Robert Taylor, 'Managing Workplace Change', *ESRC Future of Work Programme Seminar Series*, Swindon: ESRC, 2003, p. 8.
11 Michael White et al., *Managing to Change?*, Basingstoke: Palgrave, 2004, p. 61.
12 'Floating on Air', *The Economist*, 19 May 2001.
13 'A Broader View of Offshoring', *BusinessWeek online*, 31 May 2005.

WHAT WILL SUCCESSFUL ORGANISATIONS BE LIKE? WHAT WILL SHAPE THE NEXT 20 YEARS?

- Organisations will become more transparent
- They will be shaped by 'personalised scale'
- They will adapt to the growing importance of human relationships

Demands will grow for organisations to be more transparent. Though much is said about openness today, by and large organisations remain secretive – to safeguard a competitive advantage, to protect market-sensitive information, to disguise their shortcomings and for other reasons.

These concerns will remain, but at the same time withholding information will become increasingly difficult:

Trust will be more and more important. Any firm wanting to raise capital in global markets will have to explain itself with greater rigour – 'These are our core competences and this is our strategy to build on them.' As new methodologies emerge to define and demonstrate unique strengths, businesses will be expected to disclose more information.

They will also have to tell consumers more about their products, such as effects on health. Information can create trust, and trusted brands add a lot to a company's value.

Brands are a tool to help consumers navigate alternatives. If the brand is trustworthy:

- it reduces doubt;
- it makes the decision easier;
- it encourages loyalty.[1]

As now, building trust will give brands a competitive advantage.

Public expectations will continue to rise. Corporate power has created alarm in parts of global civil society – 'How can business be held to account?' Concerns are likely to mount as the world becomes better educated.

2002 research indicated that nearly 1.2 million non-profit organisations existed in India, for example.[2] As more people enter higher education, the number will grow. An expanding number of NGOs will scrutinise business and state organisations.

NGOs' greater influence will mean that they themselves will be subject to closer scrutiny – 'On what basis do you claim to speak for these people?'

Technology will make scrutiny much easier. Even now, the charity WITNESS, which concerns itself with breaches of trust in professional relationships, gives camcorders to activists around the world so that they can document human rights abuses.

> 'We are on the verge of having access to amazingly cheap and tiny cameras, about the size of a postage stamp, that can be stuck anywhere and can send messages wirelessly to a computer.'[3]

The semantic web makes it possible to collate relevant data about an organisation from across the Web so that it is displayed as one result. Activists will have a phenomenally powerful tool. Confidential e-mails can be hacked into – if you are willing to pay an expert.

Might the threat to privacy come not from 'big government', but from individuals seeking to keep track of organisations they fear?[4]

How will organisations respond? They are likely to seek a bargain with civil society – 'We'll tell you more, if you respect our right to confidentiality in certain areas.'

- ■ *A growing number will release more information,* as many are doing. RFID tags and other technologies will allow more details to be given about items for sale, for instance. Tesco, the UK retailer, is to introduce a labelling system showing how much carbon has been released to make its products.[5]

    As trust becomes more important, so will formal verification, openly communicated. Successful organisations will see these as complementary and focus on both.

- ■ *Some organisations will engage in complex communication,* taking the growing art of apology to a next stage. Rather than giving a simplistic message, they will describe pluses and minuses to gain a trust advantage.

    When trust has evaporated, former UK political adviser Daniel Finkelstein has asked:

    'Why not try saying that a new policy has a cost, that a fresh law may not work, that a reform has some risks? Why not share all the advice, the upside and the downside? Hard-bitten pols [politicians] may think me naive. But if they think it works going on as they are, then it is not me that is the naive one.'[6]

- *More organisations may try to create informed policy communities.* As some have begun to, corporations may become premier sources of information and comment about their sectors, drawing in experts and critics to address strategic questions.

    These mostly online communities would provide a public service, and a forum for senior management to get across its views and pick up warning signals. But would these communities be authentic? Or might they serve business interests so strongly that they lose credibility?

- *Might new forms of governance emerge?* Though not on the agenda now, might Anglo-Saxon capitalism evolve more complex forms of governance to hear stakeholder voices?

    Advisory boards representing consumers and civil society, for example, might help corporations (and others) respond more quickly to signs of discontent and help them retain their 'licence to operate'. Rather than adding to complexity, might dispersing information flows at the top simplify governance? Boards would have a more accurate picture?[7]

Organisations will be shaped by how they manage 'personalised scale'. This is our term for two trends that are coming together.

One is bigness. Companies go global to get economies of scale, for example, or they link two separate products to provide a more attractive combined offering (like newspapers selling discounted products): the scope of the business is bigger. The other trend is tailoring products to individuals or specific groups of customers.

> Bigness + customisation = personalised scale

Holding both trends together will be an increasing priority for organisations. *A particular challenge will be combining standardisation with customisation.* 'How can we get economies of scale from selling the same product to a global market, while at the same time gearing the product to regional and other differences?'

As already happens, some companies will resolve this tension by bolting customised features on to standardised offerings – such as a Greek salad in an Athens McDonald's, for instance.

In addition, as is becoming good practice, they will develop standardised processes for tailor-making their products. 'Are there effective techniques that we can apply across the enterprise for customising this product wherever we operate?'

Routines are at the heart of organisations. Where these routines have to be fluid so that decisions can fit the context, standardised processes are being designed to support staff in making their judgements – 'Here's a checklist to help you get it right.'

Companies might identify the basic steps in researching a market. They would then design ways to compare their processes with other firms doing something similar – 'Do these steps take us longer than this other company? Are we doing them better – we have fewer product failures? Are they costing us more (perhaps because we run more focus groups)?'

Finally, they develop a set of standards to measure how well they are comparing their activities and getting continuous improvement.

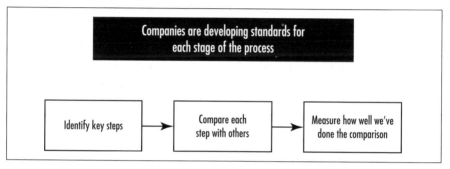

MIT researchers have developed an online library, the Process Handbook, of more than 5000 standardised processes and activities that describe the deep structure of a wide variety of business operations, and some of their variations.[8]

Standardised customisation will be one of the paradoxes of globalisation. *Customising products will also be a growing challenge.* **Customisation based on choice is becoming problematic**, such as choosing a Smart car from over a million combinations of colour, interior trim and so forth:

- you can feel overwhelmed by all the options;
- choice can be a time guzzler (especially online);
- if you choose one thing you frequently can't choose something else, so choosing may be tempered by regret;
- choice is often fraught with anxiety ('what will my friends think?');
- someone else can always afford a better choice than you.

In short, choice can make you unhappy.[9] So relying on choice to customise will meet mounting resistance. 'Don't give me more choice,' consumers will increasingly say, 'just give me what I want'.

Co-production as an alternative may have limited potential. Co-production enables the consumer and supplier to work together to produce the end product.

Some experts see this as a way forward in health care, for instance. Rather than passively consuming care, patients would jointly manage their health with professionals to get better results. A very different example may be coming soon: T-shirts with built-in TVs screening a video made by the wearer – the owner would have produced the design.[10]

Yet what will happen when co-production becomes commonplace? Individuals will welcome co-production in the one or two spheres most important to them, such as co-producing a cancer treatment. But in a time-squeezed world, won't they baulk at the time and energy required to co-produce lots of products?

Will 'personalisation' become the main form of customisation? Personalisation will involve organisations adapting more radically to individuals. Starting with the affluent and then cascading down the income range, organisations will seek to give individuals exactly what they want.

More people will afford personalisation because of higher incomes. Squeezing supply chain costs – by turning to cheaper producers abroad and using advanced technologies – will also allow companies to release funds for personalisation.[11]

Some firms will continue to research their top spenders and meet their precise demands, while offering choice between cheaper products for those who spend less.

Others will add a personal touch to the purchasing experience by selling perhaps a standard product in a personalised way. Shopping assistants who find what you are looking for and other types of 'choice manager' will become common.[12] Being treated as an individual will often mean more to a customer than buying a tailor-made item.[13]

The personal relationship between consumers and sellers will emerge as a major – often *the* major – source of value in the supply chain. To provide a personalised experience, staff who relate to customers will have greater discretion. Consumer-facing employees will drive organisations even more than they do now.

Organisations will adapt to the growing importance of human relationships at work. These relationships, captured by the somewhat elusive concept of social capital, are increasingly recognised as critical for organisational success.

Where social capital is high, it is argued, organisations can expect better levels of trust and cooperation, greater knowledge sharing, more coherence of action, lower rates of staff turnover and enhanced commitment. 'Companies thrive on good company.'[14] Social capital is set to become still more important in future.

> 'Companies will thrive on good company'

One result will be that the nature of offshoring is likely to change. Fewer jobs dealing with customers will be done abroad. Because shared culture will help in providing a high-quality buying experience, these jobs will tend to be near the market.

There are signs of this starting to happen. Some companies like Powergen are bringing back their call centres because of consumer complaints. Their forays overseas were driven too much by costs and not enough by customer experience.[15] More back-office jobs may go abroad instead.

'Tacit interactions' at work are gaining ground in the more advanced economies. These are tasks requiring workers to deal with ambiguity – there is no rule book to tell you what to do. Individuals have to exercise judgement and draw on experience.

From 1999 to 2004, these types of job grew three times faster in the United States than did employment as a whole. They comprised 70% of all the jobs created and made up 41% of total employment in 2005.[16]

Many of these complex tasks are too difficult to be done by individuals alone. Managers, sales persons, lawyers, nurses, mentors, mediators and many more have to liaise with, consult and tell others. Frequently they are part of a team – often several teams.

As a result, individuals are spending more time relating to other people at work. Skill surveys in the UK, for example, show that human interactive skills such as 'listening carefully to colleagues' have increased significantly.[17]

Managing knowledge will continue to be a growing priority as the knowledge economy matures.

In the 1990s, companies thought managing knowledge was largely about IT – technologies for 'capture and retrieval'. Since then they have realised that knowledge is basically a social activity – people learn and create new knowledge by working together.

Organisations increasingly look for ways of capturing the knowledge and experience in employees' heads so that other workers can benefit – 'I'm dealing with this problem in Australia, has anyone faced something similar?'

People who know Papua New Guinea may be brought together with experts on building oil refineries to develop new knowledge about building and running a refinery in that country: two 'domains' of knowledge are pooled to create a third 'domain'.

Storing knowledge electronically often remains vital, but these knowledge libraries are resource-learning networks, known as 'communities of practice'.[18] Members of the network use the library and contribute to it, as part of their work together.

'People are our main asset' will become *'relationships between people are our chief asset.'* New ways of measuring and improving these relationships will be developed and may lead to profound changes in how organisations think about themselves.

Some companies have begun to redefine themselves not in terms of their products, but their ability to generate and share certain kinds of knowledge: 'our core competence is not selling pensions, it's our ability to gain knowledge about the market. Can we use that knowledge for other purposes?'

More organisations will think like this about social capital – 'These are the relationships in which we have strengths. How can we get more value from them?'

Reshaping organisations to make the most of interpersonal relationships will be at the top of chief executives' in-trays.

1   Nicholas Ind, 'A brand of enlightenment' in Nicholas Ind (ed.), *Beyond Branding. How the New Values of Transparency and Integrity Are Changing the World of Brands*, London: Kogan Page, 2003, p. 4.

2   '1.18 million non-profit organisations in India ...', Press Release, 10 January 2003, **http://www.pria.org.**

3   Eamonn Kelly, *Powerful Times*, New Jersey: Wharton School Publishing, 2006, p. 35.

4   *Dilemmas of Privacy and Surveillance. Challenges of Technological Change*, London: The Royal Academy of Engineering, 2007, pp. 18, 24.

5   'You've checked the price and calorie count, now here's the carbon cost', *Guardian Unlimited*, 19 January 2007, **http://environment.guardian.co.uk.**

6   *The Times*, 4 April 2007.

7   For one radical set of proposals see Shann Turnbull, *A New Way to Govern. Organisations and Society after Enron*, London: New Economics Foundation, 2002.

8   Thomas W. Malone, *The Future of Work*, Boston: Harvard Business School, 2004, p. 151.

9   Barry Schwartz, *The Paradox of Choice. Why more is less*, London: HarperCollins, 2004.

10 'Billboards' that walk, talk, and even flirt a little', 12 July 2004, **http://www.csmonitor.com.**

11 Shoshana Zuboff & James Maxmin, *The Support Economy*, London: Allen Lane, 2003.

12 'Choice manager' is Michael Willmott's helpful term in Michael Willmott, *Citizen Brands*, Chichester: Wiley, 2001, pp. 159–160.

13 In a 2003 Future Foundation survey, 49% of respondents wanted human contact at every stage of the purchase cycle, only 5% wanted self-service at every stage and the rest wanted a combination of the two, in a variety of patterns. Melanie Howard, 'The consumer future of e-commerce', *Admap*, June 2003, p. 26.

14 See for example Ken Starkey & Sue Tempest, 'Late Twentieth-Century Management, the Business School, and Social Capital' in Cary L. Cooper (ed.), *Leadership and Management in the 21st Century*, Oxford: OUP, 2005, p. 152.

15 'Just returning your call ... to the UK', 14 February 2007, **http://news.bbc.uk.**

16 Bradford C. Johnson, James Manyika & Lareina A. Yee, 'The next revolution in interactions', *The McKinsey Quarterly*, 2005, No. 4, pp. 25–26.

17 Alan Felstead, Duncan Gallie & Francis Green, *Work Skills in Britain 1986–2001*, London: DfES, 2002, pp. 123–126.

18 See for example Ash Amin & Patrick Cohendet, *Architectures of Knowledge. Firms, Capabilities and Communities*, Oxford: OUP, 2004.

WHAT WILL SUCCESSFUL ORGANISATIONS BE LIKE? WHAT MIGHT BE THE IMPLICATIONS?

- Successful organisations will be side to side
- Variety will rule
- 'Information utilities' may be one new organisation to emerge

Successful organisations won't be top down, nor bottom up: they will be side to side. It is said that as 'command and control' recedes in the rear mirror, organisations are becoming bottom up.

But this underestimates the continuing need for senior managers who liaise with stakeholders, maintain the organisation's focus, and coordinate and manage staff. The tail-off in delayering, which we've noted, may reflect the greater demand for management in a more complex world.

Successful organisations will come to rely on three groups of people:

- *Practitioners* will increasingly become researchers. As they deal with customers, coordinate supply chains, operate factories and carry out myriad other tasks, researching best practice will be a growing priority. Even more than now, they will form communities of practice to share and create knowledge.
- *Senior managers* will relate to stakeholders, secure agreement on goals, and design and maintain systems to achieve these goals. On top of vision and values, leadership will be increasingly about systems design.
- *Integrators* will stand between practitioners and senior managers. They will capture knowledge created by practitioners, and use it to develop standardised processes for dissemination throughout the organisation. They will also make sure these processes advance the goals agreed with stakeholders.

   They will funnel the shared learning of practitioners to senior managers ('our experience is showing that this goal is not achievable'), and turn the expectations of top management into frameworks for structuring practitioners' knowledge.

'Side to side' does not mean the end of hierarchy – there will still be a top. Rather, it points to the replacement of 'command and control' with a collaborative mindset. Senior managers, integrators and practitioners will need to keep listening to each other.

They will also have to work with information coming from all sides of the organisation – from consumers, suppliers, shareholders, partner organisations and civil society.

These 'side to side' organisations will take different forms:

- *market-based* – with the market contract at their heart;
- *hierarchical* – with the employment contract at their heart;
- *networked* – with trust and shared aims at their heart.[1]

Demands for greater transparency will help bring about 'side to side' organisations. Senior managers will have to be even more skilled than now in handling external relationships and these relationships will take up more time.

'Standardising customisation' will be another driver. It will create jobs – in-house or outsourced – that are about integrating and standardising knowledge. As a third driver, practitioners will spend longer learning from each other.

Within this broad direction of change, variety will rule. Alongside some of today's forms of organisation will be many new ones. The following types of organisation are likely to spread, but doubtless there will be surprises too:[2]

- *The virtual corporation* will rely on a network of market-based contracts to develop, manufacture, market, distribute and support its offerings. It will hardly be an organisation at all – more a network of contractors held together by legal bonds. It will be pioneered by entrepreneurs who can pull together a variety of skills to grasp an opportunity.
- *The network organisation* will be semi-virtual, in that it will rely on external suppliers for many of its activities. But it will build more enduring, 'thicker' connections through joint venture agreements, formal alliances, interlocking shareholdings or long-standing contracts. It will tend to have a larger 'strategic centre', able to coordinate and direct the evolution of its activities.
- *The boundary-less organisation* will use both external and internal networks. Relying on joint ventures and alliances, the boundaries between the organisation and its external partners will be highly porous. Information will flow freely across its 'borders' and people will work easily on either side. But there will also be a strong commitment to internal networks. Global corporations increasingly embody this approach.

- *The project-based (or team) organisation* will assemble temporary groups of people according to the needs of each project. Sometimes the project or team will be the basis for the whole organisation, so that when the project is over the organisation dissolves, as in the TV industry. More often these teams and projects will operate within a more stable organisational framework.
- *The modular (or cellular) corporation* will comprise discrete units (or cells) that can be assembled into all sorts of combinations or simply transferred outside. Modules will be combined and recombined easily because they rely on common standards or procedures, such as unified information technology, consistent reward and career structures across the organisation, or uniform planning, investment appraisal or innovation processes.
- *The process-based (or horizontal) organisation* will build on complete processes rather than traditional functional tasks. It will be the equivalent of a hierarchical organisation turned on its side. Managers will look across narrow departments along the horizontal track of meeting customer needs, rather than simply up and down according to traditional, vertical reporting lines.

'Information utilities' may be one new organisation to emerge.[3] Controlled by their members, these utilities would hold electronic data on large numbers of people, such as where they live, their buying habits, perhaps health records and so on.

Individuals would allow this information to be stored in return for tailor-made services offered on the basis of the information they provided.

To save me surfing the net or searching the shops, for example, the information utility would use advanced software to do the looking for me. If I gave it permission, it would draw my attention to products that fitted my buying pattern. It would shield me from unwanted advertising.

With my consent, it might earn me a small income by selling anonymous information about me (and other members) to market research firms that helped organisations personalise their products. It would secure favourable deals on bulk orders – for insurance, perhaps.

These utilities would be a classic example of personalised scale. They would combine various kinds of bigness, not least large numbers of members and

> 'Information utilities would be a classic example of personalised scale'

access to a wide range of products. This scale would allow them to serve their members in highly personalised ways.

Though some way off, might specialist firms managing supply chains evolve into information utilities? And might these utilities be one of many new organisations that will transform everyday life?[4]

---

1   We are grateful to Professor Tom Ling for these categories.
2   These categories are based on Richard Whittington & Michael Mayer, *Organising for Success in the Twenty-First Century*, London: CIPD, 2002, pp. 6–8.
3   John Taylor, 'The information utility' in Helen McCarthy, Paul Miller & Paul Skidmore (eds.), *Network Logic. Who governs in an interconnected world?*, London: Demos: 2004, pp. 179–188.
4   John Hagal III & Marc Singer, *Net Worth*, Boston: Harvard, 1999.

CHAPTER 10
WHO WILL WIN THE 'WAR ON TERROR'?
THE STORY SO FAR

- Security has become a global priority
- New forms of terrorism have emerged amid 'new wars'
- Several developments have encouraged the spread of Islamist terrorism
- Al-Qaeda is a new form of terrorism
- Today's terrorist threat is 'real, here, deadly and enduring'

Security has become a global priority. As the world has locked more closely together, a threat to one is now a threat to all. In 2004 a United Nations 'High-level Panel' identified six clusters of threats facing the planet:

- war between states;
- violence within states, such as civil war;
- poverty, infectious disease and environmental degradation;
- nuclear, radiological, chemical and biological weapons;
- terrorism;
- transnational organised crime.[1]

New forms of terrorism have emerged in the context of 'new wars'. Whereas traditional wars have been fought between states, using conventional forces, new wars – in the Balkans, the Caucasus, Central Asia and Africa – have occurred largely within states.

Unlike traditional wars, they have often lacked clear beginnings or definable ends. They have commonly involved a mixture of war, organised crime and large-scale violation of human rights. Frequently there have been conventional forces on one side (Soviet troops in Afghanistan for example) and unconventional fighters on the other.[2]

New wars have often been a strategic response to the organised forces of the modern state. Rather than attacking these forces head-on, opponents have used tactics ranging from hit-and-run to taking hostages.

They have sought to use their base amongst the people to gain an advantage over regular forces, whose training and equipment is ill-suited to this type of conflict. Once they have weakened the state, groups often turn on each other, as in post-invasion Iraq.

From the standpoint of the terrorist, terrorism is an effective form of 'war amongst the people'.[3] Hidden among civilians, they can use military-like violence without facing a military response.

A number of developments have encouraged the spread of Islamist terrorism, against the background of the unresolved Israel-Palestinian conflict and Arab resentment at American support for Israel.[4]

The Egyptian Sayyid Qutb helped lay the foundations of modern Islamist thought. During the 1950s he developed a radical philosophy of Islam as a complete system of morality, justice and governance. Sharia laws and principles should be the sole basis of government and every aspect of life.

All non-Islamist states were illegitimate because they lacked shari'a law. A revolutionary vanguard should use Jihaad to bring about Islamist states, starting with his home country Egypt.

One of Sayyid Qutb's students was Ayman al-Zawahiri, who became Osama bin Laden's number two. Al-Zawahiri and his fellow Egyptian jihadists believed that they should overthrow the 'near enemy' – Middle East regimes run by apostate rulers – to achieve Qutb's goals.

Bin Laden took the next step, persuading al-Zawahiri that the root of the problem was not the 'near enemy' but the 'far enemy' – the US, which propped up the status quo in the Middle East.

Saudi Arabia has exported its strict brand of Islam, Wahabbism. Since the early 1970s, it has used petro-dollars to fund Islamic schools and religious centres around the world. In many poor areas of Pakistan, Indonesia and elsewhere, religious schooling of this type is the only option for children. A small, purist sect gained global reach.

Wahabbis see themselves as a movement to restore Islam from what they perceive to be deviancy, heresy and idolatry, such as watching television, listening to music or innovations in religion.

The Saudi export of Wahabbism eventually bore fruit with the advent of the Taliban, who were influenced by Wahabbist doctrines. The spread of Wahabbism expanded the global constituency receptive to the ideas of bin Laden and helped parts of Pakistan and Afghanistan to become training grounds for al-Qaeda terrorists.

The Soviet Union's invasion of Afghanistan in 1979 became a rallying point for Muslim fighters across the world. The Afghan war radicalised a generation of Arab militants (not least the group around bin Laden), who kept in touch with each other, gained battlefield experience and came to believe that they had played a big role in the destruction of the Soviet Union.

The defeat of the Soviet Union dispersed these fighters to their home countries, where some continued to fight the 'holy war' as a struggle against their secular governments – in the Philippines, for example.

A growing number of Muslims were radicalised by other conflicts. Following the collapse of Communism, conflicts involving Muslims proliferated in countries like Bosnia, Kosovo, Chechnya and Tajikistan.

Along with fragile states like the Sudan and Taliban-ruled Afghanistan, they attracted Muslim fighters from overseas, who returned home or moved on to other struggles.

Publicity given to these conflicts strengthened the impression among some Muslims that Islam the world over was under attack. This had a great influence on a number of young British Muslims, for example.

Particularly important was the first Iraq war. To support its invasion, the US stationed troops in Saudi Arabia and left them there subsequently, largely to support sanctions against the Saddam Hussein regime.

For bin Laden, this amounted to American presence on holy soil – the land of Mecca and Medina. He described it as the greatest aggression against Islam since the death of the Prophet in 632.[5]

Bin Laden's forces merged with the Egyptian Islamic Jihad, led by Ayman al-Zawahiri, in the late 1990s to form what is roughly the present-day al-Qaeda.

The 'globalist' bin Laden, who believed in confronting his enemies anywhere regardless of borders, came together with 'localist' leaders like al-Zawahiri, who had concentrated on Islamist struggles within national borders: al-Zawahiri's motto for a while had been 'the road to Jerusalem is through Cairo.'

The 'globalists' gained a larger number of foot soldiers, while local struggles were linked to the global goal of evicting the US from the Middle East.

In 1998 bin Laden and his colleagues issued a fatwa that greatly influenced Islamist groups. The fatwa removed the distinction between civilians and military personnel, and declared that killing Americans and their allies was a duty for any Muslim, who can do it in any country where it is possible.

The fatwa followed a period in the early to mid 1990s, when Israel had expelled many leading Palestinian terrorists to Lebanon. There the Palestinians had come into contact with Iranian-sponsored terrorists, who used car bombs, bombs strapped to individuals and other suicide tactics.

Many of these exiles eventually returned to Lebanon and the occupied territories, where they tried these new techniques and gained increased legitimacy. Bin Laden's fatwa encouraged his followers to do the same.

Policies of America and its allies after 9/ll have given Islamist terrorism a huge fillip. 'It is enormously important to terrorists' sense of themselves that they be considered and treated as soldiers.'[6] Declaring a war on terror elevated the stature of al-Qaeda in a way it could never have done itself.

The 2003 invasion of Iraq and its aftermath led to widespread coverage of civilian casualties, which has been a powerful recruiting tool among Muslims.

Baghdad was the historic centre of the Abbasid Caliphate (750 to 1250 in the Western calendar), the most sustained leadership of the community of Islam, and is now easily represented as being occupied by neo-Christian forces.

Paramilitary radicals from outside Iraq are receiving combat training in urban guerrilla warfare and will be able to take this experience into other al-Qaeda operations.[7]

A comparison of terrorist attacks between 9/11 and the invasion of Iraq on 20 March 2003, and then from 21 March 2003 to 30 September 2006 found that worldwide annual attacks increased seven-fold – to nearly 200 – after the Iraq invasion. Excluding attacks within Afghanistan and Iraq, the number had still increased by 35%.[8]

> 'Terrorist attacks worldwide increased seven-fold after the Iraq invasion'

Al-Qaeda-linked groups are increasingly active in volatile parts of the Middle East outside Iraq. The deputy leader of al-Qaeda, Ayman al-Zawahiri, has urged supporters in Iraq to extend their 'holy war' to other Middle Eastern countries.

He has conjured a vision of an Islamic state comprising Lebanon, Palestine and Syria. Al-Qaeda sympathisers appear to be fighting in all three countries. In Gaza, for example, militants disillusioned with Hamas are said to be drifting to al-Qaeda.[9]

Al-Qaeda is a new form of terrorism, different to previous terrorist groups. *It is more religious* – at least in terms of its goals. Though religion was an important dimension of terrorism in Northern Ireland for example, the aims of the IRA were essentially secular – to re-unite Ireland. The IRA did not aim to create a Catholic state, in the way that bin Laden seeks to establish Islamic states within the Middle East.

It is more global. The events of 9/11 and subsequent attacks in Bali, Madrid, London and elsewhere have shown al-Qaeda to be a global force. Whereas the Malayan communists were a danger to Malaya in the 1950s but no one else, al-Qaeda has demonstrated that it is a global network, capable of attacking countries from outside.[10]

A striking feature of the 7/7 London bombings was that there seem to have been no local grievances that the alleged bombers were exploiting.

Sidique Khan and Shehzad Tanweer, two of the alleged bombers, grew up in suburban Britain, not in the Gaza strip. They may have had support from a handful of extremists in the mosques near their homes, but they did not kill themselves for a local cause.

The grievances were external – they were about American presence in the Middle East and US support for governments that had betrayed Islam. Instead of starting local and going global, the norm for terrorism, on 7/7 terrorism started global and went local: a global cause enrolled local recruits.[11]

It is more violent. Suicide bombings have introduced a whole new dimension into terrorism. The events of 9/11, other attacks and al-Qaeda's known interest in weapons of mass destruction have demonstrated a willingness to hit civilians on a far larger scale than have previous terrorist groups.

The resulting public revulsion against terrorism has brought a collapse in support for 'old terrorism'. After 9/11 the IRA recognised that it had no option but to complete the peace process. ETA, the Basque terrorist group, has found its position almost untenable.[12]

Whereas terrorist groups were mostly constrained in their use of violence against civilians, there seem to be no limits to al-Qaeda's ambitions.

It is more diverse. Al-Qaeda has evolved from a centralised organisation into a loose network of cells, which are united by a hatred of the West. The motives of these cells are increasingly varied:

- some hate the American presence in the Middle East;
- others, from the West, are driven partly by feelings of alienation – of not belonging to the country in which they live;
- others identify with global Islam and feel rage at the lack of respect their faith commands in the world;
- others, in parts of Asia, are pursuing long-running local disputes.

Some operatives are highly devout: others are committed to Islam as a political ideal, but don't follow the strict tenets of the faith. Al-Qaeda is very post-modern.

Today's terrorist threat has been described as 'real, here, deadly and enduring'.[13] In 2006 MI5 and the police were aware of some 200 al-Qaeda-related terrorist groupings or networks in the UK. They comprised over 1600 identified individuals who were actively plotting or facilitating terrorists acts in Britain or overseas. There must be many more people the security services didn't know about.

According to opinion polls conducted in the UK since July 2005, more than 100,000 British citizens believe that the 7/7 London bombings were justified.

'More and more people are moving from passive sympathy towards active terrorism through being radicalised or indoctrinated by friends, families, in organised training events here and overseas, by images on television, through chat rooms and websites on the Internet.'[14]

In late 2006 the security services were aware of 30 al-Qaeda-related plots in the UK to kill people and damage the economy. Other countries from Spain to France to Canada and Germany also face a new terrorist threat.

Will terrorism be managed effectively?

---

1 *A more secure world: Our shared responsibility*, Report of the Secretary-General's High-level Panel on Threats, Challenges and Change, New York: United Nations, 2004, p. 2.

2 Richard Devetak and Christopher W. Hughes, 'Globalisation's Shadow: An Introduction to the Globalisation of Political Violence' in Richard Devetak and Christopher W. Hughes (eds.), *The Globalisation of Political Violence: Globalisation's Shadow,* Routledge, 2007 (forthcoming)

3 This phrase is used to describe contemporary warfare by former Deputy Supreme Allied Commander in NATO, Rupert Smith, *The Utility of Force*, London: Penguin, 2006, part three.

4 A lot of research has been summarised by Peter Bergen, 'What were the causes of 9/11?' *Prospect*, September 2006, pp. 48–51 and Pete Lentini, 'Beheading, Hostage Taking and "The New Terrorism": The Transformation of Tactics and the Globalisation of Violence' in Richard Devetak and Christopher W. Hughes (eds.), *The Globalisation of Political Violence: Globalisation's Shadow,* Routledge, 2007. The summary that follows draws on these two, except where other sources are cited.

5   Michael Scott Doran, 'Somebody else's civil war', originally published in *Foreign Affairs*, January/February 2002, now available on **http://evatt.labor.net.au.**

6   Louise Richardson, *What Terrorists Want*, London: John Murray, 2006, p. 217.

7   Chris Abbott, Paul Rogers & John Sloboda, *Beyond Terror*, London: Rider, 2006, p. 35.

8   Peter Bergen & Paul Cruikshank, 'The Iraq Effect: War Has Increased Terrorism Sevenfold Worldwide', 1 March 2007, **http://www.motherjones.com.**

9   *The Sunday Times*, 27 May 2007.

10 John Gray, *Al-Qaeda and what it means to be modern*, London: Faber & Faber, 2003, p. 81.

11 Louise Richardson, *What Terrorists Want*, London: John Murray, 2006, p. 168.

12 Asta Maskaliunaite, 'Old violences, new challenges: the adaptation of Basque ETA to its changing environment' in Richard Devetak and Christopher W. Hughes (eds.), *Globalisation's Shadow: The Globalisation of Political Violence*, Routledge, 2007.

13 The phrase was used by Peter Clarke, head of the anti-terrorism branch of the Metropolitan Police in August 2006.

14 'The international terrorist threat to the UK', speech by the Director General of the security service, Dame Eliza Manningham-Buller on 9 November 2006, **http://www.mi5.gov.uk.**

WHO WILL WIN THE 'WAR ON TERROR'? WHAT WILL SHAPE THE NEXT 20 YEARS?

- Desire for respect will continue to drive Islamist terrorism
- Advances in global communications will facilitate Islamist terror
- Al-Qaeda's future depends largely on the outcome of clashes within Islam
- How the West responds to terrorism will be hugely important

Desire for respect will continue to drive Islamist terrorism. Bin Laden often talks about the humiliation inflicted on Muslims by the West. Revenge is a natural response. This is especially true in the Middle East, where vengeance is a matter of honour and commanded by the Q'ran in cases of transgressions against God. Revenge is a strong motive behind terrorism in general.[1]

Muslims' sense of humiliation is deep-seated and will not be easily reversed. As in recent years, it will be fuelled by:

- *Centuries of decline,* symbolised by the carve-up of the once-powerful Ottoman Empire after the First World War. Since the Second World War neither socialism nor Arab nationalism have delivered their promises of prosperity and social justice.

    The continuing economic failure of much of the Muslim world is reflected in this astonishing statistic: the non-oil incomes of all the Gulf states add up to less than the GDP of Finland.[2] There are few signs of a step change.
- *The state of Israel.* Palestinians have a profound sense of injustice that goes back to their experience of *Al-Nakba,* which is their word for what they regard as their catastrophe – the displacement of large numbers of refugees as a result of the 1948 war, which established Israel.[3]

    This sense of catastrophe is shared by other Muslims, and has been compounded by Israel's many military victories and its continued occupation of the West Bank. For many Muslims, bound together through the global community of Islam (*umma*), the presence of Israel symbolises their impotence.

    Hezbollah's perceived success against Israel in 2006 restored some pride, but Arab grievances remain deeply ingrained. Will a Palestinian-Israeli settlement be more achievable in the next 20 years than it has been in the past?

■ *The alienation of some Muslims in the West.* Three of the four 9/11 pilots and two of the key planners became more militant while living in the West. A quarter of 'the 79 terrorists responsible for five of the worst recent anti-Western terrorist attacks ... had attended colleges in the West.'[4]

Many Islamist terrorists living in the West are in their late adolescence or early 20s, when confusion around identity may produce a crisis about who one is. Solidarity with *umma* and joining the struggle to restore the group's honour will give potential terrorists an identity and purpose. Their view of Western society as shallow and materialistic in contrast to Islam will reinforce an 'enclave mentality'.

'The sense of duty to a brotherhood of peers is, many psychologists agree, the single most important reason why otherwise apparently rational people can be persuaded to kill themselves and others.'[5]

Advances in global communications will strengthen and facilitate Islamist terror. As now, these communications will support resilient networks, comprising multiple cells, some supervised by al-Qaeda and others loosely inspired by it.

Cheap travel will enable Muslims in the West to travel to al-Qaeda training camps, currently in Pakistan. There, separated from family and friends back home, potential suicide bombers will be immersed in intense training that creates a powerful sense of belonging to the group.

As with current practice, their field of view will be narrowed, so that everything is interpreted through a single religious lens. Repetition will make new ideas comfortable. Tactics and techniques will be taught, so that individuals return home equipped to plan their atrocities.

Even more important will be advances in media communications. Al Jazeera, the most famous of many Arab-language satellite TV stations, had an estimated 35 million viewers in the early 2000s.

Internet penetration is expanding rapidly in the Arab world. As more people use more media in more ways, the media as a terrorist weapon will become even more important than today.

Al-Qaeda has already used it to great effect. By showing beheadings live, reading the wills of suicide bombers and broadcasting statements, terrorists have been able:

■ to strengthen the overall 'narrative' that holds al-Qaeda together;
■ to demonstrate members' commitment to the cell and the cause;

- to add to the expanding myths and histories of groups and individuals – stories that can be passed on;
- to gain publicity for their views and aspirations.

Astute use of the media has been an important factor behind the growing support for al-Qaeda.[6]

The media will further strengthen Muslim identification with *umma*, the worldwide community of Islam. Attacks on Muslims elsewhere in the world will be seen as attacks on the whole community.

Further advances in media technology and improved access will bring the struggle for Islam in other countries even closer to home. Chat rooms, blogs, social network sites and other developments will allow a combination of rumour, fact and story to spread across the Muslim world. Al-Qaeda says that 50% of its war is conducted through the media.[7]

In addition, were the security services to make suicide bombings increasingly difficult, the Internet may offer al-Qaeda an alternative means of disrupting the West.

In early 2007, the British police reportedly uncovered a plot by al-Qaeda cells to bomb a high-security facility in Docklands. The buildings housed the channel through which almost all Internet information passes in and out of Britain.[8]

Might we see an evolution from 'old terrorism' (such as the IRA) to 'new terrorism' (based around al-Qaeda) to 'Internet terrorism', in which al-Qaeda cells or their successors adopt a new approach?

Al-Qaeda's future depends largely on the outcome of clashes within Islam.[9] This is a more helpful perspective than talking about a clash between civilisations, as some have done. Within contemporary Islam, the course of four debates in particular will influence the amount of support for al-Qaeda.

One is between Sunni and Shia Muslims, which centres on the nature of authority. Broadly, Shi'ites believe that authority derives from within Muhammad's family, notably Ali (his cousin and son-in-law), whereas Sunnis say that authority derives from Muhammad's disciples.

This difference influences how parts of the Q'ran and some of the traditions of Islam are interpreted, raising issues that can be highly emotive. Anti-Shia paranoia is spreading across the Middle East, fuelled by mobile phone video clips allegedly showing Shias trying to convert Sunnis.[10]

Bin Laden's primary foes have been Arab regimes that don't stick closely to his extreme fundamentalist theology, especially Saudi Arabia. But bin Laden and his close colleagues are Sunni Muslims, who have contempt for Shias.

Will they intervene increasingly on the side of Sunnis? Their determination to prevent Lebanon falling into the hands of the Shi'ite Hezbollah movement, for example, is said to explain al-Qaeda's move into the country during 2006-07.[11]

Despite American efforts, the conflict between Iraq's Sunnis and Shias could well escalate over the next few years, reeling in Shia Iran and Sunni Saudi Arabia in a proxi-war.

Al-Qaeda's Iraq operatives have set up a self-styled Islamic State of Iraq, which – despite a backlash by Sunnis in 2007 – could be embroiled increasingly in a Sunni-Shia conflict, along with a series of tribal clashes.

> 'Al-Qaeda's Iraq operatives have set up a self-styled Islamic State of Iraq'

Within al-Qaeda, there have been complaints that Iraq could detract from their wider war on the US and its allies. Might al-Qaeda fissure as some factions go after the West, others get bogged down in Iraq and elsewhere in the Middle East, and others tear themselves apart in debates about their Iraq strategy?

A second debate is between 'secular' Muslims and the Salafis. 'Secular' Muslims – including many Arab regimes – seek to accommodate Islam in the modern world.

Strongly opposed to them is the Salafiyya movement among Sunni Muslims. It is not a unified movement, but includes for example the Wahabbi ideology of the Saudi state, the Muslim Brotherhood in Egypt, the Taliban and the followers of bin Laden.

What these Salafis have in common is the belief that Muslims have deviated from God's plan, not least in compromising with the materialism of the modern world. The solution is once again to follow the Prophet Muhammad.

The Salafiyya movement, strengthened by Saudi Arabian-sponsored schools, has created a mindset receptive to the ideas of bin Laden. How far the movement flourishes, therefore, will influence the amount of support for al-Qaeda.

Worldwide, more Muslims live in countries where they are in a minority (like India and Indonesia) than in countries where, as the majority, they can form an Islamic state. As many are doing, these minority Muslims are likely to develop theologies that allow a more flexible response to modern society than the Salafis permit.

Might accommodationist views – already strong in Muslim countries with 'secular' states – gain ground within Islam? Sufism, a mystical and pietistic strand of Islam, might help to resource this. Could the sheer numerical weight of minority Muslims eventually pull Islam away from the Salafiyya movement? If so, how soon would this happen?

In the meantime, Salafi extremism may prove increasingly unpopular among a growing number of Muslims, weakening support for terrorist cells – witness the growing opposition of Sunni tribal leaders in Iraq to al-Qaeda brutalities in the country.

A cleavage has opened within the Salafiyya tradition – between extremists like bin Laden and relative moderates such as the Wahabbis allied to the Saudi state. Extremist Salafis believe that the strict application of *shari'a* (Islamic law) is necessary to ensure that Muslims walk on the path of the Prophet.

Moderates would normally agree, but bin Laden has accused the Saudi royal family of betraying its Wahabbi doctrines by compromising with the West, in particular by allowing American troops on Saudi soil.

How this debate runs will be a third influence on the amount of support for al-Qaeda. Will the Saudi Wahabbis be able to distance themselves sufficiently from the US to draw the sting of bin Laden's criticisms, or are they so enmeshed in the global economy that they will always be open to censor?

Say the royal family was overthrown and extremist Salafis seized power: would a Taliban-type regime damage the economy, alienate the public and massively discredit al-Qaeda?

A fourth debate has occurred within al-Qaeda in the past, and could easily wrench the network apart in future. Today's al-Qaeda represents a lose amalgam of those who favoured attacking apostate regimes within the Middle East (the 'near enemy') and bin Laden's followers, who believe in concentrating on the 'far enemy' – the US, which supports many Middle Eastern states.

Bin Laden won the debate in the late 1990s largely because attacking Arab governments, like Egypt's, had proved unsuccessful.

He argued that the US was inherently weak. America had withdrawn from Lebanon in 1983, after the attack on the barracks that killed 241 US servicemen. It had withdrawn from Somalia 10 years later, after 18 American soldiers were killed in Mogadishu.

Attacking the United States and its allies would weaken their resolve, force them out of the Middle East (so that they could no longer prop up governments like the Saudi royal family) and create conditions for establishing Islamist states, faithful to the Prophet.

Despite bin Laden's ascendancy, the debate resurfaced in 2005–06, in a dispute between al-Qaeda's Abu Musab al-Zarqawi (who originally favoured attacking the 'near enemy') and his mentor, Abu Muhammad al-Maqdisi.

Al-Maqdisi argued that the Iraq war was rapidly becoming a 'crematory' for the flower of Islamist youth. No energies were left for Islamist revolution elsewhere in the region. Though US forces killed al-Zarqawi in June 2006, he won the debate by arguing that the Iraq war was weakening the United States and building support for the jihadist movement.[12]

But will bin Laden's strategy be vindicated? Withdrawal of the US and its allies from Iraq and Afghanistan (where foreign troops have a poor record) would certainly be seen as a success by bin Laden, whose followers are active in both countries.

But what would happen if plots against the West were regularly foiled, and if the occasional success failed to dislodge the United States from the Middle East? Would there be a clamour for a change of tactics?

How the West responds to terrorism will be hugely important. Much of the post-9/11 strategy has played into terrorist hands. Declaring a 'war on terror' has made it easy for al-Qaeda to prevent the West winning: just one bomb will deny the West an overall victory.

At least as important has been American rhetoric that has dehumanised the country's opponents, such as using 'collateral damage' to refer to innocent civilians killed in Afghanistan or Iraq. This fuels a mirror reaction among supporters of Muslim militants, who deny the humanity of Westerners killed in terrorist attacks.

The invasion of Iraq and the post-war debacle have radicalised Muslims round the world. American withdrawal before establishing a stable democratic state (increasingly likely) would confirm bin Laden's view that the US can be forced out of the Middle East.

A prolonged war in Afghanistan would also continue to radicalise Muslims. Eventual defeat for the West – a distinct possibility – would further boost bin Laden's strategy.

There are signs of a slight shift in the West's approach, which has polarised between the Atlanticist view ('it's a war') and the European one ('it's a criminal justice issue'). Both sides seem to be drawing into the middle.

Europeans are signed up to the threat posed to the West by Islamist terror. The Americans are putting greater emphasis on intelligence and influencing Muslim opinion rather than relying so heavily on military means.

The 2008 Presidential election will provide an opportunity for the United States to move further in this direction, though it will be far from easy.

The strategy could include a change of rhetoric. Just as President Kennedy's 1963 State of the Union address very effectively reached out to the Soviet Union and helped to ease tensions, might the US find language to reach out to the global Muslim community?[13]

Demonstrating respect, and replacing the notion of 'war' with the idea that the US and its allies are tackling a form of organised crime would be a great start. Terrorists crave the status of soldiers, which 'war on terror' language confirms.

There has been a softening of rhetoric by the British prime minister, Gordon Brown, who has dropped the term 'war on terror'. But would the American public accept this new understanding of the terrorist threat?

Might the US take stronger measures to win the support of Muslims? In addition to a more pro-Islamic rhetoric, these could include:

- toning down support for Israel;
- a strong push to secure peace between Israel and the Palestinians;
- heavy investment in high-profile humanitarian projects in Muslim communities across the world;
- withdrawal of the allies from Afghanistan, and
- forswearing any future military intervention in Islamic states.

This might encourage Muslims to begin to disown the extremists.

But would America's pro-Israel lobby allow these moves in an Arab direction? How far would the aggressive strand in American politics (witness the strength of the gun lobby) allow the United States to de-escalate the violence?

And if al-Qaeda cells were seen to be flourishing in – for example – Taliban-run regions of Afghanistan, could any US president rule out military intervention? Opponents would ask, 'Why aren't you bombing their camps?'

Security forces are likely to get increased support, on top of the additional sums spent since 9/11. Might security forces gain ground against terrorism as a result of:

- advances in surveillance and other technologies;
- closer international collaboration;
- a larger number of recruits, especially from Muslim backgrounds?

In chapter 11, we argue that law enforcement agencies will have some distinct advantages over organised crime, including sophisticated forms of managing knowledge. Much the same will be true of counter-terrorism.

Huge resources within the US and other militaries are being channelled to combat terrorism, and this will lead to big advances in technology.

In a few years for instance, using existing technologies, large crowds in an airport or on the tube may pass rapidly through a series of security detectors that automatically 'see' dangerous weapons or 'smell' traces of explosives and chemical agents.[14]

As is beginning to happen, computers will store ratings of the threat posed by individuals. People who provide the necessary information and get low scores will pass through security more quickly.[15] New techniques will make it easier to identify and track suspects.

Will terror eventually be subdued by superior intelligence?

1   Louise Richardson, *What Terrorists Want*, London: John Murray, 2006, p. 117.

2   Peter Bergen, 'What were the causes of 9/11?' *Prospect*, September 2006, p. 50.

3   Scilla Elworthy & Gabrielle Rifkind, *Making Terrorism History*, London: Rider, 2006, p. 47.

4   Peter Bergen, 'What were the causes of 9/11?' *Prospect*, September 2006, p. 51.

5   Scilla Elworthy & Gabrielle Rifkind, *Making Terrorism History*, London: Rider, 2006, p. 36.

6   Pete Lentini, 'Beheading, Hostage Taking and "The New Terrorism": The Transformation of Tactics and the Globalisation of Violence' in Richard Devetak and Christopher W. Hughes (eds.), *Globalisation's Shadow: The Globalisation of Political Violence*, Routledge, 2007.

7   'The international terrorist threat to the UK', speech by the Director General of the security service, Dame Eliza Manningham-Buller on 9 November 2006, **http://www.mi5.gov.uk.**

8   *The Sunday Times*, 11 March 2007.

9   For an introduction to some of the issues discussed in the following paragraphs, see Michael Scott Doran, 'Somebody else's civil war', first published in *Foreign Affairs*, January/February 2002 and now available on **http://evatt.labor.net.au.**

10 Rachel Aspden, 'History of a conflict' *New Statesman*, 12 February 2007.

11 *The Sunday Times*, 27 May 2007.

12 Dean Godson, 'A new year's resolution for the chattering classes', *The Times*, 27 December 2006.

13 President Kennedy called on the US to examine its own attitudes and to avoid forcing adversaries into a choice between humiliating retreat and nuclear war, and praised the Soviet Union for the enormous contribution and sacrifices it had made during the Second World War. The speech deeply moved Khrushchev, the Soviet leader, and was followed within just six weeks by a Partial Nuclear Test Ban Treaty between the two countries.

14 *The Times*, 1 November 2006.

15 The US has begun to do this. *The Times*, 2 December 2006.

WHO WILL WIN THE 'WAR ON TERROR'? WHAT MIGHT BE THE IMPLICATIONS?

- Who will win the 'war on terror'?
- What would happen if the terrorists had some notable successes?
- What will be the impact of increased surveillance?

Who will win the 'war on terror'? As we have noted, the concept of 'war' is not easily applied to new terrorism. How could opponents of al-Qaeda be sure they had won? What would a victory look like? Might keeping terrorism at bay – with occasional attacks – be the best we can hope for?

The proliferation of terrorists, their growing sophistication and the public impact of a single attack make the struggle against terrorism extremely difficult. Strong forces are driving al-Qaeda-related terrorism – not least:

- feelings of humiliation within the Muslim world;
- global publicity through modern media;
- the radicalisation of Muslims following the invasion of Iraq.

But the dice are not entirely loaded in al-Qaeda's favour. This is because:

- latent divisions within the al-Qaeda network could eventually pull it apart;
- the US and its allies may learn from the mistakes of Iraq;
- the security services will improve their techniques and will be extremely well resourced.

The security forces constantly warn that overcoming Islamist terrorism will take many years. There is little reason to think they are wrong – unless al-Qaeda implodes into rival factions.

Might al-Qaeda gradually disintegrate as internal strains pull it apart? Cells that already gain strength from local conflicts, as in the Philippines, might simply become another faction in these local struggles. Al-Qaeda would decline as an overarching political force.

Might other cells slide into organised crime, as some terrorists have done in Northern Ireland? Terrorists often rely on criminals to secure forged documents, launder money and provide other support. Switching from terrorism to crime might be tempting for terrorists whose original objectives seem unrealistic.

What would happen if the terrorists had some notable successes? These might include:[1]

- another 9/11;
- five or six simultaneous suicide 'truck bombs' aimed at civilians (perhaps killing 100 each time);
- detonating a tanker full of liquefied natural gas at a harbour terminal (the explosion could be 55 times larger than the bomb that destroyed Hiroshima);
- releasing nerve gas into the air intakes of large public buildings;
- the chemical poisoning of metropolitan sewage plants;
- using computer hackers to shut down key infrastructure, such as an airport, or to spread deadly viruses indiscriminately.

How would people react? Often it is assumed that people will only tolerate today's level of risk. If risks significantly increase, people will change their behaviour.

But experience shows that as risks grow, public tolerance of those risks frequently increases too. IRA bombings in London and 7/7 added to the perceived risk of moving about in the capital, but did not markedly change long-term behaviour. Might the same be true of terrorist strikes in future? Much might depend on the nature of the attack.

A one-off event could cause a large, but temporary disruption. People might travel less, as after 9/11 for example, or parts of the infrastructure might go out of use.

But after a while life would return to normal – travel would pick up and the infrastructure would be repaired. The economic (and perhaps human) costs could be enormous, but no big change in behaviour would occur in the long term.

A series of localised attacks might bring longer, but still temporary disruption. Gradually individuals and organisations would adjust to the new risk and life would go back to normal, just as everyday life continued in Northern Ireland for much of the 1970s to 90s, despite terrorist attacks.

If bombs in tourist resorts became fairly regular, for instance, individuals might still holiday abroad, reckoning that the risk to them as individuals was small enough to accept.

A series of catastrophes might change behaviour significantly. For example, a succession of aircraft bombings over a longish period might substantially change the perception of risk involved in air travel.

Business travel might decline, and be replaced with more video-conferencing and other forms of e-communication. The long-run increase in international tourism would slow.

But if those bombings eventually came to an end, behaviour would gradually revert to its pre-bombing norm. Will the impact on long-term behaviour of terrorist attacks depend less on their size and more on whether they can be sustained?

What will be the impact of increased surveillance? New surveillance technologies are being developed rapidly and linked together.

For instance, partly in response to the terrorist threat, a growing number of countries are introducing or considering national electronic ID card systems. These systems will use iris scanning, facial recognition and other biometric techniques to identify individuals. The results will be linked to databases of selected information.

There are fears that erroneous information (perhaps the result of computer hacking) could allow individuals to be mistakenly held as terrorist suspects. In a 2004 poll, 41% of Canadians thought they would not be fairly treated if they were wrongly accused of terrorist activity.

'The multiplication of stories of those who have been wrongfully apprehended, detained and even tortured since 9/11 only serves to underscore the dangers of automating [ID] processes.'[2]

Similar fears will continue to be voiced as a variety of surveillance technologies are improved and new ones introduced.

But it won't just be governments (and companies) that increase surveillance. Surveillance technologies – sometimes building on technologies used against terrorists – will also be available to individuals and NGOs.

Might one of the effects of terrorism be to hasten the arrival of the transparent society? Authorities would more easily keep watch on individuals and individuals will be able to keep a closer eye on organisations.

Life would be more like the traditional village, in which everyone knew everything about everyone, except the village would now be in the city and knowledge would be global.

---

1 Grant T. Hammond, 'The Revolution in Security Affairs', *World Future Society Conference*, 1 August 2004.

2 David Lyon, 'Identity cards: social sorting by database', *Internet Issue Brief No. 3*, Oxford Internet Institute, November 2004, p. 8.

CHAPTER 11
WILL GLOBAL CRIME GET THE UPPER HAND?
THE STORY SO FAR

- 'Global crime' describes transnational crime
- There have been three major developments
- Global crime has encouraged global cooperation
- How big a threat is global crime?

'Global crime' describes what is technically known as transnational crime. This is crime carried out by global trading and financial networks, which engage in the provision of prohibited commodities and services.[1] Terrorism, which is connected to global crime, is discussed in the previous chapter.

Crime across borders is nothing new – think of smuggling on the Cornish coast. Some would say that global crime is the same serious crime that continues to occur at national level, only it now has a stronger international edge.[2] But others think that something qualitatively new has emerged. A larger number of crime groups are centred in no one jurisdiction, but operate in many.[3]

There have been three major developments since the late 1980s. *Globalisation has increased transnational crime.* 'Make legitimate business easier, less regulated, better supported by transport and communications, and organised crime will lap up the benefits as well.'[4]

Global crime has been associated with an expansion of people trafficking, for example, counterfeit drugs, money laundering and terrorism, which uses criminal links to support its activities.[5]

Similarities have emerged between criminal groups and legitimate global corporations:

- global crime groups network with other organisations, as do global corporations;
- they form joint ventures and strategic alliances;
- they use the same accountancy and other management techniques;
- they are strongly embedded in local communities: global 'specialists' make use of local 'opportunists'.[6]

Global crime is the shadow side of the global economy.

Fragile states have fuelled the rise of global crime. The collapse of the Soviet Union allowed state enterprise managers, government bureaucrats, party officials, military officers and illegal traders under the old regime to take advantage of the opportunities created by liberalisation.

In the 1990s, an estimated three-quarters of privatised firms and commercial banks were compelled to pay between 10% and 20% of their turnover to mafia organisations.[7] Crime has spilled across the borders of many Eastern European states.

During the 1990s a number of African governments, who relied on patron-client relationships, received insufficient financial aid to maintain these relationships. Some governments developed new sources of revenue through illegal ventures such as money laundering, smuggling (of arms, diamonds, timber, drugs and consumer goods) and the plundering of resources in neighbouring countries.

Strongmen set up parallel governments in some 'failing' states, financing schools, mosques and other public infrastructure, while engaging in illegal cross-border trade.[8]

Global crime groups have increasingly made use of advanced technology. In particular, they use the Internet for fraud, theft, extortion schemes, money laundering, to rig gambling on online sites and to connect with hackers, who assist their operations.[9]

From 1990 it took 15 years to assemble a worldwide library of 100,000 computer viruses. In the next two years the number tripled. Instead of producing a single virus, hackers now build a command centre and control millions of 'zombie' PCs without their owners' knowledge. Hackers can mount mass frauds and blackmails without overloading their systems.

The online black economy, centred on credit-card fraud, corporate blackmail and insider share dealing is thought to be worth $8 billion a year.[10]

Global crime has encouraged global cooperation in response.

In some cases, countries have been 'named and shamed'. In 2000, for instance, the Financial Action Task Force, a body set up in 1989, identified 15 jurisdictions with grossly inadequate efforts to combat money laundering. Some of those named feared their legitimate businesses would suffer if they failed to respond, and took decisive action.[11]

Some steps have been taken to harmonise national laws. For example, at a global level the UN Convention Against Transnational Organized Crime came into force in 2003.

- It provides a common definition of organised crime.
- It obliges countries to establish money laundering, corruption and certain other activities as criminal offences.
- It offers 'what is potentially a worldwide framework for cooperation against organized crime.'[12]

At a regional level have been measures like the EU's Second Money Laundering Directive, adopted in December 2001, which provides for a common regulatory framework across the Union to help reduce this type of activity.

Collaboration between law enforcement agencies has enhanced their capacity to tackle global crime. Europol, for instance, became fully operational in 1999 and coordinates cross-border policing and criminal investigations in the EU. Tackling terror has also encouraged greater cooperation.

Better collaboration with the private sector has been a significant trend. For example, to help combat money laundering in the UK, Service Level Agreements have been reached between police agencies and the Association of British Insurers and other industry associations.

The World Customs Organization has created formal partnerships between national customs agencies and private carriers to address narcotics and contraband smuggling.[13]

How big a threat is global crime? Pessimists would say that it represents an alternative form of globalisation. Criminals take part in the global economy by playing within protectionist rules.

These rules are meant to keep economic activities in the hands of a specific group of people instead of allowing competition. They are fundamentally opposed to liberal versions of globalisation and represent a growing threat.

Certainly, some estimates suggest that transnational crime is remarkably extensive:

- the 1997 *World Drugs Report* estimated that organised drug trafficking was worth around $400 billion annually, about 8% of world trade and equivalent to the world's textile industry;
- international estimates suggest that an astonishing 500,000 women were illegally trafficked into the EU in 1995;
- the International Monetary Fund has estimated that money laundering – not all of which is transnational – may comprise 2% to 5% of global GDP.[14]

But might these be exaggerations? It is almost impossible to map accurately the extent of global crime because of its secretive nature. Official bodies have an incentive to opt for the highest estimates to bolster the case for more resources to tackle crime.

The estimates just cited are quite old: have things improved since? The 2004 *World Drugs Report* suggested that there had been a degree of containment of the illicit drug trade, with a 30% cut in coca cultivation between 1999 and 2003.[15]

While global crime has expanded, the level of crime experienced by individuals in the West has been falling. In the United States, for example, the 2005 violent crime rates were less than half those of the peak year, 1994. Property crime fell by about half over the same period, having been in long-term decline since 1975.[16]

England and Wales experienced a 44% drop in all forms of crime between 1995 (when crime peaked) and 2006, with a flattening of the trend since 2004–05.[17]

How do we explain the increase in global crime and the simultaneous decline in 'local' crime?

- *Is global crime being managed quite effectively?* Maybe it is not as serious as some people think? In which case, rising global and shrinking local crime would not be such a paradox. Local crime would be falling because global crime was being contained.

■ *Or is global crime not reflected in these surveys,* which simply measure whether individuals have been victims of crime? Excluded from the figures are forms of international crime that don't affect people directly (like money laundering), or don't show up in the statistics unless people are caught: if you take drugs, there's no 'victim' to tell the police.

In February 2007 Sir Stephen Lander, head of the Serious Organised Crime Agency (SOCA), said that 85% of British banknotes were thought to be contaminated with heroin, cocaine or other 'Class A' drugs.[18]

1   Shona Morrison, 'Approaching Organised Crime: Where Are We Now and Where Are We Going?', *Trends & Issues,* Australian Institute of Criminology, No. 231, July 2002, p. 4.
2   John Broome, 'Transnational crime in the twenty-first century', paper presented at the *Transnational Crime Conference* convened by the Australian Institute of Criminology in association with the Australian Federal Police and Australian Customs Service, Canberra, 9–10 March 2000.
3   Alan Wright, *Organised Crime,* Cullompton: Willan, 2006, pp. 23–24.
4   Bargi Bhattacharyya, *Traffick. The Illicit Movement of People and Things,* London: Pluto, 2005, p. 77.
5   Jennifer L. Hestermann, 'Transnational crime and the criminal-terrorist nexus: synergies and corporate trends', Maxwell Air Force Base, Alabama, 2004, pp. 27–52.
6   Margaret Beare, 'Structures, strategies and tactics of transnational criminal organisations: critical issues for enforcement', Paper presented at the *Transnational Crime Conference* convened by the Australian Institute of Criminology in association with the Australian Federal Police and Australian Customs Service, Canberra, 9–10 March 2000.
7   John Gray, *False Dawn. The Delusions of Global Capitalism,* London: Granta, 1998, p. 155.
8   Duffield, Mark, *Global Governance and the New Wars,* London: Zed Books, 2001, pp.170–178.
9   Phil Williams, 'Organized Crime and Cybercrime: Synergies, Trends and Responses', 13 August 2001, pp. 3–4, **http://www.iwar.org.uk.**
10 Figures quoted by Eva Chen, Chief Executive of Trend Micro, 20-year veteran of the anti-virus battle and Japan's most powerful businesswoman. *The Times,* 7 April 2007.
11 Phil Williams, 'Organised Crime and Cybercrime: Synergies, Trends and Responses', 13 August 2001, p. 5, **http://www.iwar.org.uk.**
12 'The response to international crime', **http://www.fco.gov.uk** (downloaded 1 November 2006).
13 Michael Levi & Mike Maguire, 'Reducing and preventing organised crime: An evidence-based critique', *Crime, Law and Social Change,* 41, 2004, p. 422.
14 Figures quoted by Alan Wright, *Organised Crime,* Cullompton: Willan, 2006, pp. 51, 98, 196.
15 Cited by Alan Wright, *Organised Crime,* Cullompton: Willan, 2006, pp. 79–80. Wright notes that some analysts are sceptical about the optimism displayed in the report.
16 Findings of the National Crime Victimization Survey, **http://www.ojp.usdoj.gov.**
17 Alison Walker, Chris Kershaw & Sian Nicholas, *Crime in England and Wales 2005/06,* London: Home Office Statistical Bulletin, July 2006, p. 1.
18 'Soca: One Year On', speech delivered by Sir Stephen Lander, Chair of the Serious Organised Crime Agency, Centre for Crime and Justice Studies, Kings College, London, 13 February 2007, **http://www.kcl.ac.uk.**

WILL GLOBAL CRIME GET THE UPPER HAND?
WHAT WILL SHAPE THE NEXT 20 YEARS?

- There will be plenty of opportunities for global crime
- The number of potential criminals will grow
- Success against crime in one context will displace it to another
- Law enforcement agencies will tackle global crime more effectively
- There will be limits to what enforcement agencies can achieve

There will be plenty of opportunities for global crime, making it attractive to potential criminals.

Growth of the global economy will increase the possibilities. It will inflate the demand for smuggled goods and other illegal products.

In 2006 only 500,000 consumers in China had credit cards.[1] As China's middle class grows to approaching 600 million by the 2020s[2], the number of credit cards will soar. This will hugely increase the opportunities for credit-card fraud by criminals working across national borders. Insurance fraud involving automobile accidents, health-care billing scams and life-insurance schemes will flourish.

Increases in cross-border trade and movements of people will create new openings for crime. Higher volumes of traffic – whether it is people travelling through airports or individuals having their credit-card details checked – will help criminals hide their illicit transactions.

In 2003 Interpol warned about expanding the EU to 25 members. Removing border restrictions would enable Eastern European criminal gangs to operate more easily throughout the Union.[3]

The expansion of commercial Internet sites will increase the opportunities for extortion, such as threats to disable a site if conditions are not met.

New types of crime will emerge. For example, online games set in virtual worlds are spreading rapidly. In 2006, 40 million people in China and South Korea subscribed to the game 'Mu', with an average of 500,000 people playing at any one time.[4]

As we noted in chapter 2, many of these games are becoming parallel economies, in which players sell entertainment, things they have made and a variety of services. As these virtual economies mushroom, there will be plenty of new opportunities for crime.

In 2006 one such game, *Second Life,* was hit by a rogue program that allowed users to make exact replicas of objects inside the game. Unique creations became available to everyone, wreaking havoc with the in-world economy.[5]

Apparently, police in Britain, Belgium and Holland are considering whether users of *Second Life* may be committing a crime if their character – known as an avatar – sexually assaults or stalks another.[6]

Weak states will continue to create conditions in which transnational crime flourishes. Offenders are less likely to be caught in countries with ineffective governments,

> 'Will avatars in *Second Life* be committing a crime if they sexually assault another avatar?'

such as Somalia, Afghanistan and in parts of Eastern Europe.

But helping these states build governing capacity is hard. They need support, yet the abundant capabilities offered to the international community often lead to 'capacity sucking out' rather than 'capacity building'. Foreign experts replace locals, who don't gain the necessary experience.[7] Many weak states may remain weak.

New methods of crime are inevitable. Enhanced security on the Internet, for instance, could increase thefts of desk-top computers, laptops and mobile devices, which would then be used to compromise security. Will offenders bribe or blackmail staff more frequently to break high-level encryption?

Criminal techniques will improve. As one example, software may be instructed to maximise revenue from selling intellectual property, without respecting ownership rights. The software would 'steal' material off websites and sell it on.[8]

How crime is defined will influence the amount of opportunities available. Legislation like the US ban on online gambling will increase the opportunities for crime, while the decriminalisation of illegal drugs would have the opposite effect.

As governments increasingly cooperate in tackling crime, securing agreement on what represents crime could become highly contentious in some cases. How would the US react if a large number of Americans went 'offshore' for their online gambling, legally generating perhaps billions of dollars for foreign companies in an activity banned at home?

The number of potential criminals will grow. Global crime networks often sub-contract work to individuals on the edge of the legitimate economy. These contractors dispose of smuggled goods and provide other support to earn incomes not available from legitimate sources.[9]

Worldwide, the supply of this labour could increase massively. Dr. Ifzal Ali, chief economist of the Asian Development Bank, has warned of a 'huge global oversupply of labour', particularly in China, India and Russia.

India could be heading towards an employment crisis because of the increase in its working age population, which is expected to grow by 71 million between 2006 and 2011, reaching 762 million.

Many young people, Dr. Ali claimed, will not have the skills to work in factories, call centres and high-tech companies – 38% of Indian children who have completed four years of schooling cannot read a small paragraph with short sentences.[10]

The global pool of young people who are unemployed or only spasmodically in jobs could provide an expanding source of labour for organised criminals.

Successful action against crime in one context will lead to its displacement to another, as happens now. This will make reducing the overall level of crime difficult. For example, as offending becomes harder:[11]

- *Crime may shift to other locations.* Computer chip credit cards in the UK, for instance, will encourage fraudsters to target countries that do not have chips.
- *Crime may shift to new targets.* As large organisations (often in the public sector) invest heavily in security, will electronic crime move to smaller, private-sector companies?
- *Criminals may turn to other types of crime.* 'Target hardening' in the case of Internet crime might encourage offenders to move to the drug trade, people smuggling or other types of activity, or to develop new types of online crime.

Law enforcement agencies will tackle global crime more effectively, on the other hand, and this has the potential to keep crime at manageable levels.

Better cooperation between agencies will increase their overall effectiveness. Agencies will continue to work more closely together – globally, within regions such as the EU and within individual countries. Countries will increasingly pool criminal records.

Collaboration with the private sector, such as credit-card companies, will strengthen too, as business becomes increasingly responsible for monitoring and reducing organised crime.

Fears that the terrorist/criminal nexus will tighten will be one of the spurs to better cooperation at many levels.

Crime prevention and enforcement will become more sophisticated. As criminals develop new techniques, so will agencies combating crime.

Prevention strategies in particular will be more systematic. Once a crime has been solved, for instance, agencies will more often analyse the sequence of events that led up to the crime. They will identify steps that would make it harder for these events to be repeated.[12]

Sophisticated uses of knowledge management will be further developed. Secure online databases of what works well and who has tackled a similar problem will help enforcement agencies adopt good practice.

Local enforcement will remain vital because of the strong links between global and local crime – indeed, some experts think that the local dimension is so key that the notion of global crime has been overworked.[13] The quality of local enforcement should improve as police forces share good practice.[14]

True, criminals will also share expertise. But might enforcement agencies have an advantage? Lack of trust between criminal groups will limit the sharing of knowledge among offenders.

Political bosses, on the other hand, will pressurise enforcement agencies to overcome problems of security and trust, as the importance of exchanging good practice is increasingly understood.

With more experts contributing their knowledge, will enforcement agencies create new knowledge faster than their criminal opponents? Might winning this race prove decisive in the long term?

Technology will assist law enforcement agencies. This will also be true for offenders, but the benefits of scale may eventually give enforcement agencies a technological edge. These benefits may come (perhaps slowly) from the shared development of technologies, as agencies round the globe work more closely together. Defence spending – especially in the United States – increasingly focuses on terrorism. Huge sums will be invested in technology research that will benefit the fight against global crime generally.

'56% of firms in Saudi Arabia plan to introduce iris scanning and fingerprint recognition in their offices'

We could see the widespread deployment of CCTV cameras, linked to databases, that will use facial recognition technology to seek out known criminals.[15]

The US military is experimenting with 'smart dust' – thousands of tiny microphones, cameras, and heat and vibration sensors deposited in a specific area. They are all wirelessly connected to each other and give 'total awareness' of the location. Sensors are being developed that can 'sniff out' drugs, human traffic and other illegal cargoes.

A 2005 survey found that 56% of firms in Saudi Arabia planned to introduce iris scanning and fingerprint recognition for security in their office buildings.[16]

Criminals will find ways round these and other innovations, of course, and will use technologies for their own purposes.

But in our connected world, linking technologies together and to large stores of information will bring particular benefits. Will enforcement agencies, with their mandates to cooperate, better achieve these linkages than more fragmented criminal groups? And might this give them an advantage over organised crime?

There will be limits to what enforcement agencies can achieve, however. Much will depend on how well they are resourced. Massive amounts of infrastructure are needed for Internet monitoring, for instance.

As the number of criminals expands, some fear that agencies will be swamped by the sheer volume of crime.

An official in Nigeria's Economic and Financial Crimes Commission is reported as saying that Nigerian Internet fraud has become 'something huge' because the authorities delayed before taking it seriously. The same could happen in Britain, he warned, if it makes the same mistake.[17]

Success in tackling global crime will also produce diminishing returns. If enforcement agencies are successful, the risks of crime will go up. Some offenders will shift to alternative crimes, so that reducing one type of crime may increase another. Others may become more ingenious, making them harder to catch.

Techniques can be highly imaginative: to cross the Iranian desert, smugglers have used camels addicted to opium. The camels travel unaccompanied from one fix to the next.[18]

Individual battles against global crime will be won, but not an overall victory.

1 An estimate by Experian, the credit information company, *The Times*, 22 November 2006.
2 Chinese Academy of Social Science report, quoted in the *China Daily News*, 27 October 2004. The Academy's report expected 40% of China's 1.4 billion people in 2020 to be middle class. Middle class is defined as families with assets of roughly $18,000 to $36,000.
3 *The Times*, 17 November 2003.
4 Eamonn Kelly, *Powerful Times*, New Jersey: Wharton School Publishing, 2006, p. 118.
5 *The Times*, 25 November 2006.
6 *The Times*, 13 May 2007.
7 Francis Fukuyama, *State Building. Governance and World Order in the Twenty-First Century*, London: Profile, 2004, pp. 139–140.
8 *Dilemmas of Privacy and Surveillance. Challenges of Technological Change*, London: The Royal Academy of Engineering, 2007, p. 22.
9 Adam Edwards, 'Understanding Organised Crime', *Criminal Justice Matters*, 55, Spring 2004, p. 31.

10 Jo Johnson, 'Engaging India: Demographic dividend or disaster?', *Financial Times*, 10 November 2006, **www.ft.com.**

11 These examples are taken from Russell G. Smith, Nicholas Wolanin & Glenn Worthington, 'e-Crime Solutions and Crime Displacement', *Trends & Issues in crime and criminal justice*, 243, Australian Institute of Criminology, January 2003.

12 Michael Levi & Mike Maguire, 'Reducing and preventing organised crime: An evidence-based critique', *Crime, Law & Social Change*, 41, 2004, p. 431.

13 We are grateful to Dr. Alan Wright for pointing this out.

14 More police, targeting minor misdemeanours and changes in how police were evaluated, managed and given information may have contributed to more than a third of the three-quarters drop in New York's serious crime over 15 years. Franklin E. Zimring, *The Great American Crime Decline*, Oxford: OUP, 2007, pp. 135–168.

15 The UK's Vehicle Crime Intelligence Service is rolling out checkpoints that use number recognition cameras to identify stolen vehicles, including those being used to commit crime.

16 Eamonn Kelly, *Powerful Times*, New Jersey: Wharton School Publishing, 2006, pp. 24–31.

17 Michael Peel, *Nigerian-Related Financial Crime and its Links to Britain*, London: Royal Institute of International Affairs, 2006, p. vi.

18 Loretta Napoleoni, *Terror Inc. Tracing the Money Behind Global Terrorism*, London: Penguin, 2003, p. 218.

WILL GLOBAL CRIME GET THE UPPER HAND?
WHAT MIGHT BE THE IMPLICATIONS?

- Global crime will increase, but by how much?
- The expansion of global crime will pose a number of threats
- Transnational crime risks corroding society

Global crime is set to expand over the next 20 years, but by how much? More opportunities for crime, a large increase in the supply of potential criminals and the ability to switch from blocked activities to new ones could produce a very substantial increase.

Yet if law enforcement agencies are well resourced and collaborate effectively, they could have an edge over their opponents. This would put limits on the growth of transnational crime. Global crime need not spiral out of control.

The expansion of global crime will pose a number of in-your-face threats.
The criminal/terrorist nexus will strengthen. As now, organised crime groups will provide terrorists with services such as kidnapping, protection and the means to earn an illegal income. Terrorists will provide organised criminals with a market for these services and for weapons.[1]

Ahmed Ressam, a member of the Armed Islamic Group (with ties to bin Laden) who was arrested in December 1999, planned to buy a Californian petrol station with his colleagues and use it to obtain credit-card numbers secretly. A camera would have been used to photograph people punching in their pin numbers.[2] The supply chain involved in the operation would have involved criminal groups.

As global crime groups innovate and exploit new opportunities, terrorism will be harder to beat.

Global crime will sometimes weaken the power of the state. In securing their goals, as now global crime groups will jeopardise the rule of law in some countries by intimidating and corrupting public officials.

Drug cartels have undermined democracy in Columbia. Some regions of Russia and the newly independent states have fallen under the influence of criminal organisations.[3] In countries with very weak governments, whole areas may be controlled by criminal groups, who provide basic infrastructure and levy taxes.[4]

Will global crime groups also exert a growing influence on officials in countries with strong governments – 'Cooperate, or we'll randomly fabricate your patient records'?

Global crime will push up the costs of legitimate business. Further regulation – to check money laundering, for example – will increase the costs of financial transactions. Companies will have to spend more on security arrangements.

One panel of experts rated commercial espionage by corporate spies as the biggest upcoming threat to business from Internet crime.[5] As security is tightened, criminals may resort to more extreme measures, such as extortion – 'We'll disrupt your supply chain if you don't help us'.[6]

> 'Global crime may be a particular problem for medium and small companies'

Will credit-card and other forms of fraud become so widespread that consumer confidence in the financial system is put at serious risk?

Global crime may be a particular problem for medium and small companies. Government departments and large corporations will be able to afford heavy investment in security and to keep up with the latest technology. Criminals may switch to less protected, smaller firms. What strategies will the latter adopt to make themselves secure?

Transnational crime risks corroding society in more insidious ways.

It may expand the unregulated exercise of state power. Enforcement agencies, under defined conditions, are increasingly allowed to disrupt criminal networks before there is sufficient evidence to bring offenders to trial. The risk of making a mistake and damaging an innocent person is – rightly – thought to be outweighed by the risk of a serious crime.

But is there a danger that enforcement agencies will be given too much discretion, with a growing risk to innocent people?

Examples from South Africa, Spain, the Thai-Burma border and Australia have illustrated how refugees have often been placed beyond the reach of judicial systems and their rights violated.

- Decisions by border police were frequently arbitrary.
- Deportations occurred in violation of international law.
- Asylum seekers arriving at remote islands outside Australia's migration zone were not allowed to bring legal action challenging their treatment by the Australian authorities.[7]

While global crime may weaken the state in some cases, in others might it increase state power? More law officers may behave in ways that are sometimes illegal.

Global crime may encourage xenophobic identities. In Britain, for instance, media discussions about crime tap into popular fears of the 'other'. Criminals are a big threat and must be 'put away'. Global crime is described in ethnic terms – Jamaican Yardies, Afghan warlords, Nigerian fraudsters, the Russian mafia and so on.

The undesirable and criminal 'other' is identified with a particular nationality (or several nationalities), and everyone in that nationality risks being tarred with the same brush.

A Chatham House report recorded how 'one Lagos banker has described how the level of crime linked to Nigeria already leads holders of the country's distinctive green passport to be "victimised" anywhere they go in the world'.[8]

Identity is frequently defined in relation to other people – 'He's the bad criminal and I'm the good, law-abiding citizen'. Seeing global criminals as foreigners helps British people to define themselves as good in contrast to certain nationalities, who are bad.

But this is a distortion of reality. Not only is it a small minority of any national group that engages in crime, but British people do so too! Drugs from Afghanistan are handled locally by British citizens. The proceeds are cycled through British banks. The trade to Britain would not exist if there was no demand.

The likely expansion of global crime risks strengthening a racialist dimension in personal identities.[9]

Global crime may reinforce 'masculine' conceptions of crime. Crime is done mainly by men, often in cultures where masculinity is proved through aggression, control and violence.

These same values tend to dominate the agencies that tackle crime, and are reflected in the language used, such as 'fighting crime' and 'the war on drugs'. In Britain at least, the public generally favours 'tough' measures to combat crime, including the violence that goes with imprisonment.

The masculine culture surrounding crime has made it hard to gain public support for crime reduction approaches that rely on different values. These alternative strategies include:

- prevention – to tackle the social conditions that give rise to crime;
- harm-reduction, such as public health measures to reduce drug taking;
- the re-habilitation of offenders.

To an extent, these are all part of the policy-mix in most countries, but resources tend to be skewed towards 'tougher' measures. Might a more balanced approach have greater success?

1 Shona Morrison, 'Approaching Organised Crime: Where Are We Now and Where Are We Going?' *Trends and Issues*, 231, Australian Institute of Criminology, July 2002, p. 5.
2 Jennifer L. Hesterman, 'Transnational Crime and the Criminal-Terrorist Nexus: Synergies and Corporate Trends', *Research Report*, Maxwell Air Force Base, Alabama, 2004, p. 41.
3 Alan Wright, *Organised Crime*, Cullompton: Willan, 2006, p. 53.
4 Mark Duffield, *Global Governance and the New Wars*, London: Zed Books, 2001, pp. 166–167.
5 Sheridan Morris, *The future of netcrime now: Part 1 – threats and challenges*, Home Office Online Report 62/04, 2004, p. 16.
6 'I recently had a conversation with someone very senior in a giant multinational who had just had a plant in India shut down because they would not pay bribes,' wrote Hamish McRae in *The Independent*, 6 October 2004.
7 Sharon Pickering, 'The Globalisation of Violence Against Refugees' in Richard Devetak & Christopher W. Hughes (eds.), *Globalisation's Shadow: Globalisation and Political Violence*, Routledge, 2007.
8 Michael Peel, *Nigeria-Related Financial Crime and its Links with Britain*, London: Royal Institute of International Affairs, 2006, p. v.
9 See James Sheptycki, 'Against Transnational Organised Crime' and Kyle Grayson, 'Discourse, Identity, and the U.S. "War on Drugs"' in Margaret E. Beare (ed.), *Critical Reflections on Transnational Organised Crime, Money Laundering and Corruption,* Toronto: University of Toronto, 2003, pp. 120–170.

CHAPTER 12
HOW WILL THE WORLD MANAGE CLIMATE CHANGE?
THE STORY SO FAR

- The world is warming dangerously and humans are largely to blame
- The scientific evidence has hardened
- Alongside the science has come energy security
- A sea-change in world opinion is occurring
- Adapting to climate change is rising up the agenda

The world is warming dangerously and humans are largely to blame. In simple terms, the sun's energy warms the earth's surface and the atmosphere. Because the earth's surface is warmer than outer space, it emits infrared radiation, which cools the planet.

However, water vapour, carbon dioxide and other 'greenhouse gases' like nitrous oxide and methane absorb part of this radiation and re-emit some of it downwards. This 'greenhouse effect' warms the earth's surface and cools part of the atmosphere.

Between the mid twentieth century and 2006, the global average surface temperature increased by about 0.55°C. This may seem a small amount, but it was a much faster increase than in the previous half century. Eleven of the 12 years from 1995 to 2006 rank among the 12 warmest years since 1850.[1]

This warming partly reflects a 'natural' shift in global temperatures, perhaps comparable to the unusually warm years around 1000 and — in the opposite direction — the 'Little Ice Age' of the 1700s.

The more important factor, most climate experts agree, has been the unprecedented increase in human fossil fuel consumption as the world's population has grown and incomes risen. Changes in land use, such as a decrease in the areas under forest, have made a smaller but significant contribution.

In early 2007 the Intergovernmental Panel on Climate Change (IPCC), which seeks to reflect the consensus among climate scientists, reported that 'there is new and stronger evidence that most of the warming observed over the last 50 years is attributable to human activities.'[2]

Despite this broad agreement, considerable uncertainties remain. The diagram overleaf illustrates the cascading effects of these uncertainties. Each uncertainty builds to the next. When you get to impacts at a regional level, the uncertainty is substantial.

The cascading effects of uncertainty

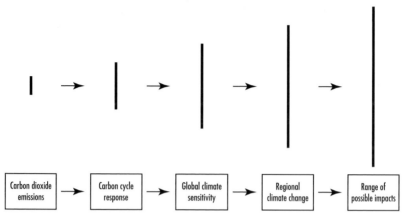

| Carbon dioxide emissions | → | Carbon cycle response | → | Global climate sensitivity | → | Regional climate change | → | Range of possible impacts |

Source: Stephen H. Schneider & Janica Lane, 'An Overview of "Dangerous" Climate Change' in Hans Joachim Schellnhuber et al. (eds.), *Avoiding Dangerous Climate Change*, Cambridge: CUP, 2006, p. 15.

The scientific evidence has hardened. The number of climate scientists doubting that humans are largely to blame for climate change has steadily fallen. Few would now dispute the consensus view.

The science academies of 11 of the world's most powerful countries issued an unprecedented declaration in 2005: the scientific understanding of climate change was sufficiently clear to justify nations taking prompt action.[3]

The world is rapidly approaching dangerous climate change. In 2007 the IPCC reported that the most recent scientific research reinforced the concerns expressed in its previous reports.

It expected the globally averaged surface temperature to increase by 0.4°C over the next two decades. By 2100, increases could range from a 'best estimate' of 1.8° above the 1980–99 average to 4.0°C.[4]

Anywhere in this range would bring a high risk of 'dangerous' climate change, including:

- large-scale eradication of coral reefs, which have the highest biodiversity of any marine system (hundreds of millions of people rely on reefs for fishing, subsistence foods and tourism);
- melting of the Greenland ice-cap, which could raise global sea levels by around 7 metres;

- the collapse of part or all of the Amazon rainforest, which would accelerate climate change by releasing huge amounts of carbon dioxide into the air;
- hundreds of millions of people at risk from water shortage, hunger, malaria, coastal flooding and weather extremes, such as hurricanes and storms;
- the depopulation of entire islands in the Indian and Pacific Oceans;
- international tensions sparked by millions of environmental refugees;
- the possible shut-down of the Gulf Stream (at high-end-of-the-range temperatures), bringing a much colder and more severe climate to Northern Europe;
- stronger feedbacks (climate change would feed further climate change), with a risk that global warming develops an 'internal' momentum, beyond human control.[5]

Where in the IPCC's range we end up will depend, for example, on how fast the global economy grows, how far it relies on fuels that emit carbon dioxide and the extent to which forests are destroyed or replanted.

To hit the lowest end of the range, the first IPCC scenario, the basis of the world economy would have to shift quickly from energy-intensive manufacturing to 'energy-lite' services and information. One glance at today's industrialisation of China shows how improbable this is.

The most likely way to keep global warming to 2.4°C, the IPCC's next lowest scenario, would be to switch rapidly to non-fossil energy sources or introduce clean and resource-efficient technologies.[6] Either would involve technologies that are currently very expensive, which would meet consumer resistance.

Yet if temperatures rose by 2.4°C or more, the effects could be dire. The world could experience some of the more extreme impacts of dangerous climate change. That is why climate scientists are so concerned. Time is rapidly running out for the world to take action.

To avoid the worst of these consequences, the costs of 'climate change' technologies need to be brought down fast. Consumers must also be persuaded to foot the higher bills.

Action is now urgent. The momentum behind climate change is becoming increasingly hard to stop. Even if all greenhouse gas emissions halted today, past emissions would warm the world by 0.5–1°C over several decades, bringing temperatures close to dangerous levels.

If annual emissions of all greenhouse gases were to stay at 2006 levels, by 2050 greenhouse gas concentrations in the atmosphere would reach close to 550ppm (parts per million) of carbon dioxide equivalent (CO_{2e}). This would commit the world to a warming of 2–5°C compared to the pre-industrial era.

Though there is no scientific consensus about what 'dangerous' means in relation to climate change, the policy community has broadly accepted that temperature increases of fewer than 2°C compared to pre-industrial levels would avoid dangerous climate change.

Temperatures in the middle of the 2–5°C range would be higher than at any time over the last 3 million years – far outside the experience of human civilisation.[7]

Keeping temperature rises to below 2°C would require greenhouse gas concentrations of no more than 450ppm CO_{2e}. This would be just 20ppm higher than in 2006. The world will reach 450ppm in less than 10 years. Even at that level, there will be more than an evens chance of exceeding 2°C.[8]

The UK Government's Stern Report, which has attracted wide attention, thought a target of 450–550ppm CO_{2e} was feasible. This would almost certainly imply temperature increases above 2°C.[9]

Though details are debated, the thrust of the science is that the world is fast reaching a point where it could be too late to avoid a planet-wide catastrophe. Hurricane Katrina in 2005 helped to convince many Americans that the science is real.

Alongside the science has come energy security, which has helped push climate change up the international agenda. (See chapter 13.)

The world's reliance on the Middle East for oil creates high-level security dilemmas. They have come sharply into focus at the start of the new century.

- America's oil-dependent economy is vulnerable to rising energy prices, which have shot up since 2003.
- An Iran with nuclear weapons would raise the stakes for Israel, yet the US is constrained from defending its ally by risks that a conflagration will disrupt the region's oil supplies.
- Saudi Arabia could have a key role in combating Islamist terror, but the US can put limited pressure on the kingdom because of the world's dependence on Saudi oil.
- China has been furiously striking oil and gas agreements to protect its long-term supplies.
- Europe is worried about its growing gas dependence on Russia, which may not prove reliable.

■ Most of the world's oil and gas comes from potentially unstable parts of the world.

To become more energy secure, consuming countries would have to increase energy efficiency, develop renewable alternatives to oil and gas, and find ways of cleaning coal so that they could tap the world's abundant supplies, often within their own borders, without causing unacceptable pollution.

These measures would also top any expert's 'action list' on how to reduce global warming. Securing energy and mitigating climate change go hand in hand.

A sea-change in world opinion is occurring, as science and energy security have come together.

In the United States, for instance, the East and West coasts have tended to be more concerned about global warming than have states in the middle. Yet some leaders within the evangelical right, heavily represented in middle America, have begun to support measures to mitigate climate change.[10]

Business has been signing up to the climate change agenda. 'Clean tech' is now the fifth largest home for venture capital investment in the US, running behind biotech, software, medical and telecoms.

By September 2006, 360 of the world's top 500 companies had joined the Carbon Disclosure Project, under which they disclose their greenhouse gas emissions.[11] The 2007 Davos World Economic Forum announced the formation of the Climate Disclosure Standards Board, which will encourage these disclosures to take a standardised form in annual reports.[12]

In February 2007 an informal meeting took place of legislators from the G8 rich countries, plus Brazil, China, India, Mexico and South Africa. They agreed that developing countries would have to set targets for cutting greenhouse gas emissions, as well as rich ones.

Previously, developing countries have said that this would be unfair, since rich nations are responsible for by far the most emissions. The United States has replied that it could never sign up to targets unless developing countries did so, too — its companies would be at a disadvantage.

Though not binding on governments, might the changes of view reflected by these legislators herald a more serious willingness to limit greenhouse gas emissions?

In March 2007, the EU reached a 'ground-breaking' agreement to cut carbon emissions by 20% by 2020, and by a further 10% if the United States and China (among others) agreed to cut their emissions too. By demonstrating that it is possible to 'go green' and grow its economy, Europe hopes to spur other countries to act more urgently on climate change.

At the summit of world leaders later in the year, President Bush reversed his previous position and showed a willingness to join the Kyoto process for reaching a global agreement on climate change. He allowed the possibility of a global target (cutting emissions 50% below 1990 levels by 2050) to be included in the communiqué, even though targets had once been an anathema to him.

The debate has moved on from a question of evidence (are humans responsible for climate change?) to a question of management (what are we going to do about it?).

Adapting to climate change is rising up the agenda. While public debate concentrates on mitigating climate change, the world is starting to adapt to the reality of global warming.

In the UK, a 2005 survey found that 60% of farmers thought that the growing season was lengthening. Farmers were grazing their livestock on natural feeds for more months, cutting winter feed requirements.[13] New crops have begun to appear, such as olives in the South West.

> 'The debate has moved on from a question of evidence to a question of management'

In Australia, ravaged by a six-year drought, the Federal government has declared the viability of the Murray-Darling basin to be at risk. The basin accounts for more than 70% of the country's irrigated croplands and pastures.

In January 2007 the prime minister, John Howard, announced a $A10.5 billion (£4 billion) programme to restore the nation's dwindling rivers. Howard, a climate change sceptic, acknowledged that the southerly weather systems which bring rains to Australia were failing. Australia's climate was getting hotter.[14]

Although the world has begun to adapt to climate change, with some exceptions, adaptation remains a low priority for policy makers: will this alter in the years ahead?

1 IPCC, 'Climate Change 2007: The Physical Science Basis. Contribution of Working Group 1 to the Fourth Assessment Report of the Intergovernmental Panel on Climate Change. Summary for Policymakers', 2007, pp. 5–6.

2 IPCC, 'A Report of Working Group 1 of the Intergovernmental Panel on Climate Change: Summary for Policymakers', 2007, p. 10.

3 'Joint science academies' statement: Global response to climate change', **http://nationalacademies.org.**

4 IPCC, 'Climate Change 2007: The Physical Science Basis. Contribution of Working Group 1 to the Fourth Assessment Report of the Intergovernmental Panel on Climate Change. Summary for Policymakers', 2007, p. 13.

5 See especially Rachel Warren, 'Impacts of Global Climate Change at Different Annual Mean Global Temperature Increases' in Hans Joachim Schellnbhuber et al (eds.), *Avoiding Dangerous Climate Change,* Cambridge: CUP, 2006, pp. 93–131.

6 IPCC, 'Climate Change 2007: The Physical Science Basis. Contribution of Working Group 1 to the Fourth Assessment Report of the Intergovernmental Panel on Climate Change. Summary for Policymakers', 2007, pp. 13, 18.

7 Figures are taken from Nicholas Stern, *The Economics of Climate Change. The Stern Review*, Cambridge: CUP, 2006, pp. 3–15.

8 Nicholas Stern, *The Economics of Climate Change. The Stern Review*, Cambridge: CUP, 2006, p. 339.

9 Nicholas Stern, *The Economics of Climate Change. The Stern Review*, Cambridge: CUP, 2006, pp. 330, 338.

10 *The New York Times*, 8 February 2006.

11 *The Times*, 28 October 2006.

12 *The Times*, 27 January 2007.

13 *UK agriculture and climate change*, London: National Farmers' Union, 2005, p. 2.

14 *The Times*, 27 January 2007.

HOW WILL THE WORLD MANAGE CLIMATE CHANGE? WHAT WILL SHAPE THE NEXT 20 YEARS?

- Only tough and costly action will avert dangerous climate change
- Technology will cut the costs of mitigating climate change
- Will the world be willing to bear these costs?
- The balance of vested interests will be a key influence on climate policy
- The world could adopt three approaches to mitigating climate change

Only tough and costly action will avert dangerous climate change. The Stern Report, which has become a bible on climate change policy within UK government circles, called for atmospheric concentrations of greenhouse gases to be stabilised at between 450 and 550ppm CO_{2e}.

To achieve this, annual greenhouse gas emissions would have to peak and then start to fall within the next 20 years. Otherwise, the reduction required later would be unrealistically high.

At present, annual global emissions are over 40 gigatonnes of carbon dioxide equivalent ($GtCO_{2e}$). Having climbed higher, they would have to fall to between 25% and 75% of current levels by 2050, to stabilise concentrations at the Stern level.

Since the earth can absorb only 5 $GtCO_{2e}$ a year, today's 40 $GtCO_{2e}$ would eventually have to be cut by 87.5% (to 5 $GtCO_{2e}$).

Agriculture alone accounts for more than 5 $GtCO_{2e}$, and it seems relatively hard to reduce emissions in that sector. So well after 2050, stabilisation is likely to require the complete decarbonisation of all other activities. In addition, some carbon will have to be taken out of the atmosphere, by increasing the land under forests for example.[1]

Major changes in energy and land use will be essential over the next 50 years. These changes will have to start soon if the goal of 450 to 550ppm CO_{2e} is to be achieved. There will be a need for:

- *greater energy efficiency.* More than half the energy the world generates is wasted – 65% of coal burnt in a power plant is lost to heat, for example. Could the world become twice as energy efficient by the middle of the century?[2]
- *cleaner ways of using carbon.* To keep greenhouse gases below 550ppm CO_{2e}, Shell works with models assuming that nine in ten of rich countries' coal

and gas-fired power stations will capture and store carbon dioxide by 2050; half the power stations in non-OECD nations will do so.[3]

■ *alternatives to carbon.* Though carbon fuels – oil, coal and gas – are likely to remain dominant sources of energy by the mid century (see chapter 13), wind power, solar energy and other renewables will be increasingly important.

To secure these changes, the price of carbon will have to rise — either by taxing greenhouse gas emissions or through global 'cap and trade': emissions would be capped at a certain level and users wanting to exceed their cap would buy extra quotas from those who kept below. Either way, large emitters of carbon dioxide would pay extra, encouraging them to emit less.

Alongside a higher global price of carbon, richer nations will need to meet poorer countries' concern about fairness. The latter argue that having industrialised first, the West is responsible for the bulk of global warming and should pay most to slow it down. Developing countries can least afford the cost of cutting emissions.[4]

Unless these fairness arguments are addressed, China, India and others will be unlikely to join a global agreement on climate change. Richer nations will have to respond with financial and technological support.

The Stern Report estimated that to stabilise greenhouse gases in the atmosphere at around 450–550ppm CO_{2e} would cost the equivalent of 1% of global GDP in 2050, give or take 3%. Reflecting the huge uncertainties involved, at the extremes the global economy could be either boosted by 2% or might fall by 4%.[5]

Technology will cut the costs of mitigating climate change. Rapid innovation would wind down the costs of energy efficiency, alternatives to carbon and cleaning carbon fuels.

Yet despite the increased prominence of energy security and climate change, public and private spending on energy R & D has fallen since the 1980s.[6] The sector's relatively low R & D is due to:

■ *market failure,* a root problem. The environmental costs of driving a car are not paid by the motorist, but are shuffled on to future generations who will have to meet the expense of adapting to climate change. So today's market for climate change products is much reduced.

■ *the long-term nature of many investments.* It can take many years to develop a cleaner aircraft engine or to pay off the initial cost of a power plant. This pushes up the risk of developing something new ('Will the market have changed by the time we're done?').

    In addition, who would invest in a coal-fired power station with a life of 20 years or more and then write off that investment by switching to wind farms?

■ *a shortage of early adopters.* In the IT market, for example, there are a significant number of people ready to pay a high price for a new product. Companies can recoup the costs of innovation by charging the higher price.

    But power generation is different. Few consumers have proved willing to pay extra for carbon-free electricity. Innovating companies have to sell at the standard price, greatly lengthening the time before they recover their costs.

■ *infrastructure.* National grids are usually based on centralised power plants. They are not geared to distributing energy from a multiplicity of small sources, such as ground source heat or solar panels. Large-scale renewables may be at a disadvantage if they are sited a long way from the grid.

    Storing carbon dioxide from fossil fuel power stations may be expensive if CO_2 has to be pumped down specially installed pipelines to destinations far away. Innovation becomes less attractive.

■ *market distortions.* World energy subsidies were an estimated $250 billion in 2005, of which subsidies for oil products were $90 billion.[7] Usually a limited number of firms, sometimes only one, dominate electricity markets. This reduces competition and the pressure to innovate.

    Governments will need to raise the price of carbon to make innovation more profitable. Even more than today, they will also need to support the deployment of new products — for example through:

■ tax incentives;
■ capital grants for demonstration projects;
■ guaranteed prices;
■ quotas, such as requiring power stations to buy a fixed proportion of their energy from renewable sources;
■ subsidies;
■ public sector procurement policies;
■ planning and building regulations;
■ cutting government support for high-emission technologies.

These measures have been tried in different countries and proved effective. Not many realise for example, that with strong government support, China had become the world's largest producer of renewable energy by 2005.[8]

However, a big drive to speed up energy innovation would involve substantial extra costs – higher energy prices to consumers and the spending of public money.

Will the world be willing to bear these costs? The answer will depend on a number of factors.

The scientific evidence will be crucial. As we have noted, the evidence continues to mount that humans are contributing to climate change, which is reaching – some would say it has already reached – dangerous levels.

Scientific evidence led to the 1987 Montreal Protocol to end the production of CFCs and other ozone-depleting substances. Might science encourage the world to act with similar urgency on climate change?

'No regrets' policies will play a key role. This is a term for measures to address global warming that would also be desirable on grounds other than climate change.

Energy security is the obvious example. China, Europe, the United States and other big importers of oil and gas could rely more heavily on domestic sources of power if they could produce 'clean' coal (which could be burnt without emitting much carbon dioxide) or develop non-renewable fuels like solar power. They would become less dependent on the Middle East and other volatile parts of the world.

Other 'no regrets' include cutting business costs through greater energy efficiency and adopting non-carbon sources of motor fuel to reduce pollution. Atmospheric pollution is a massive problem in Beijing and elsewhere, as more affluent urban populations switch from bicycles to cars. 400,000 Chinese die each year from respiratory diseases caused by pollution.[9]

Might the economic debate muddy the waters? Stern argues that action must be taken now to mitigate climate change to avoid the much higher human and economic costs if we wait.

But other economists claim that a richer world tomorrow will be more able to afford the costs of tackling climate change than we are today. More technologically advanced societies will be better placed to address the challenges.

They argue for a 'climate policy ramp', in which policies to slow global warming gradually ramp up over time. Future societies would use their greater wealth to invest in more effective and cheaper technologies.[10]

For example, University of Calgary researchers are trying to capture carbon dioxide from the atmosphere and store it underground. If the technology works at a reasonable cost, industrial-sized facilities could be built on desert oil fields to scrub CO_2 from the air and pump it into the seams from which oil was extracted.[11]

This is one of thousands of ideas scientists are working on to tackle climate change. Wouldn't it be better to wait for the inevitable breakthroughs, some economists ask, when the world will have more money to invest in them?

This argument could confuse the scientific message that the world is warming fast and that higher temperatures could trigger carbon cycle feedback mechanisms. If action is delayed, we could have 'runaway' climate change, in which feedbacks from previous climate change propel even more change.

Consumer resistance may remain the stumbling block. Stern makes the reasonable point that if mitigating climate change entails a possible 1% loss of global GDP by 2050, this would be small beer compared to the rich countries' expected 200% growth in output between now and then.[12]

But the challenge is not that simple.

- *The pay-off from 'no regrets' measures takes time.* For example, using less energy in your home requires up-front spending on insulation and the like, but these costs won't be recovered through lower energy bills for several years.

  Cutting imports of oil and gas to improve energy security would require high levels of investment in alternative and more expensive supplies, yet would take some time before having a marked impact.

  Consumers suffer the initial costs but don't get the full benefits till later.

- *Acting now would take 30 to 50 years to slow climate change.* Even if you sliced back carbon emissions today, it would be between three and five decades before global temperatures were significantly lower. Meanwhile, in the Northern Hemisphere the summers would get hotter, the winters wetter and floods would increase.

  This is a hard sell for politicians – 'Don't worry about the pain folks, you'll see the climate benefits in 30 to 50 years. Meanwhile, things will get worse!'

- *Rich consumers would be making sacrifices for the poor,* especially in the short term. Though the whole world will suffer from climate change, poor countries will suffer most in the next few years.

  Temperature rises beyond 2°C, increasingly on the cards, are likely to reduce crop yields in most tropical and sub-tropical regions, whereas crop yields in parts of the Northern Hemisphere may actually increase for a while.[13] The global South will be least able to afford the cost of adapting to climate change.

Yet 'psychic numbing' neutralises compassion for people who are remote from us. Some psychologists believe that we have evolved to care for ourselves and people who are close by. There was no adaptive or survival value in protecting people on the far side of the planet.

Modern communications make us more aware of crises thousands of miles away, but we still react as we would have long ago. This psychic numbing will make it hard for consumers in rich countries to back climate change measures for the sake of humanity as a whole.[14]

■ *Rich-world consumers remain reluctant to change lifestyles* to mitigate climate change – look at the anxiety when fuel prices jump! Very often identity is bound up with consumption, so that shifting consumer behaviour is far from easy: identities are at stake.

Change may be even more difficult in the developing world, where cars and 'white' goods are still relatively scarce. Given the scarcity value of these goods, material possessions tend to be a much higher priority than climate change.

Difficult trade-offs lie ahead. Pushing the world to mitigate climate change will be the scientific evidence and the 'side' benefits of measures with 'no regrets'. In the opposite direction will be the argument for a 'climate policy ramp' and consumer resistance.

The balance of vested interests will be a key influence on climate policy. In the United States, interests could line up as follows.

Supporters of measures to mitigate climate change:	*Opponents of mitigation measures*
• Environmentalists, including some on the religious right.	• Consumers who experience higher energy prices.
• States like California and New York and a number of cities that are ahead of the game in tackling climate change.	• Businesses which fear that global agreements on climate change could put them at a competitive disadvantage – for example, if American carbon caps were tougher than for China and India.
• Business with a stake in environmental products – from energy efficiency to renewable sources.	• The Federal Reserve, which may worry that climate policies will push up prices.

- Energy producers and high users of energy, who will welcome clarity about the long-term price of energy.

- Farmers who see the opportunities from growing biofuels, or who benefit from the rising price of corn and other products as land is switched from food to energy crops.

- Oil, motor and other companies, traditionally opposed to (or lukewarm about) mitigating climate change. Recognising the shift in political weather, they will lobby Washington for climate-change legislation so that they can then help to shape it,[15] and they will grab the handouts that will become available for carbon-cutting technologies.

- The State Department and those with an interest in national and homeland security, who will see the strategic benefits of reducing American dependence on imported oil.

- The Treasury, which would receive additional revenue from either a carbon tax or the auctioning of carbon-emission quotas within a cap-and-trade scheme. (Government would keep the income from auctioned quotas. Firms would recoup their costs by raising prices and/or selling their unused allocations.)

- Commercial bodies which fear that higher inflation will lead to slower economic growth, outweighing the immediate business benefits of mitigating climate change.

In China, there will be similar differences of interest.

Supporters of measures to mitigate climate change	Opponents of mitigation measures
- Those concerned about the effects of climate change on Chinese society, such as pollution in the cities and water	- Consumers who experience higher energy prices.

shortages, which are already acute in some areas.

- Businesses that see an opportunity to use China's cheap labour to produce climate-change products for a potentially vast world market.

- Companies that see an advantage in leap-frogging their Western competitors by adopting new, emission-cutting technologies.

- Farmers who see gains in switching to biofuels, or who benefit from the higher price of traditional crops as others do so.

- The Chinese government, which would get extra revenue from a carbon tax or auctioning emission quotas.

- Regional governors who are rewarded on their ability to secure economic growth and may fear that climate change policies will slow growth in their regions.

- The Communist Party which may fear that higher energy prices will fuel inflation and slow growth, making it harder to cut unemployment.

- Supporters and opponents will line up in similar ways in other countries. In each case, the balance between the two will affect how that particular country approaches climate-change negotiations.

The world could adopt three broad approaches to mitigating climate change.
A carbon tax. This could, in theory, be the cornerstone of a global agreement. Along with other mechanisms, countries would impose a common tax on carbon emissions, which would encourage consumers to reduce their usage. Governments could use the revenue to cut other taxes.[16]

But some countries would see this as outside interference with their tax policy – if it is alright to negotiate a worldwide carbon tax, why not introduce a 'development' tax on financial flows to alleviate global poverty? Why not harmonise tax policies to eliminate unfair competition? European countries have failed to agree a carbon tax. So why should it work globally?

Cap and trade. This would build on the Kyoto Protocol, which was signed in 1997 and is due to be renegotiated between 2009 and 2012. Kyoto contains provisions for carbon trading, but a truly global cap-and-trade scheme would go much further.

All countries would agree targets to cut their greenhouse-gas emissions. National targets would be translated into quotas that would be auctioned to individual organisations – initially, the main emitters of greenhouse-gases – and which could be traded in a global market. Governments would get an income from auctioning quotas, which they could use to cut taxes elsewhere.

Additional measures, paid for by the rich economies, would support developing countries in adopting clean technologies, extending forests (which absorb CO_2 as they grow), and taking other steps to mitigate and adapt to climate change.

Some proponents of cap and trade envisage that targets would initially be tougher for the rich countries, which emit most greenhouse gases. But they would gradually converge, till eventually – in the ideal – there was a single per person target across the world.

Setting the targets would be highly contentious, since countries' circumstances differ and each would argue for a higher limit. A high target could be tantamount to giving the country money. If the country undershot, it could sell the surplus to nations that wanted more.

Governments may also be suspicious that organisations will cheat. Corruption is widespread in many countries. Might an illegal market in fraudulent quotas emerge?

To reconcile conflicting interests, governments could well agree targets that were too generous to tackle climate change with the urgency required. Or negotiations may fail.

A patchwork of separate agreements. Some commentators think that this is most likely. In the absence of a convincing global agreement, a series of ad hoc deals would be reached. They might include, for example:

- an agreement between leading countries from the global North and South to encourage the development of clean technologies;
- the introduction of a trading scheme for air-transport emissions;
- a global agreement for emission standards in motor vehicles;
- an agreement for the aluminium sector;
- agreements that link the emission-trading schemes springing up round the world.

To progress all these deals, however, would require a high degree of political energy. But if this energy was forthcoming and a bottom-up approach gained ground, might politicians use the Kyoto framework to coordinate the various initiatives?

Maybe in 2012 a weak Kyoto II will be agreed, with generous emission targets for the United States and the large developing countries to get them involved. A further round of separate agreements might follow – such as tighter emission standards for motor vehicles – to provide some of the bite missing from Kyoto II. Might this lead to a more punchy Kyoto III?

Questions for a Kyoto II agreement

Time frame? Short (focusing on robust institutions and frameworks), medium (charting an outline course for several rounds of negotiation, each bringing stronger commitments) or long-term targets?

Top down or bottom up? Globally negotiated national targets, or country pledges of domestic measures, whose effectiveness would be subject to international scrutiny?

Type of commitments? Binding emission targets (countries can't overshoot)? Or non-binding targets (overshooting countries can buy allowances from countries that undershoot)? Or alternatives to targets (such as agreed industry standards for energy efficiency)?

Stringency of commitments? Initially weak commitments to encourage broad participation? Or tougher commitments, perhaps phased in?

Burden sharing? Tougher targets for developed than developing countries? Or eventual convergence of targets, with rich countries helping poor ones bear the costs? On what should targets be based – per capita GDP, per capita emissions or total emissions?

Meeting costs of adapting to climate change? Via a new UN Framework Convention on Climate Change Disaster Relief Fund, financed by industrialised countries on the basis of their historic contribution to global warming? Or through an insurance pool, perhaps financed by an emissions trading levy?

Implementation and compliance? What measures would prevent cheating?

1 All these figures are based on Nicholas Stern, *The Economics of Climate Change. The Stern Review*, Cambridge: CUP, 2006, p. 340.
2 Jeroen van der Veer, 'High hopes and hard truths dictate future', *The Times*, 25 June 2007.
3 Jeroen van der Veer, 'High hopes and hard truths dictate future', *The Times*, 25 June 2007.
4 For an introduction to the international politics of climate change, see Joyeeta Gupta, *Our Simmering Planet. What to do about global warming?* London: Zed Books, 2001, pp. 85–114.
5 Nicholas Stern, *The Economics of Climate Change. The Stern Review*, Cambridge: CUP, 2006, pp. 267–281.
6 'Do we have the right R & D priorities and programmes to support energy technologies of the future?' 13 June 2006, 18th Round Table on Sustainable Development: background paper, Paris: OECD, p. 7, **http://www.oecd.org.**
7 Nicholas Stern, *The Economics of Climate Change. The Stern Review*, Cambridge: CUP, 2006, p. 403.
8 'Renewables Global Status Report: 2006 update', Washington DC: Worldwatch, **http://www.ren21.net.**
9 Will Hutton & Meghnad Desai, 'Does the future really belong to China?' *Prospect*, January 2007, p. 27.

10 William Nordhaus, 'The Stern Review on the Economics of Climate Change', 17 November 2006, pp. 2–3, **http://www.econ.yale.edu.** Nordhaus claims that this is the consensus view among climate-change economists.

11 **http://the25milliondollaridea.blogspot.com.**

12 Nicholas Stern, *The Economics of Climate Change. The Stern Review*, Cambridge: CUP, 2006, p. 26.

13 The Working Group on Climate Change and Development, *Up in smoke?* London: New Economics Forum, 2004, p. 2. Some Russian scientists and economists have argued that Russia will benefit from moderate climate change. A. Barrie Pittock, *Climate Change. Turning up the Heat*, London: Earthscan, 2005, p. 273.

14 Paul Slovic, '"If I Look at the Mass, I Will Never Act." Psychic Numbing and Genocide', paper presented at the *Annual meeting of the American Association for the Advancement of Science*, San Francisco, 16 February 2007.

15 The United States Climate Action Partnership, a lobby group backed by companies such as General Electric, is already doing this.

16 This has been proposed for example by Joseph Stiglitz, *Making Globalization Work*, London: Allen Lane, 2006, pp. 180–182.

HOW WILL THE WORLD MANAGE CLIMATE CHANGE? WHAT MIGHT BE THE IMPLICATIONS?

- Mitigation measures will begin to transform the world economy
- Yet they will be unlikely to stop the world warming dangerously
- Adapting to climate change will shoot up the policy mast
- What might surprise us?

Mitigation measures will begin to transform the world economy over the next 20 years, however cautiously they are introduced.

As is starting to happen, a global carbon market will emerge. It will include specialists who buy and sell quotas and new investment products based on quota prices. Green taxes will spread. Companies specialising in 'climate change' products will eventually comprise a large sector of the economy.

As discussed in chapter 13, energy companies will make money from helping consumers to *reduce* their consumption. Homes and offices will have devices that record hourly energy consumption, sensors that switch off appliances and lights when not in use and solar panels, ground-source pumps and other means to produce renewable energy.

Buildings will not only become 'zero-carbon', they will sell surplus energy from their own renewable sources back to the grid.

> 'Buildings will sell surplus energy back to the grid'

Cities and some countries will introduce road charging to cut both global warming and congestion. Cars will face ever stricter emission limits and will increasingly run on alternative fuels.

When he was the UK's Secretary of State for the Environment, David Miliband was interested in the idea of giving each individual a personal carbon allowance. People with a carbon footprint less than their allowance could earn money by selling their allowance to those who need more.

Tesco is to introduce a labelling system showing how much carbon has been released to make its products. A new credit card called Ice is about to be launched that will automatically count up your carbon emissions as you make your purchases.

Why shouldn't emissions be totted up on the four main transactions that account for most of each person's carbon – electricity, gas, petrol and aviation?[1]

Yet these and other measures will be unlikely to stop the world warming dangerously. We already have climate change. The challenge is to avert dangerous climate change. A growing number of experts fear it may already be too late.

For reasons discussed, consumers may well resist tough action. In the UK, the effects of fuel protests in 2000 were felt for seven years. They halted the government's policy of raising transport fuel duties by more than inflation, so as to bear down on consumption.

In autumn 2006, Britain's right-wing *Daily Mail* predicted that families would be hit with more than £1000 worth of green taxes. It complained that 'since Britain is responsible for just 2% of carbon emission … can the public be blamed for suspecting this is all becoming a convenient excuse for higher taxes?'[2]

Even if consumer resistance is overcome, Stern seems to have conceded that early global action would be unlikely to keep temperature rises below 2°C compared to the pre-industrial period.

Momentum within the climate system may take us over the 2°C threshold, whatever we do in the years ahead. In 2006 Sir David King, the UK's chief scientist, said that a rise of at least 3°C was now almost inevitable.[3]

According to estimates at the UK's Tyndall Centre for Climate Change, a rise of 2 to 3°C could see the Amazon rainforest turn into savannah, with a huge loss of biodiversity. Vast amounts of carbon dioxide would be released into the air, which would speed up climate change.

Worldwide, an extra 0.9 to 3.5 billion people could suffer from increased water stress, millions could be displaced from the world's coastlands because of rising sea levels and cyclones, and a drop in global cereal production could make millions more people hungry – a form of 'climatic genocide'.[4]

Can we avoid a cataclysm?

Adapting to climate change will shoot up the policy mast. Though the need to adapt is widely recognised, it is generally a low priority. This will shift as climate change bites. Some land in Mediterranean countries could turn into deserts, and winter flooding will increase further north.

But the global South will bear the brunt of climate change. In 2005 several aid agencies identified the following changes *currently* happening in Africa, at least partly because of global warming. These changes will accelerate:[5]

- more flash floods;
- longer and more frequent droughts;
- decreasing and less predictable rainfall, and less distinct seasons;

- less drinking water;
- declining crop yields;
- desertification, a big problem in the Sahel (a marginal area to the south of the Sahara, from Senegal to Somalia);
- increased migration to the cities, aggravated by all the above;
- loss of traditional medicines due to the decline in biodiversity.

Climate change appears to be a factor behind the Darfur conflict. Rainfall in northern Darfur has declined by almost 40% over the past century, increasing water competition between previously co-existing peoples.[6] Does Darfur provide a glimpse of the future?

What might surprise us? Today, 'business as usual' is producing high levels of greenhouse-gas emissions. This is about to change – gradually – as mitigating climate change becomes urgent. Soon, adapting to climate change will be a priority, alongside mitigation.

Might technology save us from the worst effects of climate change, confounding the gloomy projections widespread today? A number of geoscientists are proposing systems that would strip surplus carbon dioxide out of the air.

In addition to 'mechanical' approaches like artificial trees, there may be more natural solutions. Craig Venter for example, who led the private sector human genome sequencing team, has suggested using genome analysis to identify plankton that best absorb carbon dioxide. Vast colonies of microbes would then be created to scrub the atmosphere of greenhouse gases.

Many of these ideas seem off the wall now. But remember how far technology has advanced in the past 50 years — what did computers look like in the late 1950s? Might not climate-change technologies make equivalent leaps?

This possibility is not an excuse for government inaction. Rather, it should spur governments to hasten innovation by giving bigger incentives. Plenty of solutions to climate change exist. Are we prepared to pay for them?

---

1 David Miliband, 'Get ready to be a carbon trader', *The Sunday Times*, 11 March 2007.
2 *Daily Mail*, 30 October 2006.
3 *The Times*, 15 April 2006.
4 Rachel Warren, 'Impacts of Global Climate Change at Different Annual Mean Global Temperature Increases' in Hans Joachim Schellnhuber et al. (eds.), *Avoiding Dangerous Climate Change*, Cambridge: CUP, 2006, pp. 93–131.
5 Rachel Roach, *Dried Up, Drowned Out. Voices from the Developing World on a Changing Cimate*, London: Tearfund, 2005, pp. 7–18.
6 Ben Vogel, 'Climate change creates security challenge "more complex than cold war"', 30 January 2007, **http://www.janes.com.**

CHAPTER 13
WILL WE HAVE ENOUGH ENERGY?
THE STORY SO FAR

- Will the world economy hit resource buffers?
- Oil security has shot up the agenda
- The world became less energy efficient between 2000 and 2005
- Carbon trading is bringing radical change to the energy market

Will the world economy hit resource buffers? Some fear that as the global economy motors ahead, there won't be enough aluminium, iron ore and other raw materials to support the growth. Concerns focus particularly on energy.

The consumption of primary energy – the basic forms of fuel, such as coal and oil – has risen sharply, from 8.3 billion tonnes of oil equivalent in 1995 to nearly 10.9 billion in 2006. Prices have leapt too (see charts below).

Global consumption of primary energy by type of fuel (million tonnes oil equivalent), 2006

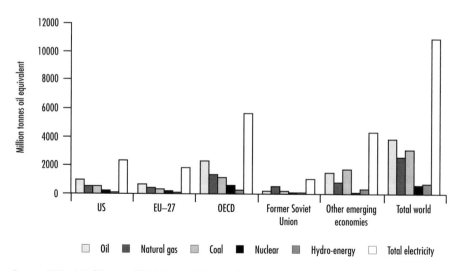

Source: *BP Statistical Review of World Energy 2007*, London: BP, June 2007, p. 41.

Spot price of Brent crude oil, 1976–2006

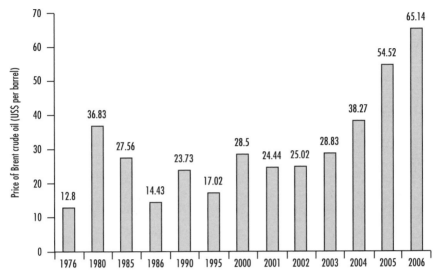

Source: *BP Statistical Review of World Energy 2007*, London: BP, June 2007, p.16.

Prices of crude oil hit a low in 1986, bobbed up and down for the next 16 years and then began to rise in 2003, averaging $65 a barrel in 2006 and touching often higher levels in the first half of 2007. (A barrel is roughly equivalent to 35 gallons.) Driving up prices were large increases in consumption, especially in China, without an equivalent jump in supply.

Tightening oil-refining capacity made the situation worse. Despite the steep growth of global demand, from 2001 to 2005 capacity expanded at less than half the rate in the previous five years.[1] Prices at the pump soared. Though crude prices eased a bit in the first half of 2007, concerns about long-term supplies remain.

Oil, coal and natural gas overwhelmingly dominate primary energy consumption. The first chart above shows how much the world has to do to cut its dependence on these fuels, which are a major source of carbon-dioxide emissions and global warming. Apart from hydroelectricity, renewable sources of energy are so small that they don't even register on the chart.

Oil security has shot up the agenda. Until around 1970, the United States could use its major oil fields in Texas and elsewhere to provide for almost all its needs. Despite new fields, domestic production fell over the next 30 years and demand rose.

America had become a massive importer of oil by the end of the century (importing about half its needs), with China expected to import the same proportion by 2010 (having been self-sufficient up to 1993).

This 'resource shift' has had a powerful effect on defence thinking. The world's top five countries with oil reserves are all in the Middle East – Saudi Arabia, Iraq, Iran, Kuwait and the United Arab Emirates.

They have two-thirds of the planet's proven reserves. Moreover, their oil tends to be of high quality and is easy to extract.[2] Russia, Iran and Qatar contain over 55% of the world's known gas reserves.[3]

Importers are rushing to secure these supplies. China has made some long-term agreements with Iran, which include the sale of arms. The Middle East is now China's fourth-largest trading partner. Chinese nuclear weapons designs were found in Libya.[4] The Pentagon is eager to 'secure' the Persian Gulf.

The world became less energy efficient between 2000 and 2005, reversing a long period of improving efficiency. Instead of needing a smaller amount of energy for each unit of economic growth, the world required more energy.

The ratio of energy growth to GDP growth fell (unevenly) from 1.16 in 1966–70 to 0.29 in 1996–2000, and then rose to 0.76 for the 2000–05 period.[5]

The need for more energy per unit of growth was due largely to the rapid industrialisation of China and India and to the fall in real terms in energy prices after the 1970s, which reduced the incentive to use energy-saving technologies.

In 2006, however, oil consumption in the more developed countries, the OECD, fell by 0.6% – the first annual drop in 20 years – even though overall these economies grew.[6] Might higher oil prices be bringing a new period of rising energy efficiency?

Carbon trading is radically changing the energy market. In Europe, under the Kyoto Protocol heavy corporate consumers of energy receive allocations allowing them to emit specific amounts of carbon dioxide. Companies giving out more than permitted have to buy extra allocations from firms that emit less.

Other parts of the world are following suit, including California and the North Eastern states of the US. Within the energy sector, two types of commodity market are emerging alongside each other – one in energy and one in emission permits. Firms will be able to make money from both. It will pay companies to sell energy to consumers on the one hand, and to encourage consumers to save energy — so that suppliers have more permits to sell – on the other.

1 *BP Statistical Review of World Energy*, London: BP, 2006, p. 18.
2 Chris Abbott, Paul Rogers & John Sloboda, *Beyond Terror*, London: Rider, 2006, pp. 28–33.
3 *Shell Global Scenarios to 2025*, London: Shell, 2005, p. 194.
4 Stephen Pollard, 'How China's secret deals are fuelling war', *The Times*, 8 August 2006. Stephen Pollard is Senior Fellow at the Centre for the New Europe, Brussels.
5 Shell International.
6 International Energy Agency sources, cited by *Wall Street Journal* (European edition), 19–21 January 2007.

WILL WE HAVE ENOUGH ENERGY?
WHAT WILL SHAPE THE NEXT 20 YEARS?

- Energy demand will grow by 50% between 2006 and 2030
- Oil reserves are likely to be adequate for some time
- A carbon future for many years looks more probable than one based on renewable supplies
- Getting fossil fuels out of the ground could be a bigger problem than having enough reserves
- Will the West's search for energy security be a key driver of change?

Energy demand will grow by 50% between 2006 and 2030, according to the International Energy Agency (IEA).[1] This assumes existing policies continue and represents a conventional view.

This growth would reflect the interaction between:

- *A larger world population,* which on the UN's 'medium' projection will increase from an estimated 6.7 billion in 2007 to 9.12 billion in 2050 (see chart overleaf).[2]
- *Global economic growth,* which will push up the demand for electricity and transport, the two largest components of energy consumption. The speed of growth is startling. In 2006, China enlarged its electricity capacity by roughly the size of the UK's entire stock of power stations.
- *Growing energy efficiency,* which will dampen the expansion of energy demand. Greater efficiency will reflect the recent rise in energy prices, future steps to mitigate climate change, advances in technology and the huge potential to improve efficiency.

  More than half the energy generated by the world is wasted. In an average car, for example, only about 20% of the petrol actually moves the car forward: the rest is lost as heat.[3]
- *Consumer reluctance to pay more for energy,* which will restrain politicians from raising energy prices to encourage more efficient use.

In Britain, for example, 'transport' was the largest item of average family spending in 2005–06, costing £62 a week out of a total weekly spend of £434.[4]

Many families spend more on their cars than their mortgages. No wonder politicians fear the impact of higher energy prices on public opinion!

Estimated and projected world population (millions), 2007–2050

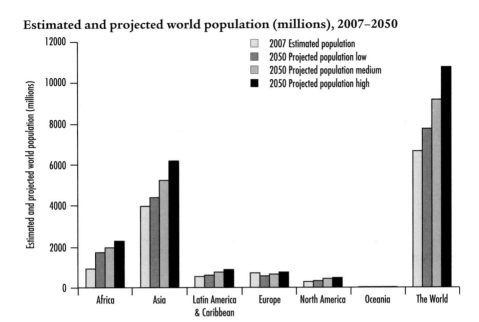

	2007	2050		
	Estimated population	Projected population		
		Low	Medium	High
Africa	965	1,718	1,998	2,302
Asia	4,030	4,444	5,266	6,189
Latin America & the Caribbean	572	641	769	914
Europe	731	566	664	777
North America	339	382	445	517
Oceania	34	42	49	56
The World	6,671	7,792	9,191	10,756

Source: *World Population Prospects: The 2006 Revision*, New York: United Nations, 2007, table I.1.

Might demand grow more slowly – and surprise us? Though there are few signs of this now, in time technology may save more energy than many expect. Environmentalist Amory Lovins believes that new technologies and more efficient use of existing technologies offer enormous energy reductions.

For example, in 2005 window coatings that transmit light but reflect heat (reducing the need for air-conditioning) were a quarter of the price they had been five years earlier.

One of Lovins' teams showed that for cars, trucks and planes, combining lightweight materials with better aerodynamics could cut oil use by two-thirds without compromising safety, comfort, performance or affordability.[5]

Imagine that to mitigate climate change and improve energy security, Western governments did more to support the development of energy-saving technologies.

Imagine, too, that they paid countries like China to adopt them – Gordon Brown and others have called for a £20 billion World Bank loan and grant facility to help developing countries invest in alternative-energy supplies and in greater efficiency. Might energy demand grow more slowly than many expect?

Will new patterns of consumption emerge, requiring less energy? For instance, might the emergence of the virtual economy, discussed in chapters 1 and 7, eventually channel a significant amount of consumption online, slowing the increase in energy use?

In the West, happiness – or well-being – is rising up the agenda. For the middle classes, research repeatedly shows that having more money does not necessarily bring contentment, whereas satisfying relationships do. Might this produce less material forms of consumption?

Might toy shops, for example, focus less on selling toys and more on teaching parents how to play with their children? Might beauty shops find a new line of business – helping customers feel beautiful on the inside as well as looking good on the outside? The increase in energy demand would slow.

Oil reserves are likely to be adequate for some time. Pessimists fear that oil supplies will peak before 2025 and then wind down. This is because 80% of today's oil comes from fields discovered before 1973, and these fields cannot last for ever.[6]

The average annual increase in proven oil reserves slowed from 4.5% in the 1980s to around 1% by 2005; discoveries replaced only about 45% of production between 1999 and 2005.[7]

Some experts think that a new set of 'supergiant' oil fields would have to be discovered to meet global demand, but no supergiant has been found since 1986. New fields are smaller than older ones. Many analysts doubt that undiscovered supergiants exist.[8]

However, there are reasons to be more optimistic.

- *Gloomy predictions have regularly been wrong.* In the late 1970s for example, at least 12 studies, by BP and Shell among others, expected oil production to peak before 2000 or soon after. All were based on false assumptions.[9]
- *Technology will increase the amounts extracted from known reserves.* Proven reserves have been increasing faster than consumption since 1971, largely because technology has expanded the capacity of existing reserves. Revisions, additions and exploration increased oil reserves by 320 billion barrels between 1995 and 2003 – a third more than total production.[10]

   A conservative estimate suggests that the volume of known reserves could be revised upwards by 350 billion barrels between 2000 and 2020. This would be enough to extend the availability of oil from these reserves by 14 years at 2000 levels of production. Assuming oil use grew at 2% a year from 2000, production is unlikely to peak till after 2030.[11]

- *'Unconventional oil', such as bitumen, exists in large quantities,* especially in Canada and Venezuela. But it has problems: capital costs are higher than for conventional wells, production requires much more energy, a lot more carbon is emitted during production and local populations can be sensitive (native Indian land rights in Canada, for instance).

   Despite these difficulties, if conventional oil becomes scarce and prices rise, unconventional sources could fill the gap.[12] Production companies have been pouring into Alberta since oil prices started to climb in the early 2000s. Might unconventional oil push back a peak in all forms of oil production to the mid century perhaps, or later?

- *An 'undulating plateau' is more likely than a peak in oil production after 2030,* according to Cambridge Energy Research Associates (CERA), a leading US energy-research company. Based on 'bottom up' field-by-field analysis, CERA believes that the world has 4.8 trillion barrels of conventional and unconventional reserves.

   Of these, 1.08 trillion barrels have been produced. The remaining 3.72 trillion barrels should allow oil production to continue to expand till at least 2030, after which it will plateau for one or more decades, as the world adapts, before declining slowly.[13]

A carbon future for many years looks more probable than one based on renewable supplies – for several reasons.

Plenty of coal and gas exists in addition to oil. Large coal deposits exist in many parts of the world. In addition, known conventional gas reserves and new discoveries could keep the production of natural gas growing at an average of 3% a year till mid century.

Non-conventional gas, such as gas from fractured shales, will become increasingly important from the 2020s, perhaps becoming the largest component of gas supply by 2070.[14]

Assuming no change in government policy, the IEA expects fossil fuels to supply some 83% of the *increase* in world primary energy demand between 2004 and 2030.[15]

Carbon capture and storage seems a promising technology. The problem with coal and gas is that they emit climate-warming carbon dioxide when they are converted into energy, mainly in power stations.

But hopes are growing that capture and storage technologies will allow 80–90% of the carbon dioxide from coal and gas-fired power plants to be kept underground. (See also chapter 12.)

Separation, capture and storage involve established technologies used by the oil and chemical industries in a number of commercial settings, yet these technologies have never been brought together to clean up electricity generation. So uncertainties exist about their use in the power industry on a wide scale.

One question is whether large amounts of carbon dioxide can be stored permanently without leaking. If carbon capture were to be the main way of tackling emissions this century and if only 1% of the captured carbon seeped back into the atmosphere, one estimate suggests that by 2100 the annual leak would be double today's annual global carbon emissions.[16]

'Will the technology be affordable?' is another question that prevents carbon capture from being a done deal.

Yet despite the doubts, this technology looks a promising way to make carbon-based electricity 85–90% cleaner. It could become commercially viable in the middle of the next decade.

The EU seems confident about the technology. It included mandatory carbon-capture fittings for gas- and coal-fired power stations in its March 2007 agreement to tackle climate change.[17]

Gas could be a route into the 'hydrogen economy'. Natural gas is the cleanest of the carbon fuels, carbon capture could clean it almost completely and huge supplies exist. A leading expert, Peter Odell, believes that natural gas will be the fuel of the twenty-first century, overtaking oil some time over the next 50 years.[18]

Supplemented by coal, gas could usher in a 'hydrogen economy', bringing about a new energy regime that is sustainable and non-polluting. Even now, the foundations of this new economy are being laid in the hydrogen-powered fuel cells that are being sold to produce power, heat and light in factories, offices and homes. Hydrogen cars are on the distant horizon.[19]

The big advantage of hydrogen is that it never runs out and doesn't emit a single atom of carbon. The large-scale use of hydrogen-powered fuel cells would massively cut carbon-dioxide emissions throughout the economy.

The trouble is that producing the hydrogen would use lots of extra electricity. With current methods of generation, this would substantially increase carbon-dioxide emissions. However, using electricity from plants employing carbon-capture technology would allow hydrogen to be produced cleanly, which would slash greenhouse-gas emissions overall.

Renewable fuels will play a significant, though relatively small role over the next 20 years. Not everyone would agree. Some experts believe that it will be renewables, such as solar power, biomass (organic matter used as a fuel) and wind farms, that will provide the electricity to blaze a path to the 'hydrogen economy'.[20]

But the development of renewables will face big constraints.

- *Expansion will start from a low base.* Renewables, including hydroelectricity, contributed about 10% to global energy production in 2006. Excluding hydroelectricity, renewables contributed less than 0.5%.

  Ramping up production from small beginnings is notoriously difficult. Knowledge and technical skills take time to accumulate. Existing technologies have to reach the end of their lives before being replaced by new ones.

- *Uncertainty about oil prices is deterring investment.* Investors want to know whether the recent rise in oil prices will be sustained, and at what level. The higher the price of oil, the more economic it becomes to invest in alternative, more expensive supplies.

  Short-term movements in oil prices are not always a good guide to long-term trends. The 1982 peak in oil prices was followed by a long period of falling prices in real terms.[21] If oil prices drop, to what extent will governments keep domestic energy prices artificially high and/or subsidise renewable producers?

- *The cost-effectiveness of renewables may peak at relatively low levels.* Germany, for instance, has the most wind farms in the world, providing up to 20% of power in some areas.

  However, the German Energy Agency claims that the cost of linking many more wind farms to the national grid would be much higher than installing modern filters at existing fossil fuel power plants. Filters would cut carbon-dioxide emissions by almost the same amount.[22]

Building wind turbines at sea is proving more difficult than many had thought. By the end of 2006, development off the UK coast had barely begun because of problems with shipping lanes, bird life and radar interference.

Runaway costs were a particular problem. US and German tax breaks for investors in wind farms had caused a shortage of turbines, while the cost of steel required to embed giant turbines 20 metres in the sea had spiralled up. Offshore wind farms were beginning to look distinctly uncompetitive.[23]

■ *Carbon capture may reduce the incentive to invest in renewables.* If carbon-capture technologies prove cost effective, investors may ask, 'Why back uncertain renewable sources when carbon capture, allied to hydrogen, can largely crack the problem of greenhouse-gas emissions?'

The IEA expects that between 2002 and 2030, renewables (excluding hydroelectricity), will more than triple as a source of electricity generation. This would be impressive growth. But by the end of the period, renewable sources would still provide just 1.7% of total energy production.[24]

■ *Finally, the nuclear industry will struggle to increase its share of total energy supply.* In OECD Europe, for example, three-quarters of nuclear energy capacity in 2004 is expected to be retired by 2030.[25] Many new nuclear plants will simply replace old ones being phased out.

Will there be enough skilled workers to build additional plants over and above these replacement ones? Might uranium shortages occur, as some experts predict, if there was a large expansion of the world's nuclear industry?[26]

The IEA expects global nuclear capacity to increase slightly by 2030, with a larger increase if public concerns about waste are overcome.[27]

Getting fossil fuels out of the ground could be a bigger problem than having enough reserves. In 2005 Shell estimated that at current savings rates, 7% of global savings (or about 1.6% of world GDP) would be required to finance energy investments between 2005 and 2025. Russia would have to invest around 5.5% of its GDP to exploit its oil and gas reserves.

Energy investment involves large upfront costs, requires long lead times before profits start to flow and occurs in a highly competitive market, in which prices jump up and down. So it is high risk. Will enough investment be forthcoming?

Producing countries may struggle to raise the necessary funds because of:

- other budget priorities;
- the limited size of their domestic capital markets;
- restrictions on foreign direct investment in oil and gas;
- the low credit ratings of national governments;
- uncertainties about long-term returns.[28]

On the other hand, the industry is making large extra profits from today's higher prices, so funds could be available.[29]

Supply bottlenecks, such as the shortage of drilling rigs and trained oilfield workers, may be a bigger problem. This was highlighted by Total's head of exploration, Christophe de Margerie, in 2006. He claimed that political constraints on getting access to OPEC reserves and sheer logistics would make it impossible to achieve the production of oil predicted for 2030.

'Take Qatar. How many projects can you have at the same time? You have more than 100,000 people working on sites. It's a big city of contractors.'[30]

In particular, the electricity generating industry, which accounts for nearly 40% of freshwater withdrawals in the United States, may find it increasingly difficult to acquire the water it needs for cooling and other purposes.

In February 2005, Governor Mike Rounds of South Dakota called for a summit to discuss how drought-induced low flows on the Missouri river were impacting irrigation, drinking water and power plants.[31] China is now building a new power station every week. With water stress already widespread, where will it get the necessary water?

'Resource nationalism' is a growing problem. A 2006 US military report warned that the extension of state control over energy production in several Latin American countries was deterring the investment needed to sustain and expand long-term production.[32] Might the same apply to Russia?

'Power stations account for nearly 40% of freshwater withdrawals in the United States'

Exploration and development in some regions could be severely hit by uncertainties about the future tax regime, fears of nationalisation, and the risk of increased political interference and regulation.

Will the West's search for energy security be a key driver of change? The world depends heavily for oil on OPEC producers, dominated by the Middle East. On current policies, OPEC's market share is expected to rise from 40% in 2005 to 50% in 2030.[33]

Though for many years the US has paid lip-service to reducing its dependence on imported oil, energy security is becoming a higher priority in the wake of the second Iraq war, the so-called 'war on terror', Iran's possible development of nuclear weapons (which would threaten Israel) and growing competition for supplies with China.

Might the US turn the oil weapon against the Middle East? A big push to develop alternative supplies would reduce American dependence on the Middle East, diminishing the need to prop up regimes in Saudi Arabia and elsewhere. This would help the struggle against Islamist terror in the long run, since a top priority for al-Qaeda is to get the United States out of the region.

Reduced dependence on the Middle East would make it easier for the US to intervene if Israel's vital interests were at stake.

Though not on the agenda now, might securing alternative energy supplies be achieved if the governments of major consuming countries under-wrote the price of oil? They might agree to tax oil imports if the price fell below, say, $50 a barrel, and to raise that threshold gradually in real terms over the long term.

This would provide investors with the security needed to expand oil extraction from Canada's tar sands, develop clean electricity using carbon capture, and encourage investment in renewable sources of supply.[34]

Backing for such an approach might come from China, already concerned about its long-term energy needs and the effects of pollution from its fossil-based power plants. The EU, worried about its growing dependence on Russian gas, might also see the advantages. In time, might consuming nations agree that this was a sensible way to help address climate change?

---

1 Executive Summary, 'World Energy Outlook 2006', pp. 37–38, **http://www.iea.org.**
2 *World Population Prospects: The 2006 Revision*, New York: United Nations, 2007, table I.1.
3 Jeroen van der Veer, 'High hopes and hard truths dictate future', *The Times*, 25 June 2007.
4 'Family Spending 2006', ONS Press Release, 18 January 2007.
5 Amory B. Lovins, 'More profit with less carbon', *Scientific American*, 293(111), August 2005, pp. 74–82.
6 'When will the oil run out? And what happens then?', *Prospect*, December 2005, p. 23.
7 *Shell Global Scenarios to 2025*, London: Shell, 2005, p. 194.
8 Sonia Shah, *Crude: the story of oil*, New York: Seven Stories Press, 2004, pp. 115–133.

9 Peter R. Odell, *Why Carbon Fuels Will Dominate The 21st Century's Global Energy Economy*, Brentwood: Multi-Science Publishing, 2004, pp. 35–36.

10 *Why the 'Peak Oil' Theory Falls Down – Myths, Legends, and the Future of Oil Resources*, Cambridge, MSS: Cambridge Energy Research Associates, 2006, summarised in Press Release, 14 November 2006.

11 Peter R. Odell, *Why Carbon Fuels Will Dominate The 21st Century's Global Energy Economy*, Brentwood: Multi-Science Publishing, 2004, pp. xxi, 36–39, 125.

12 In September 2006, Murray Edwards, vice-chairman of Canadian Natural Resources, a leading oil sands investor, claimed that tar sands projects needed long-term oil prices above US$50 a barrel (*The Times*, 23 September 2006). In 2007, prices ranged between about $60 and $70+.

13 *Why the 'Peak Oil' Theory Falls Down – Myths, Legends, and the Future of Oil Resources*, Cambridge, MSS: Cambridge Energy Research Associates, 2006, summarised in Press Release, 14 November 2006.

14 Peter R. Odell, *Why Carbon Fuels Will Dominate The 21st Century's Global Energy Economy*, Brentwood: Multi-Science Publishing, 2004, pp. xxii-xxiii, 71–100.

15 Executive Summary, 'World Energy Outlook 2006', pp. 37-38, 93–94, **http://www.iea.org.**

16 A. Barrie Pittock, *Climate Change. Turning up the Heat*, London: Earthscan, 2005, p. 185.

17 David Miliband, 'Get ready to be a carbon trader', *The Sunday Times*, 11 March 2007.

18 Peter R. Odell, *Why Carbon Fuels Will Dominate The 21st Century's Global Energy Economy*, Brentwood: Multi-Science Publishing, 2004, pp. 71–100.

19 Jeremy Rifkin, *The Hydrogen Economy*, New York: Tarcher/Penguin, 2002, p. 9.

20 See for example Mayer Hillman, *How We Can Save the Planet*, London: Penguin, 2004, pp. 109-110.

21 Toby Shelley, *Oil: Poverty, Politics and the Planet*, London & New York: Zed Books, 2005, p. 30.

22 'Anti-wind farm report dismissed', 26 February 2005, **http://news.bbc.co.uk.** Reactions to the report in Britain focused on the fact that there are many fewer wind farms in the UK than Germany, making the report irrelevant to this country, it was claimed.

23 *The Energy Challenge. Energy review report 2006*, London: Dept. of Trade & Industry, 2006, p. 99; Angela Jameson, 'Why wind generates only bluster', *The Times*, 23 September 2006.

24 'World Energy Outlook 2006', p. 68, **http://www.iea.org.**

25 Executive Summary, 'World Energy Outlook 2004', p. 34, **http://www.iea.org.**

26 Environmental Audit Committee, *Keeping the lights on: nuclear, renewables, and climate change*, London: Environmental Audit Committee, 2006, pp. 34–37.

27 Executive Summary, 'World Energy Outlook 2006', p. 43, **http://www.iea.org.**

28 *Shell Global Scenarios to 2025*, London: Shell, 2005, p. 197.

29 'When will the oil run out? And what happens then?' *Prospect*, December 2005, p. 24.

30 *The Times*, 8 April 2006.

31 Lindsay M. Green, 'Finding technological solutions to the energy-water nexus', Institute for the Analysis of Global Security, **http://www.iags.org.**

32 *Financial Times*, 26 June 2006.

33 *The Energy Challenge. Energy review report 2006*, London: Dept. of Trade & Industry, 2006, p. 78.

34 Tsvi Bisk, 'The Energy Project: Independence by 2020', *The Futurist*, January–February 2007, pp. 25-34.

WILL WE HAVE ENOUGH ENERGY?
WHAT MIGHT BE THE IMPLICATIONS?

- The world could face an oil supply crunch within five years
- Energy prices over the next 20 years look highly uncertain
- Energy supplies will gradually decentralise
- The energy-water-food-poverty nexus could prove more intractable

The world could face an oil supply crunch within five years, according to the IEA.[1] Demand is likely to rise by 2.2% a year between 2007 and 2012, faster than the 2% the IEA had previously forecast.

Supplies have recently been falling more rapidly than expected in mature areas like Mexico and the North Sea, while projects in new areas like the Russian Far East are facing long delays. The problem is not lack of oil in the ground, but the slow pace of investment to get it out.

Oil prices could reach record levels and the West could become still more dependent on the Middle East. Natural gas markets could be even tighter than at the start of the decade.

The long-run outlook for energy prices remains highly uncertain. Conventional wisdom foresees:

- demand growth driven especially by China and the emerging economies;
- supplies heavily dependent on oil, gas and coal, with renewables making a small contribution overall (despite growing rapidly);
- no 'peak' in oil production, but supplies possibly remaining tight because of difficulties in shoving up production;
- cleaner electricity generation, thanks to carbon capture;
- volatile prices, as in the past.

However, this 'business as usual' future may be challenged from several directions.

Demand might grow more slowly than expected in the long term. In particular, energy-saving technologies could have a surprising impact. Their scope to reduce demand is potentially very large.

To mitigate climate change, might Western governments provide sizeable financial support for these technologies among their own populations and in emerging economies like China?

Demand would also slow if insufficient investment, supply bottlenecks and water shortages caused energy prices to rise, with more energy saving as a result. *The hydrogen economy might arrive sooner than imagined.* Carbon capture technologies may well prove effective and re-chargeable hydrogen fuel cells are likely to fall in price.

Both developments would allow cuts in greenhouse gas emissions from the two main sources of carbon emissions — electricity generation (by using carbon capture) and transport (by using hydrogen fuel cells).

Might climate change force governments to create the conditions in which both sets of technologies advance more rapidly than now seems likely?

Energy security might encourage consuming nations to make oil prices more predictable. Consuming countries will have strong incentives to make energy security a priority – in the US to lessen its reliance on the Middle East, in Europe to reduce dependence on Russia, and in China and India to guarantee enough supplies to fuel their rapid economic development.

Might large importers create mechanisms to support a predictable and steadily rising price of oil, which would encourage the faster development of alternatives to existing supplies? Could this bring a revolution in energy markets and transform global politics?

Energy supplies will start to decentralise. The slow shift to microgeneration – the production of heat or electricity on a small scale from a low carbon source – will accelerate, though at different paces in different parts of the world.

Companies and households will begin to produce their own energy, using technologies such as:

- ground source heat pumps;
- fuel cells;
- CHP (combined heat and power; technology that produces heat and power at the same time);
- micro-wind;
- bio-energy;
- solar power.

The electricity they don't need, they will sell to the grid.

Microgeneration will be attractive to remote villages in India and other parts of the world without access to centralised grids, consumers who experience supply disruptions, consumers generally if high energy prices make it economic, and supply companies wanting to bring extra investment into the industry.

Between the mid 1990s and mid 'noughts', California added six gigawatts of power generation – equivalent to the total installed nuclear power of the state – without building a single power station. This was achieved mainly through home-based and small-scale sources, such as wind and solar.[2]

In Britain Asda, the supermarket company, is planning to install wind turbines at six of its British warehouses, as part of a strategy to power all its distribution centres with renewable energy.[3] Other companies are moving in this direction. The UK government is developing a strategy to promote microgeneration, and so are other countries.

These developments herald an important long-term trend. But how important? Much will depend on:

- how soon technological barriers are overcome, such as lack of storage for surplus energy generated by micropower;
- how quickly cheaper technologies can be developed;
- how many 'early adopters' catch on – large numbers will bring economies of scale;
- how quickly the industry scales up to meet demand;
- how effectively governments support the industry;
- whether energy prices will stay high enough to make microgeneration viable without subsidies.

In 2005 the Energy Saving Trust estimated that microgeneration could provide 30–40% of the UK's total electricity needs by 2050.[4]

Microgeneration will reinforce a new thrust emerging within the power industry. Power companies have traditionally supplied energy. But as energy saving becomes a higher priority, suppliers are having to change their business model. Instead of supplying just energy, they are beginning to provide energy services – insulation and other means of conserving energy.

Might the supply of energy form a smaller component of their activities, whilst selling and installing equipment to generate energy locally becomes steadily more important? One day, instead of supplying energy, their business may be to help consumers become energy self-sufficient.[5]

The energy-water-food-poverty nexus could prove more and more intractable. For example, electricity generation uses huge amounts of water, as we have seen. Water shortages already exist in many developing countries. Will increased electricity generation make these shortages even more acute?

In India, groundwater irrigation supports the livelihoods of 55–60% of the population, the bulk of whom rely on rice production. Pumping water creates a substantial demand for electricity. So trying to reduce energy demand in rural areas could come head to head with the need to pump water to grow food.

Resolving this will not be easy. Rationing electricity or raising prices is politically difficult. Improving agricultural efficiency per se may not be the answer, either: greater efficiency – by adding an extra crop to the rotation for instance – may simply increase the demand for water and for the energy to pump it. Cutting the demand for water by developing varieties that use less would be a long-term solution, but far from easy.[6]

More than a quarter of the world's population don't have access to electricity at all. The IEA expects little progress in reducing the number of people in this position if current policies persist. Indeed, the total could actually rise by 2030. Living standards in the developing world are unlikely to increase without access to modern energy services.[7]

Will energy crops be developed at the expense of food crops? Large-scale mono-species, industrially harvested, are often seen as the economic way forward for biofuels. But if high energy prices make large-scale biomass and other energy crops financially attractive, will farmers switch out of food production?

As has been happening, this would push up the price of food. Will energy shortages and measures to mitigate climate change force up food prices in the long term, hurting the poor most?

1 The IEA's Medium-Term Oil Market Report, reported in the *Financial Times*, 10 July 2007.
2 *Global Innovation Outlook 2.0*, IBM, 2005.
3 *The Times*, 24 January 2005.
4 'Potential for Microgeneration: Study and Analysis', 14 November 2005, **http://www.dti.gov.uk.**
5 The UK is considering introducing a carbon cap and trade scheme among energy suppliers after 2011 to support their shift from being suppliers of energy to suppliers of energy efficiency. This would also accelerate the shift to microgeneration. *The Energy Challenge. Energy review report 2006*, London: Dept. of Trade & Industry, 2006, p. 45.
6 'Water, Livelihoods & Environment in India: Frontline Issues in Water and Land Management Policy', 2nd IWMI Annual Partners' Meet Report, 2003, **http://www.iwmi.org.**
7 Executive Summary, 'World Energy Outlook 2006', p. 47, **http://www.iea.org.**

CHAPTER 14
WHAT WILL CHANGE?

- The world economy will enter a new phase
- How stable will the world economy be?
- Will an oil crunch halt economic growth?
- Climate change will impact all our lives
- Climate change could make extreme poverty worse
- Big increases in global migration are likely
- The al-Qaeda threat may not last for long
- Global crime could prove a more insidious threat
- Effective global governance will become a priority
- The world will continue to be more organised
- Will we rise to the challenge?

People often say that the world is changing rapidly. But change occurs at varying speeds. For instance:

- buildings, railway lines and other infrastructure can last for years;
- social changes may occur more quickly – attitudes to divorce and remarriage, for example – but still take time;
- technology advances rather faster, especially communication technologies;
- fashions seem to change all the time.

So when we ask, 'How will the world change over the next 20 years?' we should remember that the pace of these changes will vary greatly.

Nevertheless, in this final chapter we stick our necks out – based on all that we have said before – and highlight some of the changes we think are likely over the next two decades.

The world economy will enter a new phase as the virtual economy takes off. The virtual economy will comprise paid-for products that are created purely online.

Virtual reality will be especially important. More and more people will make a living in parallel economies like *Second Life*. When a game becomes your job, ideas about work and leisure will change profoundly. Working from home will be natural, easing the commuter rush.

Traffic models, economic models, business models and many other ways of thinking about the world may have to be revised.

Societies will be seen to have evolved from agriculture, to manufacturing, to services, to virtuality, each phase adding to and eventually dominating the phase that came before it.

How stable will the world economy be? Periodic shocks are part of economic life, but over the last quarter of a century the global economy has recovered quickly from shocks like 9/11 and continued to grow. Might this change?

Threats lie in various directions, but perhaps the biggest is that China and India will stumble. As both countries increasingly power world economic growth, the health of their economies will be a vital global concern.

China, for example, needs to sustain rapid economic growth to avoid social instability. Unemployment is a serious threat. But the environmental damage caused by this growth may produce unrest. Complaints about big-city pollution are on the rise. Water shortages, partly due to climate change, are becoming acute.

China could be trapped between a rock and hard place – needing rapid economic growth but unable to live with the consequences. Some pundits fear that major social upheavals will derail the economy. Will the West make it easier for China (and India) to manage these and other tensions?

The danger to the West is not that China and India will be too successful. There will be scope for the world's different economies to gain from each other's strengths. The bigger risk is that internal conflicts stop China and India from being successful enough.

Will an oil crunch halt economic growth? From the early 1980s to the early 2000s, cheap oil has fuelled the global economy. We have now entered a period of much higher oil prices, and the International Energy Authority believes that oil markets will remain tight for the next five years.

Some experts think that oil production will soon peak and the world will start to run out of oil. Might the next 20 years see the beginnings of shift to a non-carbon economy?

This seems unlikely. Supported by higher energy prices, new technologies will continue to extend the life of existing oil fields, make new fields viable and make it increasingly possible to tap the vast reserves of unconventional oil. Huge reserves of gas, another carbon fuel, also exist.

As in the past, energy prices are likely to level off in the medium to long term and perhaps fall in real terms.

Almost certainly, in time the bulk of carbon dioxide emitted from carbon-fuelled power stations will be captured and stored. This will be one of the big changes in the next two decades. Carbon fuels will be getting much cleaner.

Renewable sources of energy will certainly gain ground. But perhaps one surprise over the next 20 years will be how central to the world economy carbon fuels have remained. People may also have become far more aware of the interdependence between energy, water, food and poverty.

Climate change will impact all our lives. The debate has moved on from a question of evidence (are humans to blame?) to a question of management (what are we going to do about it?).

People's lives will be changed by measures to tackle global warming, such as:

- *tighter regulations* to improve insulation and make new buildings 'carbon neutral'. Energy supply companies will have stronger incentives to encourage owners to cut the carbon footprint of older buildings. They will be in the business of saving energy as well as selling it;
- *higher taxes on energy consumption,* offset by lower taxes elsewhere. As a result, all forms of transport, including air travel, will continue to get more energy efficient, which will help to keep down the cost of travel. With more people

able to afford transport and efficiencies cutting the total fuel bill, will congestion prove a far bigger constraint on mobility than cost?

■ *'cap and trade'*. Eventually, countries will probably agree quotas on their greenhouse gas emissions. Nations that exceed their quotas will buy additional allocations from those that undershoot. National quotas will be translated into quotas for individual companies and, in some countries, perhaps for individual citizens. In 20 years, will individuals in Europe be trading quotas as a matter of course, perhaps starting with quotas for household energy consumption?

■ *adapting to climate change.* This will include farmers growing new crops, extra government spending because of changes in weather (from flood defences to more maintenance because roads are cracking up), changes in holiday destinations, and measures to alleviate the additional burdens placed on the poor in Africa and elsewhere.

■ *climate change as a way of thinking.* Just as the 'cold war' gave previous generations a framework for thinking about the world, so climate change looks set to become the dominant story of the next few decades – 'Global warming is the big issue.' 'Everything' s connected to climate change.' How will this affect personal values and attitudes? How will it transform political debate?

Climate change could make extreme poverty worse. The poor will be hardest hit by changing weather patterns, such as more flooding in Bangladesh, the turning of farmland to desert in parts of Africa and China, and the elimination of Pacific island communities as they sink under water.

Though the world produces enough food, the unequal distribution of what's farmed means that more than 800 million people still don't have sufficient to eat. Will that number increase as climate change accelerates and the global population expands?

Some of the proposals to mitigate climate change could make food poverty even more acute. If biofuels spread — to cut the dependence on oil — less land may be used to grow food, which would push up the cost of eating and hit the poor most.

Yet there are signs of hope. For example:

■ Africa (the continent with the largest number of poor people) is currently experiencing faster economic growth than at any time since the 1960s;

■ the knowledge exists to reduce poverty and the lack of food. The problem is scaling up what experts know works well;

■ China is transforming Africa through massive amounts of development aid. To avoid losing influence to China, the West is likely to step up its assistance as well. More resources should be available to spread good practice.

On the other hand, though the global economy will create plenty of opportunities for Africa, as now trade and other barriers may prevent Africa from taking full advantage of these openings.

People in extreme poverty will remain largely dependent on the world's eating habits. For the rich, food is about lifestyle and consumer choice, but for the poor it is a matter of survival.

As the planet becomes wealthier and more people live in the towns, Western habits of eating may continue to spread. At a billion, mainly in the West, more people today are overfed than underfed.

> 'More people today are overfed than underfed'

On current trends, to supply the demand for meat in 2050 would require giving as much grain to the world's livestock as would adequately feed 4 billion people (over two-fifths of the predicted global population).

Yet might eating habits change? Growing concerns about health may encourage people to tailor their diets to their individual health needs. Nutrigenomics and other advances will enable them to do this. Might the rich eat *enough*, leaving more for the poor?

Big increases in global migration are likely. Among pressures behind this will be:

■ the growing demand in rich countries for care workers, technicians and other migrant labour, especially as more workers in the developed world retire;

■ a growing supply in poor countries of well-educated people, willing to move (perhaps temporarily) to higher-paid jobs abroad;

■ cheap travel and more contacts in host countries (as an increasing number of friends and family migrate), making it easier to move;

■ the continued importance to poor countries of migrants' remittances, which will encourage poor country governments to support managed forms of migration;

■ the difficulty and expense for rich countries of keeping migrants out. Better for governments to manage the inflow of legal migrants well than to face a growing number of illegal entrants, with accusations that the system is out of control;

■ mounting pressure on governments from human rights organisations, arguing that it is preferable to manage larger flows of legal migration rather than to let the abuses of illegal traffic flourish.

In many countries, these pressures will win out against exaggerated fears that migrants will take jobs and housing from local people, swamp social services and threaten national cultures. Populations will become more diverse. Questions of identity – for both migrants and host countries – will move up the agenda.

The al-Qaeda threat may not last for long. Al-Qaeda represents a new form of terrorism – more religious, more global, more violent and more diverse. It has evolved from a centralised organisation to a loose network of cells.

Though a strength, this loose diversity could be al-Qaeda's undoing. Clashes within Islam could rip the network apart. Sunni-Shia conflicts in Iraq, for example, could divert al-Qaeda operatives from attacking the West.

The debate within al-Qaeda – whether to attack the 'near enemy' in the Middle East or the 'far enemy' in the United States – could cause the movement to fissure. What if bin Laden's strategy of attacking the 'far enemy' seemed to bring few results? Might some cells switch to the 'near enemy' instead?

Disintegration of al-Qaeda – a real possibility – wouldn't mean that the terrorist threat disappeared. Many cells in the Far East, for example, already gain strength from local conflicts. If al-Qaeda declined as a global political force, these cells might identify more exclusively with their local struggles.

Other cells might slide into organised crime, as some terrorists have done in Northern Ireland. Terror would not vanish: it would become more local and criminal.

Global crime could prove a more insidious threat. Even now, money laundering may comprise 2–5% of GDP.

The future will throw up new opportunities for transnational crime.

■ Expansion of the global middle class will increase credit-card fraud, insurance fraud and other consumer-based crimes. (China's middle class could reach 600 million in the 2020s.)

■ New types of crime will emerge, especially as media technologies are used in novel ways.

- Weak states will continue to create conditions in which transnational crime flourishes.
- New methods of crime are inevitable. Will offenders increasingly bribe or blackmail staff to break high-level encryption?
- The number of potential criminals will expand as global youth unemployment rises.

On the other hand, law enforcement agencies will tackle global crime more effectively. Agencies will collaborate better, develop more sophisticated strategies and invest heavily in advanced technology.

Linking up technologies and pooling knowledge will give enforcement agencies an edge. Criminals will also collaborate, but lack of trust between criminal groups will limit the amount of cooperation. Enforcement agencies are likely to create knowledge faster than their criminal opponents, and this could prove decisive in the long term. Global crime will increase, but need not spiral out of control.

As global crime expands, the criminal/terrorist nexus will strengthen. The costs of legitimate business will rise. Companies will have to spend more on security and on complying with crime-busting regulations.

Medium and small firms will be hit especially hard. Government departments and large corporations will invest heavily in security and keeping up with the latest technology. As they do, criminals will switch to easier targets. Smaller companies that can't afford so much security will find themselves on the front line.

Effective global governance will become a priority. All that we have said highlights the need for the world to find new ways of managing the challenges that lie ahead – from dealing with the implications of the virtual economy, to maintaining stable economic growth, to energy, security, to tackling climate change, to stepping up the war on poverty, to managing migration, to bearing down on global terror and crime.

In time, an expanded G8 is likely to comprise a new apex of global governance. The G8 currently embraces the heads of states of the leading Western nations (including Russia and Japan), who meet annually.

A 'plus 5' group of countries – Brazil, China, India, Mexico and South Africa – meets informally with the G8. A possibility is that this arrangement will be formalised into a G13, with perhaps further additions later.

The G13 could well evolve gradually so that it increasingly provides the world with leadership, including leadership of the IMF, World Bank and other global institutions.

Such a development would strengthen calls for greater accountability in global governance. To what extent could these leaders genuinely speak for the world? How far would they represent the diversity of views within their own countries, let alone the variety of opinions round the globe?

Alongside effectiveness, transparency and accountability will remain pressing concerns.

The world will continue to be more organised. Organisations have been reaching into the informal parts of everyday life, from childcare to volunteering. With more regulations, more targets and more accountability, organisations themselves feel more organised.

No wonder people value space where things are less structured! They enjoy the fluidity of personal life. The common reluctance to make long-term commitments may partly reflect the enjoyment of freedom that you can't have within an organisation.

In future, will successful organisations learn how to be organised in ways that don't feel organised?

Successful organisations will come to rely on three groups of people:

- *Practitioners* will increasingly become researchers. Even more than today, they will research best practice, and form networks to share and create knowledge.
- *Senior managers* will relate to stakeholders, secure agreement on goals, and design and maintain systems to achieve these goals. Alongside vision and values, leadership will be about systems design.
- *Integrators* will stand between practitioners and senior managers. They will capture knowledge created by practitioners, and from it develop standardised processes for use throughout the organisation. They will make sure these processes advance the goals of the organisation, and warn senior managers when practitioner experience suggests that these goals should be modified.

A collaborative mindset will replace 'command and control' as practitioners, senior managers and integrators keep listening to each other, and as they work with information from all sides of the organisation – from consumers, suppliers, shareholders, partner organisations and civil society.

Successful organisations won't be top down, nor bottom up: they will be side to side — thriving on networking and collaboration.

In short: globalisation is neither simple, static nor inherently good or bad. But it offers choices about how to make the most of its benefits and reduce its disadvantages. Will we have a defensive mindset ('aren't things awful?') or a positive one ('let's do better?') Will we rise to the challenge?

GLIMPSES of tomorrow *is the Tomorrow Project's online database describing emerging social, economic and demographic trends. GLIMPSES at* **www.tomorrow project.net** *provides a 'map' of recent trends to help people answer three questions: Where have we come from? Where are we going? What do we need to think about?*

PHOTO CREDITS

INDEX